# Fundamentals of Secondary Classroom Instruction

**Earl J. Montague**
THE UNIVERSITY OF TEXAS
AT AUSTIN

# Fundamentals of Secondary Classroom Instruction

89-835

**MERRILL PUBLISHING COMPANY**
*A Bell & Howell Company*
Columbus     Toronto     London     Melbourne

**In memory of a caring teacher
and a dear friend,
J. D. (Bill) Lewis**

Published by Merrill Publishing Company
A Bell & Howell Company
Columbus, Ohio 43216

This book was set in Garamond.

Administrative Editor: Jeff Johnston
Production Coordinator: Anne Daly
Cover Designer: Cathy Watterson
Text Designer: Amato Prudente

Photo credits: All photos copyrighted by individuals or companies
listed. Earl J. Montague, pp. 7, 22, 25, 42; Merrill Publishing/
photographs by Jean Grenwald, pp. ii, 1, 141; Larry Hamill, pp. 19, 63,
183, 230; Lloyd Lemmerman, pp. 13, 39, 67, 85, 70, 104, 137, 175,
221, 225, 253, 262, 259; and Doug Martin, pp. 45, 98, 148.

Library of Congress Catalog Card Number: 86-61191
International Standard Book Number: 0-675-20555-7
Printed in the United States of America

1 2 3 4 5 6 7 8 9 — 91 90 89 88 87

# *Preface*

This book is designed for a one- or two-semester course for beginning prospective teachers. It introduces fundamental skills of instruction involved in middle school, junior high school, or high school — skills most appropriately taught just before, or concurrent with, student teaching. The contents and activities in this book would also be valuable and useful in in-service programs for teachers educated before much of the recent research on teaching and learning strategies and in programs for the alternative certification of teachers.

The skills included in this book have an effect on the involvement and learning of students. While teaching styles should and do vary, studies have demonstrated the superiority of certain behaviors in promoting student on-task behavior, improved attitudes, and/or achievement. *Not* all teaching behaviors are equally effective in promoting learning.

This book guides the teacher from simple to more complex skills. Skills introduced in earlier microteaching lessons are applied and reinforced throughout subsequent lessons. Descriptions, exercises, and microteaching lessons introduce skills and provide students with many and varied opportunities to practice those skills. The ability to apply and use the skills is emphasized over memorization of technical vocabulary or more esoteric treatments of the subject. Educational jargon is used only if it will help the student better utilize additional sources. References to research findings and additional sources of information are included in each chapter for those teachers wishing to pursue a topic more fully.

The first chapter of the book introduces the teacher to the basic principles of planning and using instructional objectives. The discussion then guides the teacher through simple instructional procedures used in more didactic or expository approaches to teaching. The choice of didactic procedures is consistent with the teacher's early conceptions of the teaching process.

Following these early lessons, which build the teacher's confidence, more complex teaching processes involved in interactions and discussions with groups of students are introduced. Since most teachers will find the use of discussions a somewhat novel method of teaching, the text provides detailed information about the concept and opportunities to practice this approach.

Later chapters provide students experience with the inductive strategy of teaching. Though they are not expected to master this strategy, they should develop some understanding of it through the information and activities provided. Finally, in addition to these basic instructional skills, this text introduces teachers to the skills involved in classroom management, behavioral management, test construction, and grading.

Teachers will master few of the skills introduced in this book during a one-semester course. They should come to recognize however, the need for additional practice (in subsequent courses or supervised classroom experiences) to develop and reinforce these skills. For although research has shown clearly that skills can be developed by the processes used in this book, the ultimate transfer to the classroom will be enhanced by supervised classroom experience during which these skills are reinforced and practiced. Expecting teachers to transfer skills to the classroom without this follow-up activity is unrealistic.

This book is not meant to be an introduction to educational foundations, nor a comprehensive treatment of various methodologies and curriculum alternatives. Rather, the skills introduced are "fundamental"; they represent a foundation on which to build subsequent skills. More complex skills needed to work effectively with special students or the gifted and talented, to adapt the curriculum to students' individual learning styles, to use new instructional technologies, to team teach, to organize cooperative learning groups, or to individualize instruction are not included. These more complex skills are not unimportant; in fact, they are essential for effective teaching. However, the basic skills that are prerequisite to higher order instructional tasks provide a firm foundation on which to build subsequent skills. As teachers develop confidence in their ability to deal with the classroom setting, their ability to adapt to more complex instructional demands is enhanced, and later instruction in more advanced methodologies is facilitated.

I would like to express my appreciation to Tony Olm (The University of Texas), Debbie Shepherd, Kathleen O'Sullivan (San Francisco State University), Elaine Horowitz (The University of Texas), Lynn Burlbaw, (The University of Texas), Kent Kruetler (The University of Texas), Diana Sanderson, John Huntsberger (The University of Texas), and John Shefelbine (The University of Texas) for their suggestions and advice in preparing these materials. Patricia Reed (Bowling Green State University), Johnny Purvis (The University of Southern Mississippi), and Willis Wells (David Lipscomb College) also deserve many thanks for their helpful comments and reviews. I want especially to thank the students involved in trying out these materials. Their patience and suggestions were particularly helpful in developing and revising this program. Finally, to my wife Barbara, I give my love and appreciation for her encouragement and support.

# Contents

# *Planning Instruction* **1**

*T*he subjects you teach are not inherently interesting or dull, easy or difficult, relevant or irrelevant to most secondary students. By the choice of content or by the way the content is introduced to students, teachers make subjects interesting or dull, easy or difficult, relevant or irrelevant. And not all content is in fact equally valuable, important, interesting, or learnable to all students. You as a teacher must make choices about what to teach from the vast amount of content you have been exposed to in university classes and in school textbooks.

Several misconceptions held by teachers may need to be corrected about choosing content. First, many teachers think their subject exists in the curriculum to prepare students for advanced study in a subject. Most secondary students will not be majoring in your field at the university level. In fact, it's more likely students will serve time in prison than major in your subject (Leyden, 1984). Should we prepare everyone for prison in case he ends up serving time? Should we devote our entire energies preparing everyone to major in our field? The answer to both questions is obviously "no."

Second, teachers tend to perceive their courses as being justified solely on the basis that they are preparation for the next course in that area. Such a rationale is a weak basis on which to make decisions about what to teach people. While this perception may be partially valid, teachers who try to prepare students for the next course commonly teach the same content as that in the next course. Carried to its logical conclusion, this rationale would have the kindergarten teacher teaching everything in the curriculum. If teachers are focusing their energies on preparing students for subsequent courses, then they are abdicating their responsibility to decide what their students should learn to the teacher at the next level. Teachers should examine the nature of their students in terms of backgrounds, interests, and abilities, and then choose to teach them what will help them most at that point in time. If some of what is taught provides students with the *prerequisite* knowledge and skills needed for further study, then include it, but not at the expense of making their current learning unrelated to their current interests and abilities.

## Role of Instructional Objectives

Research suggests that clarity of instruction is directly related to student achievement and positive attitude (Rosenshine and Furst, 1971). "Clarity" refers to straightforward objectives, classroom questions, directions, and explanations. This section will show how to create and use clear instructional objectives.

Research on learning has shown that student achievement can be enhanced if the instruction is directed toward particular outcomes (Lawson, 1974; Melton, 1978; Roberts, 1982). Analyzing what students should be able to do with the content once they have learned it is important. By starting with this analysis, the teacher will be better able to choose content and activities that will result in student learning. What students will be able to do with the content should determine the nature of the learning experiences.

For example, if I want to teach students about graphs, I will be better able to focus my instruction if I first decide what I want students to be able to do with graphs. Do I want them to be able to plot bar graphs? Do I want them to be able, given one variable on one axis of a line graph, to determine the quantity of the variable on the other axis? Do I want them to be able to draw inferences from the slope of a line graph? Do I want them to derive a mathematical expression from a graph? An affirmative answer to any one of these questions would dictate a different set of learning activities as well as different kinds of assessments of student learning.

Instructional objectives should increase student achievement and improve student attitudes toward classroom instruction by helping teachers to design learning activities that are more likely to be congruent with their instructional intent, and to design assessment instruments more congruent with their instructional intent.

## Writing Instructional Objectives

An instructional objective is *a desired outcome of learning that is expressed in terms of observable behavior or performance of the learners.* The learners should be able to do something that they could not do prior to the learning experience provided by the teacher. The observed behaviors at the end of the lesson are going to be either new behaviors or extensions of existing behaviors. An instructional objective obviously will not measure all of the possible outcomes of a learning experience, but it should measure those outcomes specifically desired by the teacher.

An instructional objective is composed of three parts:

1. a verb or infinitive defining some observable action
2. a description of the task to be performed
3. an indication of the criterion to be used to judge if students can perform the task satisfactorily

Imagine you are an English teacher who wishes to teach students about writing sentences using correct verb tenses. You could choose several possible items for students to learn, each requiring a different kind of instruction. You could choose to teach students to be "able to write ten sentences, five using present tense and five using past tense, and be able to do this with 90 percent accuracy." Notice the observable action is described by the infinitive "to write," the task is "to write ten sentences, five using present tense and five using past tense." The criterion for success would be "to do this with 90 percent accuracy." On the other hand, you might want to teach the students to be able "to identify and list ten errors of verb tense found in a 250-word paragraph and write the correct verb tense with an accuracy of 80 percent." Notice the observable actions are described by the infinitives *to identify*, *to list* and *to write*. The task is one of identifying and listing ten errors in verb tense found in a paragraph, then writing the correct form. The criterion is to do this with 80 percent accuracy.

The two objectives are different even though they involve similar content. The nature of the learning activities is also different. To achieve the first objective, the appropriate learning activities might involve practice in writing sentences using present and past verb tenses. To achieve the second objective, the activities would involve practice in analyzing sentences for verb tense errors.

When writing instructional objectives, use verbs that represent some action, such as *write, diagram, list, draw, label, name, define, demonstrate, construct, perform, sketch, design, compose, invent, choose,* or *select.* Avoid such verbs as *learn, understand, appreciate, analyze, recognize, explain,* or *remember* because they represent actions that cannot be observed, and therefore cannot be assessed.

A few nonexamples may illustrate common errors in developing instructional objectives. Nonaction verbs (representing actions that cannot be observed) should not be used. For example, "Students will gain an understanding of the major tenets of communism" is an inappropriate instructional objective. An "understanding" is not observable. Also, "an understanding of the major tenets of communism" could mean anything from a one-sentence description to a large book on the subject. This kind of ambiguity gives no guidance in the choice of learning activities.

"Students will learn to appreciate music in our society" sounds like a very desirable objective. However, knowing what to teach, how to teach it, and how to assess successful instruction cannot be determined from such a vague statement. Though adequate statements for overall goals, they need to be translated into specific learning outcomes before planning instruction.

Here are a few illustrations of correctly stated instructional objectives:

1. Students will be able to identify the situation that involves the process of osmosis from a list of four written situations, only one of which involves osmosis.
2. When given photographs of ten different kinds of hats, students will be able to list the occupation associated with each with an 80 percent accuracy.
3. When given a mixed-up sequence of eight octave registers, students will be able to arrange the eight registers in order from highest to lowest.
4. When given the photographs of ten animals, students will be able to group the animals into three groups based on different characteristics for each group and list the characteristics used to group the animals.
5. When given ten Spanish sentences, students will be able to translate at least seven sentences into English without error.

Do not be misled by this initial emphasis on how to write instructional objectives into thinking that writing instructional objectives is an end in itself. The process of writing instructional objectives involves a clarification of a teacher's instructional intent. The thinking that is required to generate and use instructional objectives is the important factor (Roberts, 1982). Being able to write them merely insures that the kind of thinking needed for clearer choices of learning activities and assessment measures has been done.

## Expressing Different Instructional Objectives

The process of teaching should be concerned with three kinds of student learning: cognitive, affective, and psychomotor.

### Cognitive Learning

Cognitive learning deals with knowledge and understanding and may involve recall, comprehension, application, analysis, synthesis, or evaluation of knowledge. Teachers should be concerned that pupils learn knowledge in ways that are useful, which implies their ability to use knowledge in some fashion beyond merely being able to recall it. Benjamin Bloom (Bloom, 1956) suggested a classification system for different kinds of cognitive learning that others have found useful (Furst, 1981; Moore, 1982). The six categories of Bloom's system are knowledge, comprehension, application, analysis, synthesis, and evaluation. The following list contains simplified definitions and an example of each. More detailed descriptions will be studied in the chapters dealing with classroom questions (Chapter 5) and test construction (Chapter 7).

1. Knowledge: The ability to remember facts in a form similar to that in which they were presented.
   *Objective:* Students will be able to list the colors of the Mexican flag correctly.
2. Comprehension: The ability to translate some knowledge into your own words.
   *Objective:* Students will be able to identify correctly eight of ten action verbs found in a list of twenty verbs.
3. Application: The ability to apply learning to new situations.
   *Objective:* Given a description of possible libel, students will be able to identify which one of four possible libel defenses would be chosen to defend against a libel suit and list two reasons supporting that choice of defense.
4. Analysis: The ability to break down a situation into its component parts and to detect relationships between the parts or a part to the whole.
   *Objective:* Students will be able to identify and list two beneficial and two detrimental effects of instituting a rating system on rock music.
5. Synthesis: The ability to organize or assemble parts to form a new whole.
   *Objective:* Students will be able to describe one way to maximize the positive effects and minimize the negative effects of genetic engineering.

6. Evaluation: The ability to make judgments based on identified criteria or standards.

> *Objective:* Students will be able to list three values that could be used to help decide whether the generation of electrical power through the use of nuclear energy should be pursued.

When planning lessons, you should think about the kinds of learning that could be promoted when teaching a particular topic or unit. Writing objectives at different cognitive levels when free to choose any topics for the objectives, as in our previous example, is relatively easy. Writing objectives at different cognitive levels concerned with the same topic is more difficult. To understand this process, examine the objectives dealing with the story "Goldilocks and the Three Bears."

- Knowledge: Student will be able to list the names of the three bears.
- Comprehension: Students will be able to list the common name of the grain that is used in making porridge.
- Application: Students will be able to list two other things the bears could have done to cool their porridge other than take a walk.
- Analysis: Students will be able to list one similarity and one difference that would likely exist between the bears' beds and those used by humans.
- Synthesis: Students will be able to write an alternate ending to the story that contains an element of surprise.
- Evaluation: Students will be able to list two values they used to write an alternate ending that contained a element of surprise.

## Affective Learning

Affective learning refers to the values, attitudes, feelings, and appreciations that may result from a learning experience (Krathwohl, 1964). Writing appropriate instructional objectives of this kind is extremely difficult but possible (Anderson, 1982; Hughes, 1982). In any event, it is essential to realize that *all* instruction will affect students' attitudes and feelings positively, negatively, or in both ways. The extent to which you can define affective outcomes and teach for them will determine the success you will have in achieving them. Using affective instructional objectives appropriately is something you will learn to do as you work directly with students. Attempting to learn some of these skills prior to experience in the classroom is possible, but most are better left until the time you are in the classroom. However, in this chapter you will be asked to consider the value and interest your content might hold for students not majoring in your field. Concern for students' interest in content to be taught should be a continuing concern. Therefore, you will be asked to consider student interest in all of your microteaching lessons. Recognize, however, that initial student interest is only one aspect of the affective domain.

## Psychomotor Learning

Psychomotor learning refers to the ability to coordinate muscular movement with sensory perception (Harrow, 1972). Simple motor skills like typing or more complex skills like talking and writing may be involved. The application of such objectives in secondary classrooms usually lies within specific content to be taught, and learning the use of such objectives is better left until you begin mastering the skills of teaching within your subject area.

### Using Instructional Objectives

Using instructional objectives involves a sequence of decision making. Of course, with more sophistication you will modify this when appropriate. The suggested sequence engages the teacher in five distinct activities.

1. Identify the major goals of instruction.

Most teachers would agree that one of the goals of education is to teach students to think more effectively. Another commonly accepted goal is to teach students to understand the major generalizations that govern the functioning of the world in which the student lives. Additional similar goals could be readily identified. On the surface this may appear to be an easy task. Recognize, however, that teachers do not have the

sole right or responsibility to establish the goals of education. Parents, through legislatures and local school boards, also have an influence on the directions education takes. The establishment of goals is the mutual responsibility of all people concerned with education.

You will need to read the literature in your field, talk to university educators, check state and local policy, and identify those goals that pertain to your field of study in the school curriculum. Ultimately, the goals established for the curriculum need to be consistent with the needs and abilities of the students. All thoughtful instruction should be guided by such goals.

> 2. Develop a list of instructional objectives for a given content area that is consistent with the set of overall goals and the needs and abilities of the students.

For example, when you teach a history lesson, defining objectives that involve nothing but the memorization of names, dates, and places would be inappropriate if one of your goals is to teach students how to think about and understand major generalizations. All objectives should be developed in the context of the long-term goals you wish to accomplish. The sum total of your instructional objectives over the course of a semester or a year should logically contribute to the attainment of your goals. Keep in mind, however, that all of your goals and objectives should be based on the needs and abilities of the real students in your classroom, not some abstract conception of students.

A statement of an instructional objective describes the task students should be able to do as a result of instruction. If students already know how to do the task defined by the instructional objective, then no instruction should be necessary. Instruction on something students can already do would not be consistent with their needs and abilities. Some form of preassessment is therefore indicated before you decide on particular instructional objectives.

Some instruction is based on the assumption that students already know certain things or possess certain abilities. If students lack this prerequisite knowledge or do not possess the prerequisite skills, then they may be unable to learn what is expected. Trying to teach something students are unable to learn is also inconsistent with goals based on the needs and abilities of students. Preassessment of the prerequisite knowledge and skills expected would help you make a decision about the readiness of students to learn.

Preassessment can take the form of written tests, oral questions, or conversations with students. If you have no knowledge of students' current abilities, then using some method of assessing those abilities prior to instruction is imperative (Hunter, 1979). This preassessment will allow you to identify objectives consistent with the needs and abilities of your students.

> 3. Plan learning activities that lead to the accomplishment of your objectives.

The nature of tasks described in your objectives should determine the learning experiences to be provided. The congruence between objectives and the students' opportunities to learn determines how well the objectives will be accomplished (Armento, 1977). While this may seem obvious, the frequency with which beginning teachers fail to accomplish this coordination between objectives and learning experiences is surprising.

Teachers hold many misconceptions about the relationships between certain teaching practices and learning outcomes. While the research base is presently limited, evidence exists to support certain practices over others. You are encouraged to keep an open mind about the effectiveness of various teaching strategies and activities. Teachers are sometimes unsuccessful not because the activity is inherently defective, but because the teacher lacks the necessary skills to use the activity effectively. To overgeneralize from your individual experiences is risky. Become a consumer of research on teaching and learning. With time you will be able to make more rational decisions about the objectives you choose to accomplish and the methods you will use to accomplish them. Some of the ideas and activities found in Chapters 3, 5, and 6 will help you in making some of these decisions.

Occasionally, you may decide to modify your objectives when you find a particularly interesting learning activity. The activity may lend itself to development of objectives different from those originally intended. If the alternate objectives have validity for the students, then they may be chosen. You are encouraged to substitute objectives when improvement of instruction is likely to result.

4. Determine the methods to be used to assess the attainment of your objectives.

You may decide to ask a few questions at the end of the lesson to get immediate feedback on students' progress. You could also decide to assign students a set of homework questions or a report of some kind. Often, you will decide to give some form of written test in addition to other methods. Again, be sure that the task required for evaluation is the same task as described in your instructional objective.

5. Assess the need for further instruction.

If students were able to perform evaluation tasks successfully, then the instruction was successful. On the other hand, if students did not perform satisfactorily, then either the instruction was inadequate or the objective overambitious. In either case, you must decide what form of additional instruction is required if the objective is one you feel should be accomplished. If the objective should be altered, do so, and reteach for it. If the objective is obviously inappropriate for your students, then drop attempts to accomplish the objective.

## Some Cautions

Some detractors would argue against the use of instructional objectives to guide instruction. What they fail to perceive is that teachers are expected to evaluate the performance of their students and communicate this evaluation to students, parents, and school personnel. In order to accomplish this evaluation, teachers must ask students to perform some task. This performance may be answering questions on a test, completing some project, or in some other way demonstrating their ability to do the task the teacher is evaluating. Each of these tasks (for example, each item on an examination) is by definition an *instructional objective*. Since most teachers are currently using instructional objectives and are likely to continue to do so, instructional objectives must be used appropriately. Most teachers make up their tests after they have completed teaching a lesson, that is, they decide on what they think students should have learned after they have taught a lesson. How much better lessons would be if teachers decided what they wanted students to learn before a lesson and provided opportunities for students to learn those things (Armento, 1977).

The instructional objectives chosen and taught do not determine all of the outcomes of learning. Students will learn many things during instruction—some intended and some not. Instructional objectives should define what you intend students to learn and what you will try to insure they do learn. You may also introduce students to additional content without the expectation that they will learn predetermined outcomes. Also, while you may have some intended outcome, the actual outcome may be quite different from the intended outcome. For example, you may intend that the students learn a given concept, but the students may learn the concept incorrectly or not at all. They may also have such a disagreeable experience that they learn to hate the content being taught. Being aware of the possible incidental outcomes of instruction is important if such detrimental outcomes of instruction are to be avoided.

Don't assume in using instructional objectives that all students must pursue the same or similar objectives. When you begin to work with students in the classroom, you will find tremendous variations in students' interests and abilities. You will need to learn how to individualize instruction by having different objectives and learning activities for different students, by having the same objectives but allowing students to pursue the objectives at different paces, or by having the same objectives but different learning experiences for different students. Individualizing the curriculum will be necessary when working with highly heterogeneous classes of students. How to individualize instruction cannot be considered a fundamental instructional skill and thus will not be dealt with at this time. Later, when working in the classroom, you will have opportunities to learn the processes involved in individualizing instruction.

Using instructional objectives will not necessarily result in higher achievement (Melton, 1978). Research findings suggest that the use of instructional objectives may not result in higher achievement when students are unaware of the objectives, and when the objectives are too easily accomplished or are too difficult to accomplish given the ability levels of the students or the adequacy of the learning experiences provided.

Instructional objectives may enhance learning if the objective is told to the students prior to instruction. However, such a practice may inhibit incidental learning, that is, learning of things not intended. Most of the time, incidental learning is advantageous and should be encouraged. Evidence suggests that giving objectives, or making the objectives clear, immediately after instruction may enhance incidental learning without depressing intended learning (Melton, 1978). Therefore, do not assume that students must be told the instructional objectives at the beginning of the lesson unless you want to emphasize the intended outcomes. Rather, insure that the objectives become clear to the students by the end of the lesson.

## Limitations of Instructional Objectives

Using instructional objectives to guide instruction has some limitations. Most teachers, when first trying to use instructional objectives, will have a tendency to teach and evaluate trivial outcomes because these can more easily be specified by instructional objectives. Specifying an outcome such as "Students will be able to list at least three of the authors from a list of the titles of four books" is easy. Teaching for and measuring this outcome is also relatively easy. On the other hand, specifying the outcome that "Students, when given two novel opposing persuasive arguments for and against nuclear power plants, will be able to identify at least two distortions in each argument resulting from the use of persuasive tactics" is not only difficult, but the instruction required for students to be able to do this would be quite complex. And any test designed to measure this outcome would be a challenge. Yet, which of the two objectives is more significant? Because significant learnings are more difficult to teach and to measure, teachers may tend to focus on the trivial. Avoid focusing on the trivial.

Another risk in using instructional objectives is that the teacher will start to believe that things that cannot or should not be specified should therefore not be taught. An art teacher may decide that visiting an art gallery would be a nice experience for students, but may not have any specific outcomes in mind, only an intuitive sense that such a visit could be a valuable experience. In this case, what the individual derives from the experience should be left to the individual to seek out. Should the teacher deny students this experience because specific outcomes for the group cannot be specified? Not at all. These experiences should be provided.

Sometimes something unexpected happens that becomes a teachable moment. Taking advantage of such moments, even though the learning outcomes have not been previously specified and may be uncertain, is recommended. Teachers can and should use such occasions to provide students valuable learning experiences without being concerned about specific outcomes. As long as this does not become the primary mode of instruction, taking advantage of these moments is an appropriate occasional alternative.

## Planning As a Key to Effective Instruction

All teachers need to plan instruction. How well this is done will largely determine the quality of instruction. Studies have shown that thoroughness of planning, along with the use of instructional objectives, results in

1. more teacher flexibility when teaching a lesson,
2. more clarity in the instruction,
3. more student on-task behavior, and
4. less student disruptive behavior.

Planning is the key to effective instruction. Thorough planning does not mean just writing a lesson plan. Planning means thinking about your goals, identifying objectives congruent with your goals, choosing learning experiences likely to achieve your objectives, thinking about and writing key questions and directions, choosing and/or writing evaluation instruments, and planning all of the processes that go into instruction. Typically, teachers fail to grasp the extent to which lessons need to be thought about before, during, and after lesson plans are written. Writing lesson plans takes a small fraction of the time needed for adequate planning. Thinking about the contents that go into a lesson plan and actually implementing plans are necessary parts of effective planning. The extent to which all contingencies are anticipated prior to lessons will determine the smoothness with which instruction occurs.

Planning can be thought of as both long- and short-range. At the beginning of the school year, semester, or six-week period, the teacher must plan ahead. Such long-range planning should include consideration of

1. broad goals to be accomplished,
2. choice and sequence of content,
3. tentative time frame,
4. curriculum and other materials that will be needed,
5. field trips, outside people, or other resources,
6. how goals will be assessed, and
7. identification of any long-range learning experiences to be used.

At times teachers are expected to develop plans around major themes, topics, or problems. Such plans, commonly referred to as *unit plans,* are developed in the context of long-range plans. Since all of the microteaching lessons introduced in this book will not require long-range planning, the development of your skills in unit planning will need to wait until such time as you enter the classroom. Learning such skills at the time you are called on to practice them is more efficient than learning them in the abstract.

Short-range planning can be considered daily, weekly, or in some other small unit of time and involves a consideration of those things a teacher must think about prior to the implementation of a lesson or series of lessons. Two basic areas of short-range planning need to be considered: classroom management and instructional management.

Classroom management involves thinking about a great number of managerial tasks, including the following:

1. What directions will need to be given to manage materials and students?
2. What medium will be used? When will it be turned on? When will it be turned off? What transparencies will be used? What will be on the transparencies? What sequence?
3. What will be written on the chalkboard? Where will it be placed on the board?
4. How will students be seated?
5. Where will I be? When and where will I move during the lesson?
6. When will materials be distributed? What procedures will be followed in passing out and collecting materials?
7. When will I take roll?

Instructional management involves thinking about the instructional process, and includes thinking about the following:

1. What are my instructional objectives?
2. How will I preassess students to find out what they already know and can do?
3. What activities will I use and in what sequence?
4. How will I start the lesson to get students' attention and orient them to the lesson?
5. What key questions will I ask and in what sequence?
6. What content generalizations will be taught? In what sequence?
7. What will I say and do to make transitions from one activity to the next?
8. What will I say and do to summarize the lesson?
9. What will I do to assess my objectives?
10. What will I do if some students finish the activity before others?
11. What will I do if the class period is cut short due to an interruption such as a pep rally?
12. What will I do if I don't have enough time to complete the lesson as planned? . . .too much time?
13. What kind of improvements will I be trying to make in my teaching behavior?

## Conclusion

All planning begins with a consideration of the students to be taught. Students come to you with different backgrounds and abilities. They differ in their mental and physical development and abilities, cultural backgrounds, preferences about learning activities, and emotional maturity. These and other learner characteristics should influence the goals, objectives, and methods you choose when planning.

Once you learn the fundamentals of instruction, including planning, you then need to learn the fundamentals of curriculum design. Planning the curriculum to accommodate for things such as different learning styles, cultural backgrounds, and physical and mental abilities is as crucial as the planning of instructional strategies to be used. Additional professional preparation in child development, multicultural education, special education, and curriculum design are necessary.

## REFERENCES

Anderson, L., and J. Anderson. 1982. Affective assessment is necessary and possible. *Educational Leadership*, 39:524– 525.

Armento, B.J. 1977. Teacher behaviors related to student achievement on a social science concept test. *Journal of Teacher Education*, 28 (2):46–52.

Bloom, B.S., ed. 1956. *Taxonomy of educational objectives, handbook I: Cognitive domain*. New York: David McKay.

Centra, J.A., and D.A. Potter. 1980. School and teacher effects: An interrelational model. *Review of Educational Research* 50 (2):273–291.

Furst, E.J. 1981. Bloom's taxonomy of educational objectives for the cognitive domain: Philosophical and educational issues. *Review of Educational Research* 51 (4):441–453.

Harrow, A.J. 1972. *A taxonomy of the psychomotor domain: A guide for developing behavioral objectives.* New York: David McKay.

Hughes, A.L., and K. Frommer. 1982. A system for monitoring affective objectives. *Educational Leadership* 39:521– 523.

Hunter, M. 1979. Teaching is decision making. *Educational Leadership* 37:62–64, 67.

Krathwohl, D.R., B.S. Bloom, and B.B. Masia. 1964. *Taxonomy of educational objectives, handbook II: Affective domain.* New York: David McKay.

Lawson, T.E. 1974. Effects of instructional objectives on learning and retention. *Instructional Science* 3:1–22.

Leyden, B. 1984. You graduate more criminals than scientists. *The Science Teacher* 51 (3):27–30.

Melton, R. 1978. Resolution of conflicting claims concerning the effect of behavioral objectives on student learning. *Review of Educational Research* 48 (2):291–302.

Moore, D.S. 1982. Reconsidering Bloom's taxonomy of educational objectives, cognitive domain. *Educational Theory* 32 (1):29–34.

Roberts, W.K. 1982. Preparing instructional objectives: Usefulness revisited. *Educational Technology* 22 (7):15– 19.

Rosenshine, B., and N. Furst. 1971. Research in teacher performance criteria. In *Research in teacher education: A symposium*, ed. B.O. Smith. Englewood Cliffs, New Jersey: Prentice- Hall.

---

## SUMMARY

### Definition of an Instructional Objective

An instructional objective is a desired outcome of learning that is expressed in terms of observable behavior of the learner.

### Role of Instructional Objectives

Instructional objectives help teachers

1. design learning activities that are more likely to be congruent with their instructional intent, and
2. design assessment instruments more congruent with their instructional intent.

### Parts of Instructional Objectives

1. a verb or infinitive describing some observable action
2. a description of the task to be performed
3. a description of the criterion to be used to judge the adequacy of the performance

### Three Kinds of Learning
1. Cognitive: learning dealing with knowledge
2. Affective: learning dealing with feelings and beliefs
3. Psychomotor: learning associated with coordinating muscular movement with sensory perception

### Classification of Cognitive Objectives
1. Knowledge: the ability to remember facts in a form similar to that in which they were presented
2. Comprehension: the ability to translate some knowledge into your own words
3. Application: the ability to apply learning to new situations
4. Analysis: The ability to break down a situation into its component parts and to detect relationships between the parts or a part to the whole
5. Synthesis: the ability to organize or assemble parts to form a new whole
6. Evaluation: the ability to make judgments based on identified criteria or standards

### Steps in Using Instructional Objectives
1. Identify the major goals of instruction.
2. Develop a list of instructional objectives for a given content area that are consistent with the set of overall goals and the needs and abilities of the students.
3. Plan learning activities that would lead to the accomplishment of the objectives.
4. Determine the methods to be used to assess the attainment of the objectives.
5. Assess the need for further instruction.

### Limitations of Instructional Objectives
1. Teachers tend to teach and evaluate outcomes that are trivial because these outcomes can be easily defined and measured.
2. Teachers may tend to deny students experiences if the outcomes cannot be identified and defined.
3. Teachers may tend not to deviate from a plan, and thus ignore teachable moments.

### Advantages of Planning for Instruction
1. more teacher flexibility when teaching a lesson
2. more clarity in the instruction
3. more student on-task behavior
4. less student disruptive behavior

# EXERCISE 1
## Practice in Identifying Instructional Objectives

*Directions:* Identify which of the following are inadequate statements of instructional objectives. Recognize that ambiguity in statements allows many possible instructional objectives to be derived and should therefore be avoided. Write one correctly stated instructional objective for each inadequate statement.

1. To learn the main distinctions between the Bolsheviks and the Mensheviks.
2. To gain knowledge concerning how heroin affects the individual.
3. Students will be able to identify and record all of the acronyms presented during a thirty minute national newscast.
4. Students should be able to write the correct form of the present tense of *avoir* with an accuracy of 80 percent when it is encountered in a paragraph.
5. Students will improve their critical thinking ability.
6. To teach students the methods needed to use footnoting properly.
7. To learn why communism would fail in the U. S.
8. To be able to list some of the characteristics of social insects.
9. To identify some of the relationships between philosophy and science.
10. To show the effects of smoking on the student.

# EXERCISE 2
## Justifying Objectives

The purpose of this exercise is to provide an experience that will allow you to think about the value and appropriateness of certain instructional objectives. This exercise also allows you to share your ideas with a small group of peers and them to share their ideas with you.

*Directions:*
1. Write instructional objectives for your Instructional Objectives Teaching Lesson.
2. List the reasons you feel these objectives would be interesting, useful, or in some way beneficial to those peers whom you will be teaching.
3. Come prepared to share this information with the group of peers you will be teaching. Provide a copy for each group member.

*Discussion:*
1. Pass out a copy of your objectives and the reasons for teaching them.
2. Each person should then share his/her *honest* opinion about the merits of the content and the objectives, as well as the validity of the reasons given. In addition, the appropriateness of the objectives in terms of level of difficulty should be discussed.

3. If all are in agreement that the objectives and content are consistent with the reasons, the reasons are valid, and the level of difficulty is appropriate, then no reason exists to change them.
4. If your peers do not perceive that the objectives and content are useful and appropriate, then you will need to convince them of the merits of the content and objectives, or ask them to offer suggestions about the ways the objectives could be reworded to be appropriate and have value. You will probably choose the second option.

# EXERCISE 3
## Writing Instructional Objectives at Different Cognitive Levels

The purpose of this exercise is to help you learn to think about the different kinds of instructional objectives that could be taught when teaching a particular topic. This exercise will help you view the possible outcomes of learning in ways not restricted to the memorization of knowledge.

*Directions:*
1. Choose some topic from your field of certification that would be taught through a series of lessons. Write the name of the topic at the top of the paper to be submitted.
2. Write a one- or two-sentence description of the topic.
3. Write one instructional objective that could be a possible outcome of instruction on this topic for each of the six cognitive levels: knowledge, comprehension, application, analysis, synthesis, and evaluation. Label each objective with the cognitive level of the outcome the objective is designed to describe.

*Microteaching*  **2**

*S*ince actual practice classrooms with students are not readily available to prospective teachers, other opportunities for practice teaching must be provided. In this course you will be divided into small groups and will practice basic skills by teaching your peers. This is called microteaching—teaching in a microcosm of the classroom.

Obviously, teaching a small group of peers is not the same as teaching a class full of adolescents. Teaching your peers will initially seem threatening, but that will pass. Teaching your peers will be different from actual classroom teaching. You need not worry about disruptive behavior, which should make the microteaching situation less intimidating than the regular classroom. Your peers are adults, so the choice of content and the nature of your interactions will be different from those found in the classroom. Then too, the eagerness and willingness of your peers to learn will not be representative of most high school students. In spite of these differences and the artificiality these differences introduce, however, the advantages outweigh the disadvantages in this approach to learning basic skills.

Microteaching not only limits the number of students you teach, but it also limits the complexity of the tasks you will be asked to do. This will allow you to practice a limited number of skills without being concerned with all of the complexities of the teaching process. Learning to teach can be thought of in somewhat the same way as learning how to write a novel. One doesn't learn how to write a novel in one lesson. Rather, one learns how to write one step at a time. For example, one must first learn the meaning of words and how to spell them and proceed from there. Expecting students during the early stages of learning to produce a novel would be out of the question. Microteaching lessons will limit the number of skills in much the same way. You will not be asked to teach a master lesson. Instead, you will practice limited sets of skills until they become familiar. Later, in student teaching, you will continue practicing these skills until you become competent. Microteaching lessons are artificial classroom settings.

Avoid practicing microteaching skills unthinkingly. What distinguishes an effective from an ineffective teacher is not simply whether or not he uses certain skills. The effective teacher knows when and how to use certain skills. Not all skills and strategies can be used in all settings with all students.

Learning complex skills like those being introduced in the microteaching lessons involves trial-and-error. You cannot learn enough from reading and talking prior to practice teaching to eliminate all errors. Just as you cannot learn to type or play golf without actually practicing, making errors, and correcting them, you cannot learn how to teach without making errors. Do not feel threatened when you make errors; expect them. Identifying these errors yourself or with the help of others is an integral part of the microteaching process. This focus on errors is not personal criticism. While we will want to reinforce those things you are doing well, we will not want to let errors go uncorrected just for the sake of making you feel good. Accepting constructive criticism is part of becoming a professional.

## Planning Tips

Planning microteaching lessons is similar to planning classroom instruction but with some obvious differences. At first, planning a fifteen to twenty minute lesson is going to seem strange. You are familiar with fifty to sixty minute class periods, and planning for shorter periods will seem different. Actually, when planning for fifty to sixty minute periods, thinking of that period in terms of short ten to fifteen minute segments is necessary. Teachers usually provide two or three different activities each class period in order to maintain the attention of students. Therefore, when planning for microteaching lessons, think of one sixty minute period as composed of two or three shorter activities, with only one of the activities being taught in the microteaching lesson. This is excellent practice for later classroom planning.

When planning for instruction, a teacher will identify the objectives he or she wishes to accomplish and then choose appropriate learning activities. In order for you to practice certain teaching skills in the microteaching lessons, this sequence will be reversed. Not all content and instructional strategies are equally effective in allowing you to practice certain teaching skills in an assigned lesson. Be sure to analyze the nature of the skills involved in each lesson before choosing content to be taught. Try to choose content that will fit the particular set of skills being practiced. If you have difficulty doing this, seek help from your instructor well in advance of your microteaching lesson. Your instructor can help you modify existing plans in advance, and he or she can more likely insure a satisfying experience for you.

The members of each group will be as heterogeneous as your instructor can make them to give you the opportunity of teaching a group of individuals not majoring or deeply interested in your field. The peers with which you are working, like your future students, will not be inherently interested in the content you are teaching. This should provide you many opportunities to select content appropriate for the general population and to practice motivational techniques to interest students in the content.

When choosing content for lessons, you will be restricted to one of your certification fields appropriate for a general population of adults. *You are restricted to teaching subject matter content. Do not teach topics dealing with teaching.* Your instructor will allow you some time to discuss the appropriateness of your choices of content with your peer group prior to early lessons. Since members of your peer group are not likely to be majors in your field, they will likely have little or no interest in its technical aspects. On the surface, teaching such a group may seem like a difficult task and unlike that which you will need to do as a classroom teacher, but that is exactly the kind of task you will face as a classroom teacher. Few students at the junior high or senior high school level will major in your field and most will have little or no interest in the technical aspects of your field. Too many classroom teachers fail to recognize this fact and force students to learn a great deal of meaningless content. You need to learn early the importance of making appropriate choices of content. Choosing appropriate content is not an easy task. You have had little opportunity to practice the kind of thinking necessary in choosing content appropriate for the general population since almost all of the coursework you have completed in your field was designed to meet the needs of researchers or scholars. The difficulty of selecting appropriate content will diminish but not disappear with experience and will be something you can expect to be struggling with throughout your professional career.

Another difficulty you will have is limiting the amount of content to that which can be taught adequately in the time available. *Teachers try to teach far too much content in the time available.* You will tend to underestimate the time needed for students to learn content with understanding. Memorizing nonsense symbols takes little time, but understanding content takes considerable time. In planning lessons, try to limit the amount of content to be taught to a very few ideas or concepts.

Some students, when planning microteaching lessons, tend to develop sequential lessons. While planning sequential lessons in actual teaching situations is very desirable, planning sequential lessons for microteaching lessons can be a distinct disadvantage. Sequential lessons may not provide the situations for practicing certain skills. Therefore, do not be concerned with teaching a logical sequence of content from one lesson to the next, but *approach each lesson as an independent lesson designed to allow you to practice those skills assigned that lesson.*

Since these microteaching lessons may be your first attempt at teaching, judging the amount and detail of planning necessary to teach successful lessons will be difficult. You may underestimate the amount of time needed to plan a lesson adequately. You should expect to spend *at least* three to four hours, and more typically five to seven hours, planning each lesson. Some people need to spend significantly more time than others, so defining a maximum time required is not possible.

Each of the microteaching lessons has distinct objectives identified in the "Self-Analysis" and "Observation Guide" for each lesson. When planning your lesson, attempt to achieve the assigned objectives. Trying to improve on or practice all of the possible skills involved in the teaching process would be overwhelming. Focus only on those tasks assigned for a given lesson to insure that you will be able to gain some practice in them.

A suggested format for lesson plans will be included in the description of each microteaching lesson. Following this format will help you to include all parts of each lesson.

## Model Teaching

During the class period preceding your microteaching lesson, your instructor may ask some of you to demonstrate the upcoming lesson by teaching it to the entire class in order to provide some students with the opportunity of teaching the whole class and to allow the class to see someone actually attempt to teach the lesson. Students teaching these model lessons will likely make errors not very different from those made by most students. By seeing a student teach the lesson and analyzing what the student did, the class can benefit from the mistakes. If you are called upon to teach a model lesson, you will get extra credit for, but not be graded on, your demonstration lesson and you will have the benefit of having practiced the microteaching lesson before doing it in the microteaching laboratory. This practice should help your ultimate performance. The more practice you can have in teaching large groups of students, the easier the transition will be when you move to the regular classroom.

If you volunteer to do a model teaching lesson, plan the lesson to last approximately the same time as a microteaching lesson. Do not try for perfection and plan the lesson just as you would any other lesson. Expect to make mistakes and don't worry about them. If you fail to make any mistakes, the model lesson will not be as useful.

Your instructor may also demonstrate some model teaching if he or she feels you have had limited experiences observing the skills being practiced in the lesson. Your instructor may also make mistakes. Teaching is a life-long learning process, and you should not expect yourself or anyone else to be perfect.

## Conducting Microteaching Lessons

A few simple rules should be followed during the microteaching lessons. Do not play the role of teacher, but teach and interact with your peers as adults. Avoid referring to them as you would young people.

When you are the student, act as any normal adult. Do not play the role of an imaginary student. If you feel bored, act bored. If you are interested, act interested. The only restriction on your behavior is that *you do not ask questions during lessons* unless you need to have the teacher clarify something. Each teacher has a limited amount of time, and, if you as a student interject too many questions, the teacher may not have time to finish the planned lesson.

## Microteaching Procedures

Plan a lesson for each of the microteaching lessons except when you are assigned to be an Observer. (See "The Observer.") When planning your lessons, try to incorporate the skills to be practiced as listed in the descriptions of the microteaching lessons as well as those listed in the observation guide and self-analysis.

For each microteaching lesson, some or all of you will be expected to turn in a copy of your lesson plan. Follow the format suggested for that lesson. Your instructor will tell you if the lesson plan is to be turned in prior to or following the lesson.

Once your group has arrived in the teaching laboratory, be sure to check that all needed equipment is present *and in working order.* If any piece of equipment is missing or not functioning, notify your instructor at once. Decide on the order of your presentations. When preparations are complete, divide the remaining time equally between those presenting lessons that day. Each of you should restrict the length of your lesson to the time available. The Observer has been directed to stop you when you reach the maximum time allowed. *You will be stopped at the end of your allotted time whether finished or not.* During the teaching lesson, the Observer will be busy with other tasks, so he or she will not be one of the students. Before starting your lesson, give a copy of the "Observation Guide" for the lesson to the Observer.

Following the lesson, and before the next class period, listen to a tape of your lesson or view a videotape of your lesson and complete a "Self-Analysis." You may be asked to turn in the "Self-Analysis" at the next class meeting. This "Self-Analysis" is meant to help you identify those skills you need to improve and to help

you develop the skills needed to study your teaching behavior for purposes of self-improvement. These self-improvement skills will be invaluable to you as a student teacher and as a classroom teacher.

During each subsequent microteaching lesson, you will be expected to incorporate the skills introduced in earlier lessons. Continued practice of these skills is the only mechanism available for self improvement.

Except for the lesson when you will be the assigned Observer, you will be expected to present the following lessons:

1. Unstructured Microteaching
2. Teaching for Instructional Objectives
3. Presenting I
4. Presenting II
5. Discussion I
6. Discussion II
7. Inductive Strategy I
8. Inductive Strategy II

## The Observer

Since your instructor cannot observe each of you during each of your lessons, you will be assigned the task of observing your peers during one of their microteaching lessons. Carefully directed peer feedback, as used in this approach, provides valid suggestions for improving your teaching techniques. Carefully observing several teachers attempting the same tasks and then analyzing these observations can also help you analyze your own teaching, which should enable you to make more rapid improvement on later teaching lessons.

### Responsibilities of the Observer

1. You will be assigned one group to observe during the semester. You will evaluate each person during the microteaching lesson assigned that day.
2. Besides audiotaping the lesson, you will collect data during the lesson and from the audiotape that will allow you to complete an Observation Guide for each individual. Each item on this guide should be rated as to how well the student met the stated criteria. Comparing the performance of individuals is unnecessary and undesirable. *Do not rate an individual the same in all categories.* Let the person know which skills were done well, and which may need to improve.
3. You will share your evaluations the next class period during a feedback session with the individuals you have evaluated. You will offer *at least* one specific suggestion for improvement related to the items on the "Observation Guide" to each individual.
4. Following the feedback session, you will turn in to the instructor a copy of each "Observation Guide" you completed. The suggestion for improvement made to each individual should be written at the bottom of the form. You are also responsible for turning in an audiotape of all the teaching lessons you observed. *Insuring that there is a clear recording of each person teaching is your responsibility.*
5. As observer, you will be graded primarily on *the quality of your suggestions.*

### Procedures for the Observer

Tape Recorders

1. Check out two tape recorders sometime before the class begins. Your instructor will indicate where these recorders can be found. If a videotape recorder is to be used, check out only one audiotape recorder.

2. Place a tape in each of the two recorders, and insure that both are working properly before class begins. Replace faulty recorders.
3. Do not place tape recorders on or near the overhead projector if the overhead projector is to be used during the teaching lesson.
4. Place the microphone of the tape recorder so the student's voice is recorded clearly.
5. Place your tape in one recorder and the student's audio- or videotape in the other recorder before beginning the teaching lesson.
6. Have the person doing the teaching say his or her name before beginning the lesson so that you will know who taught which lesson.
7. Give the instructor an audible tape of each lesson during the next class period.

### Timing

1. Once all preparations for the microteaching lesson are completed, determine how much time is left in the period assigned for the microteaching lesson.
2. Divide the remaining time by the number of persons doing a microteaching lesson that day. That is the *maximum time* allowed each individual student. *No student may be allowed to continue beyond this length of time.* Insuring that students do not exceed their allotted time is your responsibility.

### Preparation for Observations

1. Study your text, class notes, and the forms to be used for the microteaching lesson. You must know more about what is expected of individuals doing the microteaching lesson than they do.
2. Decide what needs to be observed during the actual lesson and what can be observed later by listening to the tape.
3. Decide how and when all data will be collected. Studying "Observing Teaching Behavior" will help you with this task.

### Feedback to Students

1. During the next class period you will again meet with the individuals you observed during the microteaching lesson. Be prepared to share your observations and evaluations with them during this feedback session.
2. The feedback session will be sequenced as follows:
   a. The person who did the teaching lesson will briefly describe what he thinks he did well and what he thinks could be improved. He may also indicate areas on which he would like some feedback.
   b. Students in the group may now offer their appraisals and suggestions to the teacher, including some discussion of the appropriateness and amount of content included in the lesson.
   c. The Observer will then provide any additional information to the teacher that he or she may have gathered. Avoid evaluative phrases such as "very good" and

"poor." The teacher is then given a copy of the "Observation Guide" as well as the observational data completed by the Observer.

3. Involve the whole group in discussing your suggestions, and encourage each member of the group to offer suggestions also. Avoid criticizing individuals. Identify helpful suggestions that will enable each individual to improve his or her teaching.

4. During the feedback discussion, focus only on those tasks found on the "Observation Guide." The individual receiving feedback cannot assimilate suggestions about every aspect of his or her teaching. Therefore, do not discuss extraneous observations and recommendations.

5. Give the instructor copies of your "Observation Guides," your observational data, and your tape recording of the microteaching lessons following this feedback session. Your instructor may need to further analyze the teaching of individuals who seem to be demonstrating extraordinary problems or who feel a need for additional assistance. Your data and tapes can be valuable to the instructor for this purpose.

## Observing Teaching Behavior

Every microteaching lesson will require you as teacher to collect data on your teaching behaviors in order to complete the Self-Analysis or as Observer to complete the "Observation Guide." Research has shown that individuals can profit from a study of their teaching behavior if the information is specific to certain tasks and is studied in a nonthreatening environment (Tuckman, McCall, and Hyman, 1966; Tuckman and Oliver, 1968). Learning the process of analyzing teaching behavior is valuable both for the microteaching lessons and for later classroom use. One reason for providing this experience is to teach you the kind of thinking involved in productive self-analysis.

### Observations

Observations need to provide the teacher with a description of what he or she is or is not doing. This description may detail verbal or nonverbal behavior. In the microteaching lessons, you will be asked to develop systematic descriptions of your own or others' teaching behaviors specific to the tasks being practiced. Descriptions must meet the following criteria:

1. The raw data will use low inference words and expressions. Avoid words and phrases open to many different interpretations, such as "enthusiasm," "participation," "involvement," "more," "less," "adequate," "not enough," "too much," "fast-paced," "many," "most," and "effective."

2. Evaluative words, such as "great," "dull," "interesting," "enjoyable," "excellent," "good," "poor," and "slow," should not be a part of observations.

3. Observations should be restricted to the tasks being practiced in that particular lesson. Since the tasks assigned individual lessons are extensive enough to challenge the best students, adding feedback on additional tasks would do nothing but overwhelm those receiving the feedback.

## Observing the Lessons

Each Microteaching Lesson will introduce you to some methods for observing specific skills. Once an observation has been described, it will not be described again. Review methods for observing skills from prior lessons before making observations on a new lesson. Some observations are self-explanatory and are not discussed. If you need additional information on how to observe for a specific behavior, check with your instructor.

### REFERENCES

Tuckman, B.W., K.M. McCall, and R.T. Hyman. 1966. The modification of teacher behavior: Effects of dissonance and coded feedback. *American Educational Research Journal* 6:607–620.

Tuckman, B.W., and W.F. Oliver. 1968. Effectiveness of feedback to teachers as a function of source. *Journal of Educational Psychology* 59:297–301.

# MICROTEACHING LESSON 1 _____
## Unstructured Microteaching

Until this course, most of you have sat passively waiting to be taught. Moving you to the front of the classroom is necessary so you can begin thinking about the teaching process. This is the purpose of this first teaching lesson.

At the start of the next class period, your instructor will take you to the teaching laboratories—small rooms where you will do microteaching lessons—and show you the facilities. He or she will also divide you into small groups to do this initial lesson.

### Description of the Lesson

Choose a topic you think would be relevant and interesting to a small group of your peers. Come prepared to teach that topic the next class period and teach it. Your lesson should last no longer than ten minutes. You will not be evaluated on this teaching lesson.

These are all the directions that will be provided. Your instructor will not help you decide on a topic, help you with any further planning, or provide any additional information about the nature of the task. You are on your own.

### Observing the Lesson

Systematic observation of this microteaching lesson will not be required. Your instructor may ask you to audio- or videotape this lesson for later analysis. Comparing your behavior on this lesson with your behavior on the last microteaching lesson will enable you to recognize your growth through the semester.


# MICROTEACHING LESSON 2 _____
## Teaching for Instructional Objectives

In this microteaching lesson you will conduct a lesson in which the students will achieve your instructional objective. Complete the following tasks:

1. Write one instructional objective (or possibly two) that could be reasonably achieved in ten to fifteen minutes.
2. Design a lesson not to exceed fifteen minutes that will accomplish this objective. Take special care to insure that the learning activity is congruent with the objective you wish to accomplish.
3. When planning and teaching the lesson, consider the following:
   a. At some point in the lesson, your instructional objective should become clear to the observer and the students.
   b. Teach the lesson using an instructional mode and instructional materials congruent with the objective.

c. At the end of the lesson, but within the fifteen minute time frame, ask the class questions that will let you know whether or not you have accomplished your instructional objectives. Plan these questions carefully so that they will be congruent with your instructional objective. Keep in mind that, in the regular classroom, you would also use some kind of performance assessment instrument in addition to the brief informal assessment at the end of a lesson.

d. Review each item on the "Observation Guide" and the "Self-Analysis," and attempt to incorporate each of these behaviors into your lesson.

4. Write a lesson plan using the following format:
   a. State your instructional objective(s) at the beginning of the lesson plan.
   b. Describe your learning activity in enough detail so the instructor can judge the congruence between your objective and the learning activity provided.
   c. List the questions you will ask to assess the attainment of the objective at the end of the lesson.

## Reminders

In examining the kinds of things that need to be considered in planning lessons, not all the questions listed in Chapter 1, "Planning Instruction," need to be considered for microteaching lessons. Though some of these items may not be of concern in your teaching lessons, think about your planning as if you were planning for a class of twenty-five students. Manage your small microteaching group as if it were a larger group. This will enable you to avoid any bad habits that could develop from working with a small group. Your lesson plans should reflect this kind of thinking throughout all of the microteaching lessons.

Look over the criteria listed in the "Self-Analysis" that define the objectives you should try to achieve for this microteaching lesson. In your planning, attempt to address each of these criteria. In addition to the contents of the lesson plan specified add any reminders you feel could help you practice the skills listed in the "Self-Analysis." Review the information in "Observing the Lesson" before collecting data from your tape.

## Observing the Lesson

The three tasks to observe in this lesson are listed on the "Self-Analysis" and the "Observation Guide." You will be asked to record additional data on the "Self-Analysis." When recording observations of your verbal mannerisms for the "Self-Analysis," recording verbatim each time you use mannerisms such as "you know" or "OK" is recommended to help you become sensitive to their use. Becoming aware of your mannerisms is the necessary first step in breaking any undesirable verbal habits. Count the number of times you use these filler words.

Recording data on the amount of teacher talk versus student talk will also be a part of the observations for this lesson. To accomplish this task, set up a small chart as follows:

Teacher Talk

---

Student Talk

---

Silence or Confusion

---

As you listen to an audiotape of the lesson, place a check mark on the chart to represent who was talking approximately every 2 seconds. (The exact time is unimportant, but try to keep a regular interval.) If no one was talking, or if many people were talking simultaneously, then place a check in the Silence or Confusion category. When you have finished listening to the lesson, count the number of checks in each category as well as the total number of checks in the categories of Teacher Talk and Student Talk combined. Use the following formula to determine the percent of teacher talk:

$$\frac{\text{Checks under teacher talk}}{\substack{\text{Total number of checks} \\ \text{teacher + student talk}}} \times 100 = \% \text{ of Teacher Talk}$$

As the Observer, you will be asked to make a judgment about the clarity with which the teacher communicated the objective. A simple method for making this judgment is to record the objective at the completion of the lesson without having been told what the objective is. After the lesson, ask the teacher to give you a written statement of his or her objective. Comparing the two will enable you to judge the clarity of the objective.

A verbatim recording of the questions asked at the end of the lesson compared with the teacher's objective will enable you to judge the adequacy of the questions in assessing the attainment of the objective. Writing a brief description of the lesson's attempt to achieve the objective should be sufficient to make the other judgments requested. If you need additional guidance in how to observe this lesson for purposes of the "Self-Analysis" or "Observation Guide," check with your instructor.

# Teaching for Instructional Objectives
## Self-Analysis

Name _____

The items in this self-analysis are designed to help you identify what you are doing well and what you need to try to improve. If you decide to try to change some teaching behaviors as a result of your analysis, do not attempt to change more than two or three behaviors simultaneously. Circle the number that represents your assessment of your behavior on each of the following tasks:

1. The teacher either stated the objectives of the lesson or in some other manner made the objectives clear by the end of the lesson.

| 1 | 2 | 3 | 4 | 5 |
|---|---|---|---|---|
| The objective was clear to all students | | The objective was clear to some students | | The objective was not clear to any students |

2. The lesson focused directly upon the achievement of the objective.

| 1 | 2 | 3 | 4 | 5 |
|---|---|---|---|---|
| The lesson was directed at accomplishing the objective | | There were a few digressions from accomplishing the objective | | There was little relationship between the lesson and the objective |

3. The teacher asked questions at the end of the lesson to assess the degree to which the students achieved the objective.

| 1 | 2 | 3 | 4 | 5 |
|---|---|---|---|---|
| The teacher asked questions that clearly demonstrated that most students achieved the objective of the lesson | | | | The teacher asked no questions to assess students' achievement of the objective |

*Listen to an audiotape of your lesson and tally the following behaviors.* (Reread the section, "Observing Teaching Behavior" in this chapter before recording this data.)

Number of times the lesson digressed from accomplishing the objective    _____

Number of questions you asked at the end of the lesson to assess the extent to which the students learned what you intended in your objectives    _____

Number of students you called on to respond to the questions assessing student learning    _____

*Answer the following items in the space provided.* State your objective and then list your reasons for choosing this particular objective to teach to this group of students. Do these reasons still seem valid to you? If not, why not?

1. Objective

2. Reasons

Were students able to demonstrate that they learned what you intended them to learn? If so, what evidence leads you to this conclusion?

What *specific* changes will you make in your behavior during the next teaching lesson as a result of your analysis?

*Additional considerations:* The items here are not directly related to the tasks assigned but are included to help you identify any general behaviors that might be interfering with your effectiveness. Listen to an audiotape of your lesson and tally the following:

Number of filler words or sounds used ("ok" "you know" or "uh")　　　　　_____

Number of times students were addressed by name (You should have used each student's name several times.)　　　　　_____

Number of times you paused for people to think about what had just been said (Pauses are important for learning)　　　　　_____

Percent of time you talked (Some student talk is desirable)　　　　　_____

What will you do before and during the next teaching lesson to modify any of these behaviors?

# Teaching for Instructional Objectives
# Observation Guide

Name _____ Observer _____

Describe the teacher's behavior and assess the effectiveness of that behavior for the following items by circling the number that corresponds to your assessment. Reread "Observing Teaching Behavior," prior to making observations for this lesson. Attach your observational data to this report. Ignore any teaching behaviors not listed here.

1. The teacher either stated the objectives of the lesson or in some other manner made the objectives clear by the end of the lesson.

| 1 | 2 | 3 | 4 | 5 |
|---|---|---|---|---|
| The objective was clear to all students | | The objective was clear to some students | | The objective was not clear to any students |

2. The lesson focused directly on the achievement of the objective.

| 1 | 2 | 3 | 4 | 5 |
|---|---|---|---|---|
| The lesson was directed at accomplishing the objective | | There were a few digressions from accomplishing the objective | | There was little relationship between the lesson and the objective |

3. The teacher asked questions at the end of the lesson to assess the degree to which the students achieved the intended objective.

| 1 | 2 | 3 | 4 | 5 |
|---|---|---|---|---|
| The teacher asked questions that clearly demonstrated that most students achieved the objective of the lesson | | | The teacher asked no questions to assess students' achievement of the objective | |

*Complete the following tasks in the spaces provided.*

4. List the objective of the lesson as you best can determine it *without* asking the teacher or looking at his or her lesson plan.

5. Offer at least one suggestion for improving this objective.

6. Offer at least one suggestion to improve the effectiveness of the lesson. Do not be concerned with all aspects of the teaching process but merely with the teacher's attempt to accomplish the tasks of the lesson. Consider only those tasks directly related to the criteria assessed.

*Presenting* **3**

*T*eaching, in the minds of many teachers, means *presenting*, that is, taking information and presenting it to the students. In practice, presenting is only one of many tasks that teachers perform in the process of teaching. While teaching is more than presenting, presenting is something you will want to do well.

To present information, you must take ideas and put them into words that communicate the essence of those ideas. Clear communication is difficult because it requires you to have some knowledge of what words mean to the students. Remember, you will probably have more knowledge about a subject than your students. Your knowledge and experiences allow you to know the denotations and connotations of words that your students may not understand. Students hearing your words will need to associate these words with what they know from their experiences. Since their knowledge and experiences will differ from yours, the meanings they derive from words they hear may be quite different from the meanings you intend. Failure to recognize this will result in a lack of communication.

## Purpose of Presenting

The basic purpose of a presentation is to introduce new information, or to summarize some activity in order to draw generalizations. For example, if students have had considerable experience with some concept or generalization, then drawing on that experience to provide new insights may constitute an effective presentation. Or, if students have just completed a set of activities, generalizations to be drawn from those activities may be presented by the teacher. Usually pure presentations are short and part of a larger lesson. Conducting lessons using only this strategy is usually undesirable and ineffective.

## Assessment of Readiness

Before presenting information to students, assessing what students know or don't know about a topic is vital (Ausubel, *et al.,* 1978). Teaching something students already know makes little sense except in certain situations where overlearning may be desirable. Attempting to teach something if the students do not possess the prerequisite knowledge and/or skills to learn the material being presented also makes little sense. Preassessment questions determine whether students possess the necessary prerequisite knowledge and/or skills. As pointed out earlier we often do this assessment at the beginning of a lesson through the use of written or oral questions.

Another aspect of preassessment, often overlooked by teachers, is determining the readiness of students to want to learn the material to be introduced—not their knowledge of the material, but rather their feelings about the material. Part of the preassessment process involves a consideration of the present level of interest students have about the topics of a new lesson. If students have little or no interest in the topics, you need to provide some initial experiences to create an interest. On the other hand, stimulating an interest in students already possessing a high degree of interest may be unnecessary.

This assessment of interest is accomplished through the use of questions dealing with how students are feeling. Questions that ask students how they feel are called *affective* questions, as opposed to questions that assess student knowledge, called *cognitive* questions. Both cognitive and affective questions should be a part of preassessment.

You may already have had some limited experience with these questions during your informal discussions with others about the appropriateness of your lessons. These same kinds of discussions should take place continually with your students.

Preassessment is not something associated only with presentations. Preassessment is something you are going to do before introducing any unit or lesson (Hartley and Davies, 1976). Regardless of the method of instruction being used, you do not want to teach something students already know, or teach something for which students lack necessary prerequisites.

## Starting the Presentation

The introduction of a lesson is crucial to pupil learning (Hartley and Davies, 1976). It should focus the students' attention on what is going to be talked about and help them see how the presentation is going to fit into a larger framework. Providing a framework for a lesson can be done by relating the lesson to students' past experiences, knowledge and interests; stating the purpose of the lesson in language appropriate for the student; and relating the lesson to past and future goals of the unit or larger topic.

Basically, the introduction of a lesson should make the students ready and eager to learn. The introduction may take the form of a statement: "We have just studied some plant structures and their functions, and now we are ready to examine some of the important roles plants play in our lives." This statement could then be followed by a question: "What could happen to our lives if suddenly there were no plants on the earth?" Or, "We have studied the definitions and read some examples of metaphors and similes. We are now going to examine the purposes these play in our language by examining what the English language would be like if we stopped using similes and metaphors."

Photographs, models, paintings, puzzles, demonstrations, or objects could also help start a class. Providing some direct experience to lead into a topic could also serve this function, and you will want to become familiar with this process. For example, if the topic of free speech was to be taught, the teacher could provide a brief experience of approximately ten minutes for the students in which all free speech was stifled. Then the teacher could introduce the topic of free speech by asking students to react to the experience just provided and contrasting that experience with a situation involving free speech.

*The process of inducing a readiness to learn is called set induction.* Research has indicated that the quality with which set induction is accomplished will affect the achievement of learners (Schuck, 1981). Providing effective set inductions is important. Four tasks to be completed during a set induction, but not necessarily in this order, are

1. relating the lesson to be taught to students' past experiences,
2. stating the purpose of the lesson in the students' language without telling them the specific objectives or contents of the lesson (Melton, 1978),
3. relating the lesson to past and future goals of the topic,
4. doing something to get the students' attention and interest.

**Conducting a Presentation**

Logical arrangement of content during a presentation is crucial. If the arrangement is confusing, then students will not understand the relationships among the elements presented (Bush, Kennedy, and Cruickshank, 1977). Two ways of organizing content are commonly used. First, content can be organized from the general to the specific. When using this type of organization, the teacher must assume that students have a clear understanding of the initial generalization. This understanding is then used as a basis for identifying more specific applications. Second, content can be organized from the specific to the general. If you are using the specific to general strategy, your students need to have had some direct experience with the specific examples being used.

For an example of the general to specific strategy, an English teacher may choose to introduce the rules governing the use of the words *who* and *whom*. An outline beginning with the generalization to be taught might look like this.

A. Generalize

*Who* acts as the subject of a main or subordinate clause.

*Whom* acts as an object of a main or subordinate clause.

B. Explain
    1. main clause
    2. subordinate clause
    3. subject
    4. object

C. Give examples. Discuss which are correct and which are incorrect.

He is the one who should go to the store.

They are the people who should be given the charity.

Whom should be allowed to go to the movie?

I like the people who are good to me.

On the other hand, the same lesson could be taught by reversing the order. The following is an outline of such a lesson.

A. Preassess the students' understanding of
    1. main clause
    2. subordinate clause
    3. subject
    4. object

B. Examine the following examples

He is the one who should go to the store.

They are the people who should be given the charity.

Who should be allowed to go to the movie?

I like the people who are good to me.

Who should receive the prize?

Whom do you like the best?

My mother is the person who went on the picnic with us.

C. Explain the use of *who* as the subject and *whom* as the object in each of the examples.

D. Now write the rules.

*Who* acts as the subject of a main or subordinate clause.

*Whom* acts as an object of a main or subordinate clause.

E. Provide the students with additional examples of sentences.

Recognizing the assumptions underlying the organization of content is important regardless of the pattern of organization chosen. If any of the assumptions is violated, students may have difficulty in understanding and learning the content. For example, if students do not understand the generalization used to generate examples, then they may misunderstand the examples (Tennyson and Park, 1980). And if students have not had experience with the examples being used to develop some generalization, they will not understand the generalization.

To avoid misunderstandings ask questions to ascertain if students understand the essential elements of the presentation. Uninterrupted teacher talk should rarely exceed two to five minutes. If the content is complex or abstract, then more frequent questions may be necessary. If in doubt whether students understand something, ask questions. Failure to follow this practice may cause you to lose contact with students during a presentation.

Asking discussion questions during a presentation will merely interrupt the flow of ideas you are presenting; avoid asking questions likely to lead to further discussion during presentations.

Clarity may be aided during a presentation by the use of examples and nonexamples with which students are familiar (Armento, 1977; Tennyson and Park, 1980). An art teacher could explain perspective by showing students a photograph of the street outside the school and pointing out the horizon and vanishing point. For a nonexample, the teacher could demonstrate how a cubist painting without a vanishing point or horizon distorts perspective. Examples chosen from the daily life experiences of students will not only add clarity, but will also help make the content more interesting and useful to the students.

Since students remain passive during presentations, presentations should be stimulating. Using audio-visual aids, including the overhead projector, the chalkboard, models, charts, or objects, and using voice control have marked effects on presentations. More instruction on making stimulating presentations will be given in the next chapter.

Presentations need to be organized well and delivered smoothly. This requires careful planning and rehearsal, particularly for beginning teachers. The extent to which you must stop and refer to notes, or hesitate in order to think of the next idea, will diminish effectiveness. You will find it helpful to outline the content to be included in a presentation for reference during the lesson. Do not make the outline too extensive, or you will have difficulty in finding the appropriate point during the lesson. On the other hand, do not make the outline too brief, or you may neglect needed ideas. Experience will indicate the appropriate amount of direction you will need for a smooth delivery.

## Note Taking

Since the information you present will need to be assimilated by the students, allow time for them to take notes. Let students know what material should be remembered from the material presented. Not all material presented will be equally important.

Some teachers have the mistaken notion that providing note taking aids, such as outlines or copies of the teacher's notes, prior to a presentation will help students. Research has shown the opposite to be true (Petrich and Montague, 1981).

Outlines or other organizational aids given students before presentations will actually lower achievement. The more students are expected to organize their own notes, the more mental involvement they will have in the activity and the higher their resultant achievement. You will need to teach students how to take notes, however. Without instruction on taking notes, students are unlikely to be successful note takers.

When writing on the chalkboard or overhead projector during a presentation, your writing should be neat and organized. Avoid using abbreviations of words you wish students to learn to use and spell. Students will have the tendency to copy only those things you have written on the chalkboard or overhead projector. If you abbreviate, they will abbreviate. If your writing is disorganized, their writing will be disorganized. Try to set a good example. If you are one of those individuals who writes poorly when writing on the chalkboard, then practice writing on a chalkboard until you improve.

## Closing the Lesson

At least two tasks need to be accomplished during the closing of a lesson. First, restate and reinforce the important generalizations to be learned from the lesson (Wright, 1970; Armento, 1977). Second, at least partially assess the attainment of the instructional objectives either by asking the students to respond verbally to questions congruent with the instructional objectives or by using some other means of obtaining feedback, such as a brief quiz or an individual writing exercise. This assessment should not be conducted merely by asking questions like "Are there any questions?" or "Do you understand?" If you want to find out if students have actually learned what you want them to learn, then ask closed questions directly assessing your instructional objectives.

Studies on learning have clearly demonstrated that students tend to remember better those things presented at the beginning and ending of a lesson (Armento, 1977; Wright, 1970). They remember less well those things in between. Therefore, include in the closing that information you want the students to remember from the lesson.

## REFERENCES

Armento, B.J. 1977. Teacher behaviors related to student achievement on a social science concept test. *Journal of Teacher Education* 28(2): 46–52.

Ausubel, D.P., J.D. Novak, and H. Hanesian. 1978. *Educational psychology: A cognitive view.* 2d ed. New York: Holt, Rinehart and Winston.

Bush, A.J., J.J. Kennedy, and D.R. Cruickshank. 1977. An empirical investigation of teacher clarity. *Journal of Teacher Education* 28(2): 53–58.

Hartley, J. and I.K. Davies. 1976. Preinstructional strategies: The role of pretests, behavioral objectives, overviews, and advance organizers. *Review of Educational Research* 46(2): 239–265.

Melton, R.F. 1978. Resolution of conflicting claims concerning the effect of behavioral objectives on student learning. *Review of Educational Research* 48(2): 291–302.

Petrich, J.A. and E.J. Montague. 1981. The effect of instructor-prepared handout materials on learning from lecture instruction. *Journal of Research in Science Teaching* 18(2): 177–187.

Schuck, R.F. 1981. The impact of set induction on student achievement and retention. *Journal of Educational Research* 74(4): 227–232.

Tennyson, R.D. and O. Park. 1980. The teaching of concepts: A review of instructional design research literature. *Review of Educational Research* 50(1): 55–70.

Wright, C.J., and G. Nuthall. 1970. Relationships between teacher behaviors and pupil achievement in three experimental science lessons. *American Educational Research Journal* 7(4): 477–491.

---

## SUMMARY

### Definition of Presenting
Presenting is essentially telling the students something you want them to know and remember.

### Purposes of Presentations
1. to introduce new information or knowledge
2. to summarize some activity in order to draw generalizations from the activity

### Three Purposes of Preassessment
1. to find out if students possess necessary prerequisite knowledge or skills
2. to determine if students already possess the knowledge and skills to be taught
3. to determine if students have an interest in learning what is to be taught

### Definition of Set Induction
Set Induction is the process of inducing readiness to learn.

### Steps in Set Induction
1. relate the lesson to be taught to students' past experiences
2. state the purpose of the lesson in the students' language
3. relate the lesson to past and future goals of the topic
4. do something to get their attention and interest

## Conducting a Presentation

1. Organize content from the general to the specific when it is clear that students understand the generalization.
2. Organize content from specific examples to generalizations when it is clear that students have had experience with the examples, or you are going to provide the experience.
3. Ask questions during the presentation to insure that students have understood important ideas as they are presented.
4. Do not ask discussion questions during a presentation.
5. Use examples and nonexamples with which students are familiar to bring clarity to ideas being discussed.
6. Introduce or change the kind of stimuli being used during a discussion.
7. Allow time for students to take notes during a presentation.
8. Let students know the relative degree of importance of the material being presented.
9. Do not provide note taking aids, such as outlines, to students prior to a presentation.
10. Write notes on the chalkboard or overhead projector as you want them to appear in students' notes.

## Closing a Presentation

1. Restate the important generalizations to be learned from the presentation.
2. Ask questions or have students complete an exercise or test congruent with your objectives in order to partially assess attainment of the instructional objectives for the lesson.

# EXERCISE 4
## Preassessment of Interest

One of the purposes of preassessment is to determine the interest students have in the material to be presented. Students' interest in a topic can be determined through informal discussions with students before the topic is introduced. In Exercise 2, you practiced this form of preassessment. The purpose of this exercise is to provide an additional experience in determining the appropriateness (in terms of amount, level of difficulty, and relevancy) of the content and instructional objectives for a group of students from a general population. Choosing appropriate content and objectives is not something that will be easy. Choosing content is a learning process that will go on throughout your professional career.

*Directions*
1. Write instructional objectives for your Presentation Teaching Lesson (Microteaching Lesson 3).
2. List the reasons you feel this content and these objectives would be interesting, useful, or in some way beneficial to those peers you will be teaching.
3. Come prepared the next class period to share this information with the group of peers you will be teaching. Provide copies for each group member.

*The Discussion:*
1. Pass out a copy of your objectives and the reasons for teaching them.
2. Each person should then share his/her honest opinion about the merits of the content and the objectives. Discuss both the level of difficulty and the amount of content to be taught.
3. If all are in agreement that the objectives and content are consistent with the reasons, the reasons are valid, and the level of difficulty and amount of content are appropriate, then there is no reason to make changes.
4. If the objectives and content are not perceived as being useful and appropriate for your peers then you will need to convince your peers of the merits of the content and objectives or ask them to offer suggestions about the ways the objectives could be changed so as to be appropriate and have value for them. The latter is probably the option you will need to choose.

# EXERCISE 5
## Preassessment of Content

One of the concerns a teacher should have prior to any presentation is the current level of experiences and understanding of the students. If students have not had the prerequisite experience or understanding to comprehend the presentation, then these will need to be provided. Asking questions that assess the adequacy of students' prerequisite knowledge and skills is essential. This exercise is to provide you an opportunity to write questions to assess prerequisite knowledge and skills.

### Directions

1. Bring to the next class period a list of your instructional objectives for your Presentation Teaching Lesson.
2. After each objective, list the questions you will ask to assess the students' prerequisite knowledge and/or experiences.
3. During the next class period your instructor will assign you to a small group of two to four students. Your task will be to review each of your objectives and the questions assessing prerequisite experiences and understandings. Arrive at a consensus on one objective and associated questions that you feel represent an effective assessment.
4. Choose one person in your group to present your objective and questions to the entire class. Your instructor may have you place this information on the chalkboard, or he or she may ask you to prepare a transparency for a presentation during the next class period. The purpose of this presentation to the whole class is to analyze the objective and related questions for adequacy. Reviewing your objectives along with related preassessment questions will insure that no misunderstandings about the process of identifying prerequisite understandings will be perpetuated. This exercise will also provide members of the class practice in judging the adequacy of preassessment questions.

# EXERCISE 6 ———————————————————
# Set Induction

Using a set induction to start lessons will facilitate student learning. This exercise is designed to provide an experience in developing set induction strategies. A set induction should include the following elements, not necessarily in the order listed:

1. relating the lesson to be taught to students' past experiences
2. stating the purpose of the lesson in the students' language
3. relating the lesson to past and future goals of the topic
4. doing something to get their attention and interest

### Directions

1. Write a brief description of the content to be taught in the Presentation Microteaching Lesson (Microteaching Lesson 3). Title this section "Content to be Taught."
2. Write the instructional objective(s) for the lesson. Title this section "Instructional Objectives."
3. Describe the set induction you could use to start a presentation on the topic chosen. Be sure that each of the elements is included in your set induction. Where your set induction involves something you are going to say, or questions you are going to ask, list each *verbatim* and in proper sequence.

4. Your instructor may ask some of you to present your actual set induction to the whole class just as it would be used in your microteaching lesson, in addition to submitting a written report.

# EXERCISE 7
# Outlining Content

Producing an outline of content to be presented is sometimes a difficult process; therefore, this exercise is designed to provide some practice and feedback before you are asked to use an outline in the teaching process.

Any outline to be used in a lesson plan should list the content in the order it is to be discussed. Include in your outline

1. important generalizations to be made,
2. brief descriptions of specific examples or points to precede or follow the generalizations,
3. verbatim lists of questions to check understanding to be included at the point they will be asked.

*Directions:*
1. Write the instructional objectives to be used in the Presentation Teaching Lesson (Microteaching Lesson 3).
2. Write a content outline following the description above just as you intend to use it in your teaching lesson.
3. Turn your outline into your instructor for his or her comments.

# MICROTEACHING LESSON 3 _____
## Presenting I

In this exercise, you will teach a lesson using the presentation method. Read Chapter 3, "Presenting," prior to planning this lesson, then complete the following tasks:

1. Plan a lesson that requires you to present new information to your peers.
2. Incorporate a set induction strategy at the start of the lesson. Since set induction is essential, feel free to spend time (but not more than a third of your time) at the start of this lesson for this task.
3. Ask some brief questions at the beginning to preassess students' knowledge of the content to be presented if you are not confident about what they currently know.
4. Ask some questions during the presentation to check student understanding of something you have said. *Do not ask questions with the intent of starting a discussion.*
5. Close the presentation by asking questions that assess students' accomplishment of your instructional objectives. Do not ask, "Do you understand?" for this purpose.
6. You will have approximately fifteen minutes available for your lesson, including time to set up.
7. Attempt to incorporate what you learned in the preceding lesson on instructional objectives; continue to teach for the achievement of a clearly defined instructional objective.
8. If you would like to make an improvement on the skills introduced during the last lesson, continue to work on them, but do not allow that effort to interfere with the tasks of this lesson. If you need help in deciding whether or not to work on some skill, or if you do not know what you can do to help yourself improve some skill, talk with your instructor.
9. The lesson plan to be presented to your instructor on the day of the microteaching lesson should:
   a. list your instructional objectives
   b. list the preassessment questions to be asked
   c. describe the set induction to be used
   d. include an outline of the content to be presented
   e. list the questions to be asked during the lesson to check immediate understanding
   f. list points to be included during your closing comments
   g. list questions you will ask at the end of the lesson to assess the attainment of the objective(s)
10. Save an audiotape of this lesson. You will be asked to listen to this tape when you plan your second presenting lesson (Microteaching Lesson 4).

### Observing the Lesson
Much of the data needed to assess this lesson will be written descriptions of what the teacher sequentially said and did. As an Observer, you may also need to make an outline of the lesson from the audiotape to enable you to identify specific aspects of the presentation that seemed out of place or were unclear. The same can be said for the set induction, unless it was strictly

verbal. In the latter case, a verbatim transcript of the set induction could be useful in offering suggestions for change. Use the same procedure as that in Lesson 2 to determine the clarity of the objective.

The additional tasks on the "Self-Analysis" or "Observation Guides" can be done by listening to an audiotape and tallying the occurrences of the behaviors being analyzed. If you have additional questions, check with your instructor before proceeding with the analysis.

# Presenting I
# Self-Analysis

Name _____

The items on this Self-Analysis are designed to help you identify those tasks you are doing well and those you may still need to improve. If you decide to try to change some teaching behaviors as a result of what you have learned about your teaching from this analysis, do not attempt to change too many things simultaneously. Usually two or three will be the maximum.

     Listen to an audiotape of your lesson and record the data that will allow you to rate or answer the following questions. Review "Observing Teaching Behavior" in Chapter 2 and "Observing the Lesson" in earlier Microteaching Lessons before you make observations for this lesson. *Attach the observational raw data to your report.* Circle the number that corresponds to your assessment of your behavior on each of the tasks to be rated.

*Skills/tasks specific to this lesson*

1. The set induction of the lesson created an interest in the lesson.

| 1 | 2 | 3 | 4 | 5 |
|---|---|---|---|---|
| Attention of the students was effectively gained | | Some attempt was made to get the students' attention | | There was little or no attempt made to get students' attention |

2. The set induction of the lesson gave direction to the rest of the lesson by relating it to past knowledge and experiences of the students and the topics to be taught.

| 1 | 2 | 3 | 4 | 5 |
|---|---|---|---|---|
| Overall direction or purpose of the lesson was clear | | Overall direction or purpose of the lesson was somewhat clear | | Direction or purpose of the lesson was unclear |

3. The teacher closed the lesson in a way that reinforced, reviewed, and clarified the objectives and the importance or usefulness of the learning outcomes of the lesson.

| 1 | 2 | 3 | 4 | 5 |
|---|---|---|---|---|
| Objectives were reinforced and the importance of the lesson to the students was made clear | | Some attempt to review the lesson and its relevance to the students was attempted | | Little or no attempt was made to review the lesson |

4. The presentation was clear and well organized.

| 1 | 2 | 3 | 4 | 5 |
|---|---|---|---|---|

Information being presented was understandable to the students at all times

Information being presented was somewhat unclear at times

Information being presented was seldom clear to the students

5. The presentation focused directly on the achievement of the objectives.

| 1 | 2 | 3 | 4 | 5 |
|---|---|---|---|---|

The presentation was directed at accomplishing the objectives

There were a few digressions from accomplishing the objectives

There was little relationship between the lesson and the objectives

6. The content was appropriate in both amount and relevancy.

| 1 | 2 | 3 | 4 | 5 |
|---|---|---|---|---|

Content was appropriate in both amount and relevancy

Content was appropriate in one but not the other

Too much and irrelevant content

*Skills/tasks applied from previous lessons*

7. The teacher either stated the objectives of the lesson or in some other manner made the objectives clear by the end of the lesson.

| 1 | 2 | 3 | 4 | 5 |
|---|---|---|---|---|

Objectives were clear to all students

Objectives were clear to some students

Objectives were not clear to any students

*Additional considerations*:   Listen to a tape of your lessons and tally the behaviors described.

1. Did I demonstrate any distracting verbal mannerisms? If so, what?  _____

2. Number of times I used distracting verbal mannerisms  _____

3. Number of times my rate of speech slowed to stress the importance of an idea (desirable)  _____

4. Number of times I paused noticeably in order to think about what I was going to say next (usually undesirable)  _____

5. Number of questions I asked to check student understanding of what was being said during the presentation                    _____

6. Number of questions I asked during the close of the lesson to assess student learning of the objectives of the lesson                    _____

*Answer the following questions in the space provided:*

What do you think you did particularly well?

What specifically did you do or fail to do that caused your lesson to be less effective than it could have been? In replying, consider only those skills or tasks assigned specifically to this microteaching lesson.

What will you do or not do differently (behaviorally) in your next microteaching lesson?

What specific changes will you make in your *lesson plan* to help yourself accomplish the changes you listed above?

# Presenting I
# Observation Guide

Name _____  Observer _____

Either record data during the teaching lesson or record data from an audiotape that will allow you to make the judgments requested in this Observation Guide. Read the section, "Observing Teaching Behavior" in Chapter 2 and "Observing the Lesson" in this and earlier microteaching lessons prior to making observations for this lesson. Analyze the teacher's behavior and assess the effectiveness of that behavior for the following items only. Circle the number that corresponds to your assessment of the teacher's behavior. Ignore any teaching behaviors not listed below. *Attach your observational data to this report.*

*Skills/tasks specific to this lesson*

1. The set induction of the lesson created an interest in the lesson.

| 1 | 2 | 3 | 4 | 5 |
|---|---|---|---|---|
| Attention of the students was effectively gained | | Some attempt was made to get the students' attention | | There was little or no attempt made to get students' attention |

2. The set induction gave direction to the rest of the lesson by relating it to students' past knowledge and experiences and the topics to be taught.

| 1 | 2 | 3 | 4 | 5 |
|---|---|---|---|---|
| Overall direction or purpose of the lesson was clear | | Overall direction or purpose of the lesson was somewhat clear | | Direction or purpose of the lesson was unclear |

3. The presentation was clear and well organized.

| 1 | 2 | 3 | 4 | 5 |
|---|---|---|---|---|
| Information being presented was understandable to the students at all times | | Information being presented was somewhat unclear at times | | Information being presented was seldom clear to the students |

4. The presentation focused directly on the achievement of the objectives.

| 1 | 2 | 3 | 4 | 5 |
|---|---|---|---|---|

| The presentation was directed at accomplishing the objectives | | There were a few digressions from accomplishing the objectives | | There was little relationship between the lesson and the objectives |
|---|---|---|---|---|

5. The teacher closed the lesson in a way that reinforced, reviewed, and clarified the objectives and the importance or usefulness of the learning outcomes of the lesson.

| 1 | 2 | 3 | 4 | 5 |
|---|---|---|---|---|

| Objectives were reinforced, and the importance of the lesson to the students was made clear | | Some attempt to review the lesson and its relevance to the students was attempted | | Little or no attempt was made to review the lesson |
|---|---|---|---|---|

6. The content was appropriate in both amount and relevancy.

| 1 | 2 | 3 | 4 | 5 |
|---|---|---|---|---|

| Content was appropriate in both amount and relevancy | | Content was appropriate in one but not the other | | Content was excessive and irrelevant |
|---|---|---|---|---|

*Skills/tasks applied from previous lessons*

7. The teacher either stated the objectives of the lesson or in some other manner made the objectives clear by the end of the lesson.

| 1 | 2 | 3 | 4 | 5 |
|---|---|---|---|---|

| Objectives were clear to all students | | Objectives were clear to some students | | Objectives were not clear to any students |
|---|---|---|---|---|

*Answer the following questions in the space provided:* Describe one thing related to the seven skills or tasks assessed in this lesson that you thought was particularly effective and that you feel the teacher would be advised to continue.

Offer at least one specific suggestion on what the teacher could have done to improve the lesson. Consider only those tasks directly related to the criteria assessed in this lesson.

*Refocusing* **4**

*I*n preceding chapters you have been introduced to several means of enhancing student learning, including using instructional objectives, preassessing students' knowledge and experiences, using set inductions, and closing lessons by reviewing important learnings and asking questions assessing objectives. This chapter introduces the process called *refocusing*, which will help you enhance student learning by helping students remain attentive.

*Refocusing is the process of interjecting stimuli into a lesson to gain, maintain or increase student attention.* Teachers need to be aware of student reactions to class activities and be able to use refocusing when it is most likely to be effective. For example, when you have talked too long, students will lose eye contact with you, move around in their seats, play with some object, or in other ways communicate that they are no longer listening. When these signs *first become apparent*, you need to regain your students' interest. As you learn to identify these behaviors when they first appear, and as you learn how to refocus attention, you will more likely be successful in keeping students on-task and in reducing misbehavior.

## General Refocusing

Teachers can provide a variety of stimuli to help students maintain attention. You may not have the opportunity to practice these extensively in this course, but they are things to keep in mind as you plan lessons.

### Classroom Environment

Students sometimes become bored with the physical arrangement in a classroom. For example, when the same students have been seated next to each other for an extended period of time, they will be less inhibited about talking with each other. While changing student seating is not an effective way to maintain good student behavior, it can be used to help students become temporarily less distracted by others.

Bulletin boards, maps, equipment, and models are also important in gaining student interest in your subject. A classroom with barren walls does little to stimulate a student's interest in what goes on in that classroom. A history classroom should look as if history is being taught there; a science classroom should look as if science is being taught there; an English classroom should look as if English is being taught there. Students walking into classrooms displaying symbols representing the content to be taught will be stimulated to think about the subject.

On the other hand, a teacher must guard against placing things in locations likely to distract students from learning. Placing students facing windows is usually counterproductive. Things happening on the outside tend to draw a student's attention away from what is happening in the classroom. Of course, you can use this by planning activities that can appropriately occur outside. Students are more likely to stay on-task when studying the characteristics of different trees, for example, if they are looking at trees outdoors rather then looking at photographs of trees.

The main criterion for arranging materials in a classroom, deciding on seating arrangements, decorating a classroom, or arranging field trips, is the degree to which the setting will make student learning easier. Decide what will stimulate students but not distract them.

## Methodology

Your choice of methodology can do much to help students maintain interest in learning. Think of classes you enjoyed versus those you dreaded. What kind of things affected your attitudes toward your classes? Very likely your attitudes were influenced by the nature of classroom activities. For example, when the teacher used the same methodology throughout a period, or the same methodology day after day, you were more likely to be bored and less interested in what occurred. Nothing is deadlier to student interest than a teacher who follows the same passive methodology every day. Some teachers have students quietly read a section in a book and fill out a worksheet on the written material; afterwards they conduct a class review of the answers, and finally, they administer a test over the material. The same pattern is used every day. It is not surprising that their students lose interest.

You have an amazing choice of methodologies, resources, and materials available to you as a teacher. Some of your options include

A. Methods
   1. field trips
      a. to see something new
      b. to collect data
      c. to explore
      d. to collect specimens
   2. laboratory activities
      a. to show and tell or verify
      b. to collect data
      c. to explore
      d. to practice skills
   3. demonstrations
      a. to show and tell or verify
      b. to collect data

c. to create interest
d. to generate problem statements for investigation
e. to explore
f. to participate in silent demonstrations
g. to present discrepant events
4. small and large group discussions
a. to identify differences in views
b. to reach consensus on views
c. to examine data and draw inferences
d. to develop plans of action
e. to brainstorm
f. to examine current events
g. to examine controversial issues
h. to review
5. tests
a. for diagnostic review
b. for achievement
c. for preassessment
d. for practical/laboratory skills
e. for performance
6. games
a. simulations
b. computer
c. small group
d. individual
7. projects—group or individual
a. model building
1. creating a model
2. replicating a model
b. making video tapes
c. making films
d. doing research investigations
1. laboratory
2. library
e. constructing dioramas
f. drawing art work or making crafts
g. making posters and bulletin boards
8. peer instruction
a. remedial
b. enrichment
9. drill and practice
a. whole class

  b. games
  c. worksheets
10. debates
11. dramatizations and skits
12. story-telling
13. reading current publications and book reports

14. oral reports
15. panel discussions
16. creative writing
17. individual study
18. guest speakers
19. individualized learning centers
20. contests

B. Applications of instructional technology
   1. multimedia learning centers
      a. small group
      b. individual
   2. films
      a. documentary
      b. fiction
      c. investigative
      d. review
      e. topic introduction
      f. motivational
      g. simulated experiences
   3. slides/overhead projector transparencies
      a. show and tell
      b. data collection
      c. data analysis
      d. simulated experiences
      e. topic introduction
   4. records or tape recorders
      a. nature sounds
      b. role playing
      c. simulations
      d. outside speakers and events
      e. interviews
      f. creating music
   5. television
      a. current events
      b. enrichment
   6. film loops
   7. computers
      a. laboratory simulations
      b. drill and practice tutorials
      c. interactive video
      d. problem solving
      e. story writing
      f. electronic communications
      g. programming
      h. robotics

Providing different kinds of activities during each class period introduces stimulus variation for your students. Different students prefer to learn in different modes (Arlin, 1975; Dunn and Dunn, 1978; Witkin, *et al.,* 1977). Some prefer visual learning; others prefer tactile, auditory, or a combination of styles. Some like to work alone, while others like to work in groups. Some students need quiet surroundings, while others need the stimulus of music. By providing a variety of learning activities you will not be catering to a particular set of students. But if you fail to provide a variety of learning activities, you can depend on having some students uninterested in lessons, off-task, and disruptive. Successful teachers vary their instructional styles and strategies (Brophy and Evertson, 1976). Varying your style is critical (Turner, 1979), and yet we do not know conclusively how teaching styles should be matched to individuals' learning styles (Levy, 1983). Given present knowledge, teachers should at least accommodate all students some of the time by using a variety of teaching activities and strategies.

## Specific Refocusing Skills

During lessons, a teacher has a variety of ways to gain, maintain, or regain the attention of students. Choosing a specific refocusing skill to use will depend on the particular situation. Let's examine some of these skills to help you incorporate them into your teaching.

### Questions

During many activities in the classroom either the students or the teacher is talking. Whenever the teacher has been talking for a while, students will begin to lose interest. Teachers are rarely able to provide enough stimulus variation in their voices to maintain student interest over long periods. When you see students losing interest in what you are saying, then one way of regaining this interest is to ask the class a question. Providing opportunities for students to talk will regain the attention of the student responding as well as those in his immediate vicinity.

### Gestures

Gestures, using the hand, arm, face, or body, can direct the attention of the student and can do much to help students recognize important ideas and facts. Since students cannot remember every word spoken and every idea introduced during a class period, they need clues about the ones that are very important or somewhat important, and the ones introduced just to elaborate, clarify, or explain. A teacher can differentiate importance by gesturing at appropriate times; for instance, walking up to the blackboard and pointing to something written while telling the students it is important will more likely convey the word's importance than merely telling them it is important.

Overuse of gestures, on the other hand, is to be avoided. The continuous use of the same gesture will cause it to lose all effectiveness. Overuse may also result in a gesture's becoming a distracting mannerism. You will need to become purposeful in the use of gestures; use gestures when you have a specific purpose in mind, but avoid using them otherwise.

## Giving Directions

When students' interest and attention stray, you can reclaim their attention by telling them to look at you, to look at what you are showing them, or to pay attention. Use words to direct their attention. Again, this is a simple tactic, but an effective one.

## Movement

When you have remained in one location of the classroom for some time, changing your location can gain students' attention. Students far from you feel the distance. Merely changing the amount of physical distance between you and these students will increase their awareness and attention. The more the teacher stays at the front of the classroom, the higher the incidence of student off-task behavior. Conversely, the more the teacher moves around the classroom, the more students are likely to remain on task. When teachers move to different parts of the room, they tend to interact with different students, which makes the students more attentive. When students are working independently or in small groups at their seats, moving near them will help them stay on task and will help you recognize more readily when students are losing interest in or are having difficulty with a task so you can respond more quickly to their concerns.

## Sensory Change

Students should be provided with a variety of stimuli in a lesson. A change in the senses being used by the student can provide such variety. For example, after a student has been listening for a while, introducing something that will require the student to use a different or an additional sensory mode, such as sight, smell, taste, or touch, helps promote attention. Recognize that some students learn better by seeing, while others may learn better through hearing. Sensory preference can be partially accommodated by using multiple sensory channels and changing the senses students are called upon to use as activities progress. While overloading sensory channels is to be avoided, expecting students to use a variety of senses during any given lesson is advisable.

## Use of Voice

A teacher's voice should not be used solely to convey information to the students. Your voice should indicate the relative importance of information, convey the feelings you may be experiencing or would want the students to experience, and serve as a source of stimulation. When students start to lose interest, you can help them regain interest by merely increasing the volume of your voice. Importance of information can be indicated by slowing your speech and raising your voice. Varying the rate, volume, and inflection of your voice will help you maintain your students' interest.

## Silence

The use of silence in unorthodox situations can be a source of stimulation for students. One of the most effective demonstrations a teacher can do is one done in silence. Another use of silence is the pause that indicates to the students that what has just been said is something important and something that takes some time to think about. You can also use silence when students are being inattentive; remain silent until the students become silent and direct their attention toward you. Attempting to talk when students are inattentive insures that some students will not hear what is being said.

## Distractors

Any tactic used to gain students' attention can become a distracting affectation or mannerism when overused and actually interfere with their learning. Other sources of distraction include verbal mannerisms, such as "you know" and "OK," and indeed, almost any verbal behavior, gestures, or movement can become distracting when overused. Use refocusing tactics when appropriate, but be careful not to overuse them.

## REFERENCES

Arlin, M. 1975. The interaction of locus of control, classroom structure, and pupil satisfaction. *Psychology in the Schools* 12:279–286.

Brophy, J.E., and C.M. Evertson. 1976. *Learning from teaching: A developmental perspective.* Boston: Allyn and Bacon.

Dunn, R. and K. Dunn. 1978. *Teaching students through their individual learning styles: A practical approach.* Reston, Virginia: Reston Publishing.

Levy, J. 1983. Research synthesis on right and left hemispheres: We think with both sides of the brain. *Educational Leadership* 40(4): 66–71.

Turner, R.L. 1979. The value of variety in teaching styles. *Educational Leadership* 36(4): 257–258.

Witkin, H.A., C.A. Moore, D.R. Goodenough, and R.W. Cox. 1977. Field dependent and field independent cognitive styles and their educational implications. *Review of Educational Research* 47(1): 17–27.

## SUMMARY

### Definition of Refocusing
Refocusing is the process of interjecting stimuli into a lesson in order to gain, maintain, or increase student attention.

### General Refocusing
1. Classroom Environment
   a. Seating needs to reduce distractions and facilitate on-task behavior.
   b. Classroom furnishings should reflect the nature of the activities being conducted.
   c. Classroom furnishings should be placed so as not to distract ongoing activities.

2. Methodology
   a. Avoid repetitious methodology.
   b. Plan several distinctly different activities for each class period.

**Specific Refocusing**
1. Questions: Whenever a teacher has been talking for an extended period and students show signs of losing attention, then the teacher should direct questions to some students.
2. Gestures: Gestures should be used to call attention to things you want students to remember.
3. Giving directions: Telling students to direct their attention to you or to some other point of interest can help them regain attention.
4. Movement: Teacher movement about the room during lessons and seatwork can help students remain attentive and on task.
5. Sensory Change: Whenever students have been required to use one sensory mode for an extended period, changing the sensory mode can help students regain or maintain attention.
6. Voice: Variety in the volume and speed of the teacher's voice can help students stay attentive and distinguish between more and less important points.
7. Silence: Unexpected use of silence can result in gaining the attention of students.
8. Distractors: Overuse of any refocusing tactic can become distracting and cause students to lose attention.

# MICROTEACHING LESSON 4
## Presenting II

This lesson will provide another opportunity to practice the strategy of presenting. When planning this lesson, review the tasks from the microteaching lesson, "Presenting I," and study Chapter 3, "Presenting," and Chapter 4, "Refocusing." Incorporate refocusing tactics into this lesson. The only difference between "Presenting I" and "Presenting II" is the use of refocusing tactics.

### The Teaching Task

1. Remember that the introduction (set induction) of a lesson is crucial to learning. Include one in this lesson.
2. A major part of the presentation will be teacher talk. Feel free to ask some questions during this lesson, but confine them to simple questions to check students' comprehension of something you just said. Do not become involved in a discussion. That is not the purpose of this lesson.
3. Attempt to incorporate what you learned in the preceding lesson on Teaching for Instructional Objectives; continue to teach for the achievement of a clearly defined instructional objective. Include a statement of this objective at the top of your lesson plan for this exercise.
4. Throughout this lesson, try to incorporate the refocusing tactics you have just learned. Be conscious of the reactions of students, and try to provide the appropriate refocusing tactic at the appropriate time. *Review your audiotape from the Presenting I lesson to see if you have any verbal mannerisms that need to be eliminated.* Focus on eliminating those mannerisms during this lesson. Use as many different refocusing tactics as the situation will allow.
5. Present new content to your peers primarily using lecture. You will have approximately fifteen minutes available for your lesson, including time to set up. Since doing the introduction is so essential, feel free to spend considerable time for that purpose but not more than five minutes.
6. Include the following parts in your lesson:
    a. a set induction
    b. a lecture
    c. a closing
7. The lesson plan to be presented to your instructor on the day of the microteaching lesson should
    a. list your instructional objectives,
    b. list the preassessment questions to be asked,
    c. describe the set induction to be used,
    d. include an outline of the content to be presented,
    e. list the questions to be asked during the lesson to check immediate understanding,

f. list points to be included during your closing comments,

g. list questions you will ask at the end of the lesson to assess the attainment of the objective(s), and

h. list notes to yourself to include refocusing skills at appropriate points throughout the lesson plan.

## Observing the Lesson

The data for this lesson is similar to that of the preceding lesson with some additional observations needed. Review the explanations for making observations in the prior lessons before you observe for this lesson.

In order to record the gestures being used during the lesson, you will need to write about them when they occur or have access to a videotape recording of the lesson. Making a distinction between purposeful and distracting gestures would be helpful. The following symbols might allow you to record gestures as they occur:

- Purposeful Pointing—PP
- Purposeful Movement of Hands—PH
- Random, Distracting Gestures—DG

You may also add a description of each kind of distracting gesture by creating symbols for each kind and recording the modified symbol rather than this general symbol.

When recording the use of sensory channels, keep a record of the time in a column on the left and the sensory channels being used by the students in a corresponding column to the right.

| Time | Sensory Channels |
|------|------------------|
| 0–2 minutes | Hearing or listening |
| 2–6 minutes | Hearing and speaking |
| 6–8 minutes | Hearing and seeing |
| 8–9 minutes | Hearing |
| 9–10 minutes | Hearing and speaking |

# Presenting II
# Self-Analysis

Name _____

The items in this Self-Analysis are designed to help you identify those things that you are doing well and those things that you may still need to improve. Reread the section "Observing Teaching Behavior" in Chapter 2 and "Observing the Lesson" in this and earlier microteaching lessons prior to making observations for this lesson. Observe a videotape of your lesson if one is available. Record data that will enable you to make the assessments requested. Circle the number that corresponds to your assessment of your behavior on the tasks listed. *Attach your raw observational data to your Self-Analysis report.*

*Skills/tasks specific to this lesson*

1. The expression of the teacher's voice was effectively modified during the lesson.

| 1 | 2 | 3 | 4 | 5 |
|---|---|---|---|---|
| The teacher varied his or her voice to focus and/or maintain attention | | The teacher varied his or her voice only occasionally | | The teacher rarely varied his or her voice during the lesson |

2. Gestures were used to emphasize major points or to focus the students' attention to some location.

| 1 | 2 | 3 | 4 | 5 |
|---|---|---|---|---|
| Gestures were effective in focusing students' attention at a variety of times during the lesson | | Gestures were occasionally used to focus attention | | Gestures were either not used or those that were used were not effective in focusing students' attention |

3. Students were required to use several sensory channels during the lesson.

| 1 | 2 | 3 | 4 | 5 |
|---|---|---|---|---|
| The lesson required students to use at least two different senses, each for about equal times | | The lesson required students to use at least two senses, but one predominated | | Students were required to use only one sensory channel |

*Skills/tasks applied from previous lessons*

4. The set induction of the lesson created an interest in the lesson.

```
1               2               3               4               5
L_____|_____|_____|_____J
```

| Attention of the students was effectively gained | Some attempt was made to get the students' attention | There was little or no attempt made to get students' attention |

5. The set induction of the lesson gave direction to the rest of the lesson by relating it to past knowledge and experiences of the students and the topics to be taught.

```
1               2               3               4               5
L_____|_____|_____|_____J
```

| Overall direction or purpose of the lesson was clear | Overall direction or purpose of the lesson was somewhat clear | Direction or purpose of the lesson was unclear |

6. The teacher either stated the objectives of the lesson or in some other manner made the objectives clear by the end of the lesson.

```
1               2               3               4               5
L_____|_____|_____|_____J
```

| Objectives were clear to all students | Objectives were clear to some students | Objectives were not clear to any students |

7. The lesson focused directly upon the achievement of the objectives

```
1               2               3               4               5
L_____|_____|_____|_____J
```

| The presentation was directed at accomplishing the objectives | There were a few digressions from accomplishing the objectives | There was little relationship between the lesson and the objectives |

8. The lecture (presentation) was clear and well organized.

```
1               2               3               4               5
L_____|_____|_____|_____J
```

| Information being presented was understandable to the students at all times | Information being presented was somewhat unclear at times | Information being presented was seldom clear to the students |

9. The teacher closed the lesson in a way that reinforced, reviewed, and clarified the objectives and the importance or usefulness of the learning outcomes of the lesson.

| 1 | 2 | 3 | 4 | 5 |
|---|---|---|---|---|

Objectives were reinforced and the importance of the lesson to the students was made clear

Some attempt to review the lesson and its relevance to the students was attempted

Little or no attempt was made to review the lesson

10. The content was appropriate in both amount and relevancy.

| 1 | 2 | 3 | 4 | 5 |
|---|---|---|---|---|

Content was appropriate in both amount and relevance

Content was appropriate in one but not the other

Content was excessive and irrelevant

*Additional considerations: Record the number of tallies.*

1. Number of times I paused to allow students time to think about what had been said _____

2. Number of times I changed the volume of my voice noticeably to emphasize an expression _____

3. Number of filler words or sounds like "OK," "you know," or "uh" that were used _____

4. What were the gestures I used repetitiously, if any, that could be considered distracting? _____

*Answer the following items in the space provided.*

List of sensory channels students were called upon to use (list all in sequence as they occurred and the duration of each):

What *specific* changes will you make in your behavior during the next teaching lesson as a result of your analysis?

What specific changes in your *lesson plans* will you make to help yourself accomplish these changes during your next lesson?

# Presenting II
# Observation Guide

Name _____ Observer _____

Either record data during the teaching lesson or record data from an audio- or videotape that will allow you to make the judgments requested in this Observation Guide. Read the section, "Observing Teaching Behavior" in Chapter 2 and "Observing The Lesson" in this and earlier microteaching lessons prior to making observations for this lesson. Analyze the teacher's behavior and assess the effectiveness of that behavior for the following items. Circle the number that corresponds to your assessment of the teacher's behavior on the tasks. Ignore any teacher's behaviors not listed below. *Attach your raw observational data to this report.*

*Skills/tasks specific to this lesson*

1. The expression of the teacher's voice was effectively modified during the lesson.

   1     2     3     4     5

   The teacher varied his or her voice to focus and/or maintain attention

   The teacher varied his or her voice only occasionally

   The teacher rarely varied his or her voice during the lesson

2. Gestures were used to emphasize major points or to focus the students' attention to some location.

   1     2     3     4     5

   Gestures were effective in focusing students' attention at a variety of times during the lesson

   Gestures were occasionally used to focus attention

   Gestures were either not used or were not effective in focusing students' attention

3. Students were required to use several sensory channels during the lesson.

   1     2     3     4     5

   The lesson required students to use at least two different senses, each for about equal times

   The lesson required students to use at least two senses, but one predominated

   Students were required to use only one sensory channel

*Skills/tasks applied from previous lessons*

4. The set induction of the lesson created an interest in the lesson.

| 1 | 2 | 3 | 4 | 5 |
|---|---|---|---|---|

Attention of
the students was
effectively
gained

Some attempt
was made to get
the students' attention

There was little
or no attempt made
to get students'
attention

5. The set induction of the lesson gave direction to the rest of the lesson by relating it to past knowledge and experiences of the students and the topics to be taught.

| 1 | 2 | 3 | 4 | 5 |
|---|---|---|---|---|

Overall direction
or purpose of the
lesson was clear

Overall direction
or purpose of the
lesson was somewhat
clear

Direction or purpose
of the lesson was
unclear

6. The teacher either stated the objectives of the lesson or in some other manner made the objectives clear by the end of the lesson.

| 1 | 2 | 3 | 4 | 5 |
|---|---|---|---|---|

Objectives were
clear to all
students

Objectives were
clear to some
students

Objectives were
not clear to
any students

7. The lesson focused directly on the achievement of the objectives.

| 1 | 2 | 3 | 4 | 5 |
|---|---|---|---|---|

The presentation
was directed at
accomplishing
the objectives.

There were a few
digressions from
accomplishing
the objectives

There was little
relationship
between the lesson
and the objectives

8. The lecture (presentation) was clear and well organized.

| 1 | 2 | 3 | 4 | 5 |
|---|---|---|---|---|

Information being
presented was
understandable to
the students at
all times

Information being
presented was somewhat
unclear at times

Information being
presented was seldom
clear to the
students

9. The teacher closed the lesson in a way that reinforced, reviewed, and clarified the objectives and the importance or usefulness of the learning outcomes of the lesson.

| 1 | 2 | 3 | 4 | 5 |
|---|---|---|---|---|

| Objectives were reinforced, and the importance of the lesson to the students was made clear | Some attempt to review the lesson and its relevance to the students was attempted | Little or no attempt was made to review the lesson |
|---|---|---|

10. The content was appropriate in both amount and relevancy.

| 1 | 2 | 3 | 4 | 5 |
|---|---|---|---|---|

| Content was appropriate in both amount and relevancy | Content was appropriate in one but not the other | Content was excessive and irrelevant |
|---|---|---|

*Answer the following items in the space provided.*

Describe one thing related to the ten criteria above that you thought was particularly effective and that you feel the teacher would be advised to continue.

Offer at least one specific suggestion about what the teacher could have done to improve the lesson. Consider *only* those tasks that are directly related to the criteria assessed.

*Questioning* **5**

*T*he use of questions is an important part of teaching. Effective questioning is essential for conducting a variety of activities and tasks in the classroom. The purposes of questioning students include

1. to preassess students' knowledge prior to instruction,
2. to determine students' current understanding during a lesson,
3. to assess the attainment of objectives at the conclusion of a lesson,
4. to determine students' understanding of procedural directions,
5. to increase student involvement in the lesson, and
6. to provide students with opportunities to think about a topic in more depth, through discussions.

Checking for student understanding throughout a lesson insures better communication and clarity of instruction. Checking for understanding of directions reduces confusion and resultant off-task behavior. The effect of increased involvement in the lesson will be to increase student time on-task and student achievement. Providing opportunities to think about the content of a lesson will increase student understanding of the content. Increased depth of understanding may make the application of what is learned more probable.

## Questions

A teacher can ask many different types of questions during classroom instruction. Different types of questions may serve different functions. Being able to utilize certain types of questions at appropriate times is a valuable skill.

One way of analyzing questions is to consider their effect in promoting student responses. If a teacher asks a question that has only one correct answer, called a *closed* question, then a teacher can assess something specific a student knows. This kind of question will result in a restricted and usually relatively short response on the part of the student. Examples of this kind of question would be:

What is the capital of the United States?

What is the verb in this sentence?

What is the definition of *mineral?*

What is the English translation of *avoir?*

What is the name of a five-sided figure?

What is the probability of flipping heads again if a penny being flipped has just come up heads five times in a row?

What is the product of 23 times 54?

Closed questions are important for finding out whether students have understood something specific. Closed questions are usually asked at the beginning of a lesson for purposes of preassessment, during a lesson to check understanding of something that has been said or taught, and at the end of a lesson to assess students' learning. They may also be asked during a lesson to check student understanding of some directions just given.

Questions that call for one of a limited number of possible correct answers are commonly called *convergent* questions, that is, they converge on a particular set of answers. While convergent questions will likely result in slightly more student talk than closed questions, responses will still be rather limited. Some examples of convergent questions would be

What is one of the phases in mitosis?

Who was one of the last five Presidents of the United States?

What were three effects on the lives of the unemployed during the Great Depression?

What is one of the Spanish words for *child?*

Convergent and closed questions, which call for specific correct answers, pose some threat to students because they can be embarrassed by incorrect answers. This threat may prevent some students from volunteering to answer and getting involved in the lesson. Convergent and closed questions reduce students' opportunities and willingness to present their beliefs and opinions. If getting students to talk and think is a major concern in a given lesson, then teachers should ask less threatening questions that call for longer answers.

Since getting students to state their beliefs and opinions is an essential part of effective discussions, questions that allow several possible correct answers, called *divergent* questions, may be helpful in fostering more willingness and ability to respond. Some examples of divergent questions are

What are some similarities between plants and animals?

What are some of the differences between folk and classical music?

What are some of the conditions that likely led to the development of impressionistic art?

What kinds of rules do different ball sports have in common?

The least threatening kind of question of all, and the kind of question that would allow any student to respond, is the question that has no correct or incorrect responses—the *open* question. Open questions are valuable in encouraging student responses. Since there are no correct or incorrect answers, students can respond without embarrassment. An answer need only relate directly to the question to be appropriate. Some examples are

What are some things that could happen if medical science suddenly enabled the average life span to be 100 years?

What are some possible detrimental effects that could occur if English were the official language of a state?

What are some of the reasons you prefer some foods over others?

What are some of the possible effects of prejudice on the person holding the prejudice?

If a teacher wants to find out if students know certain facts, then closed and convergent questions are appropriate; however, if a teacher wants to encourage students to talk, then divergent and open questions are appropriate. The appropriate use of a question is determined by its function.

## Cognitive Levels of Questions

Another way of analyzing questions is to consider their use in the kinds of cognitive thinking students are able to demonstrate. During the instructional process, determining what students know, and the extent of this knowledge, is crucial to effective instruction. Studies have shown that many teachers restrict the cognitive level of their questions to the memory level; they merely ask students to repeat memorized facts (Centra and Potter, 1980; Clegg, 1971; Gall, 1970). The ability to repeat memorized facts is not a good indicator of a student's understanding of a topic. In fact, it is fair to say that if rote memorization is the extent to which students understand a topic, then they will not be able to apply the knowledge of that topic. That knowledge is therefore meaningless or useless (Ausubel, 1963). The constant use of memory questions conveys the message to the students that memorization is the kind of learning important to the teacher. If a teacher wants students to be able to use knowledge in any meaningful way, then the teacher must provide opportunities to use knowledge in the ways intended, in addition to mere memory, through teacher questions.

Classifying questions according to their cognitive level may be useful in helping you generate more effective questions in your classroom. The sequence in this classification also implies different complexities of understanding. Demonstrating comprehension of something would be more complex than merely knowing something (memory recall), applying something would be more complex than merely comprehending it, and analyzing something would be more complex than applying it. The cognitive levels suggested by Benjamin Bloom (Bloom, 1956), from less complex to more complex, are as follows: knowledge, comprehension, application, analysis, synthesis, and evaluation.

## Knowledge

Questions at the knowledge level ask students to remember facts about or ways of dealing with specifics. Some examples of questions about specifics are

What is the distance from the earth to the moon?

Who is the President of the United States?

What are the colors used in the Mexican flag?

What is three times four?

Questions about facts can include questions about rules, past trends, sequences, criteria, classifications, or generalizations.

• Examples dealing with rules:

What is the rule for proper use of _____?

What does the symbol _____ mean?

What kind of question should a teacher use to start a classroom discussion?

• Examples dealing with past trends:

What are two conditions that caused inhabitants of Texas to fight for independence from Mexico?

What has been the relationship between rising interest rates and the number of homes purchased?

What changes in the ethnic population of the United States are likely to occur from now until the year 2,000?

- Examples dealing with sequences:

    What are the steps involved in calculating an average value of a series of numbers?

    What are the stages a space shuttle goes through on launching?

- Examples dealing with criteria:

    What are three characteristics of a good teacher?

    What are the criteria used to judge the quality of a cut of beef?

    What conditions cause sleet to fall?

- Examples dealing with classifications:

    What are the names of the five senses?

    What are the stages of mitosis?

    What are the endings for the present tense of the verb *avoir*?

- Examples dealing with generalizations:

    What is the generalization describing the attraction and repulsion between magnets?

    What is the relationship between infidelity and divorce?

    What is the effect of campaign spending on the likelihood of a candidate's being elected?

## Comprehension

Comprehension questions help a teacher assess students' understanding of a literal message. This assessment can be done by asking students to translate, interpret, or extrapolate.

- Examples dealing with translation:

    Translate *el brazo* into English.

    Define the word *temperature* in your own words.

    What does the phrase "_____" mean?

    What is the name of the formula "NaCl"?

- Examples dealing with interpretation:

    What is the message implied in the sentence "_____"?

    What is the main idea conveyed in the word "_____"?

    What does the rising line on this graph represent?

- Examples dealing with extrapolation:

    Based on the past relationship between the outside temperature and the number of boats on the lake, what would probably happen if the temperature rose another 10 degrees?

    Given the rate of growth of the population to date, what will the population probably be at the end of next year?

    From the growth rate of the plant shown in the graph, what will the height of the plant be at the end of next week?

## Application

Questions at the application level assess the ability of students to apply the knowledge they possess without having been told the particular application they are to identify. Application questions ask students to identify solutions to problems, or in some other fashion demonstrate their ability to use knowledge in a novel or new circumstance.

- Examples of application questions:

    What is one way you might be able to put out an alcohol fire?

    What are three situations in which open questions would be appropriate?

    Recite three sentences using the correct present tense of the infinitive *to be*.

    What chemical compounds would result from the decomposition of the chemical _____ ?

## Analysis

Analytical questions assess students' ability

1. to examine a novel or new situation and break it into its component parts,
2. to identify the elements making the whole,

3. to identify the possible relationships that could exist between the parts, and
4. to recognize principles that might govern the operation of the whole.

• Example dealing with new situation and breaking it into its component parts:

> From an examination of this painting, identify some of the methods used by the artist to distort perspective.

• Examples dealing with identification of elements:

> What were the assumptions made by President Reagan when he stated that intelligence photographs indicated the presence of missiles on board the ship *El Torro*?

> From a study of the photograph of a farm, describe the most likely prevailing climate, and list those observations that led you to that conclusion.

> What factors influenced the outcome of the social experiment with communes in the United States at the turn of the century?

• Examples dealing with relationships between elements:

> What are some effects of the socioeconomic level of a community on its customs?

> What are some possible functions of acids used in the process of making steel?

> What are some of the possible causes of the recent drought in central Texas?

> What are the differences between the distinguishing characteristics of health quacks and legitimate health practitioners?

> What would happen if we changed _____?

• Examples dealing with principles:

> In what ways has the artist of this painting used color and value to emphasize despair and grief?

> What might cause a person to commit murder?

> What are the possible basic religious beliefs of those individuals advocating the death penalty?

> What would likely happen to transportation as we know it if suddenly there was no friction?

## Synthesis

Synthesis questions require students to organize knowledge in order to arrive at unique (for them) solutions or products of thought. Synthesis questions allow students to demonstrate their creativity.

- Examples include

> In what ways could our electoral system be modified to reduce the influence of large contributors on the outcomes of municipal elections?

> What would be an example of an open question that could be used not only to begin a discussion, but also to stimulate student interest in the topic?

> What kind of things could be done to reduce the incidence of drunken driving?

> What are some contributions art makes to enrich the lives of people who are not practicing artists?

## Evaluation

Evaluation questions require students to make judgments about relative values and to identify the bases for their judgments. Students are asked to analyze a novel or new situation, compare the situation with certain criteria or standards, then use the results of this analysis to make decisions about the degree of fit between elements in the situation and the criteria. This process is fundamental to decision making in life, and this level of understanding is essential for making wise decisions. When students' understanding reaches this level, they are able to use the knowledge in ways likely to have significance in their lives. A few examples illustrate evaluative questions.

> What are some assets and liabilities of the use of nuclear processes for the generation of electrical energy, and what are the criteria used to decide the difference between assets and liabilities?

> What criteria can be used to determine the value of poetry in the lives of people, and what are some of the values?

> What vocations are most appropriate for a person primarily interested in helping people solve their problems, and what factors help one choose a particular vocation?

> Which is more important for the welfare of individuals, protecting the environment or providing continued employment for workers, and what criteria help one decide?

> What knowledge is of most value to students we are teaching, and what criteria do we use to decide?

What are some of the distinctions between health quackery and legitimate medicine, and what possible benefits could result from an individual's ability to make the distinction between the two?

What would be a better way of _____, and what criteria can be used to decide?

## Uses of Cognitive Questions

Do not become overly concerned with the classification of cognitive questions into the categories just described. Bloom's taxonomy helps teachers determine the nature of the questions they tend to ask. Most educators think that effective teachers use a variety of cognitive questions. Early research studies indicated that using higher level questions in the classroom had little effect on achievement (Andre, 1979; Winne, 1979; Medley, 1979; Centra and Potter, 1980). Andre suggested that if teachers communicate that they expect their students to achieve higher level objectives; then students perceiving their task as one of acquiring as much as possible from instruction will be influenced little by higher level questions. On the other hand learners who only want to get through the instruction with the least amount of effort will be more affected by higher level questions. Later, more careful analyses of prior research (Redfield and Rousseau, 1981) found that when teachers predominantly use higher cognitive level questions, gains in achievement are positive. At present it appears that if the objectives and the tests used to measure achievement are essentially knowledge level, then the use of higher cognitive level questions will do little to aid achievement, and in fact, could be detrimental. On the other hand, if the objectives and the tests used to measure achievement deal with higher cognitive levels, then the *predominant* use of higher cognitive level classroom questions may result in achievement gains.

As is the case with any classification, questions do not always fall easily into the designated categories. Use this classification to guide the formulation of questions when planning lessons. Planning questions that are clear, that will serve the purpose intended, and that will assess not only knowledge levels of understanding but also higher levels is important.

## Formulating Questions

Clarity in phrasing questions is critical for effective questioning (Land, 1980; Gall and Gillett, 1980). The two predominant problems teachers have in phrasing questions are asking questions that call for only two alternative answers (e.g., yes or no) and questions that are ambiguous.

Ambiguity can lead to frustration for you and your students; therefore, stating questions with clarity is essential for effective interactions. When the intent of the question is unclear to students, fewer students will be willing to respond, students will attempt to guess at answers, students will ask the teacher for clarification, and lessons will tend to lose clarity. For example, what responses would be expected from the teachers asking the following questions?

> Tell me about a sonata.
>
> How is sound made?
>
> What do you know about life?
>
> How did the War of Independence begin?
>
> What exercises are good for you?

Obviously, the teachers asking these questions have not made the intent of the answers clear. The nature of the responses expected is so open-ended that students would find answering these questions difficult.

Asking questions that call for one of two alternative answers also rarely reflects the teacher's intent. For example, the question "Should immigrants to the United States be forced to learn English before they are granted citizenship?" calls for a "yes" or "no" answer, which is probably not the response the teacher really wants. In all likelihood an ambiguous follow-up question, "Why do you think that?" will be asked. A better question (and one that probably reflects the teacher's true intent) would be "What are some of the reasons for or against the proposition that immigrants to the United States should learn English before they are granted citizenship?" Ambiguous questions or those calling for one of two alternative answers will cause the student to guess or will require an immediate follow-up question by the teacher. In either case the intent of the questions would be unclear.

Here are some additional examples of undesirable phrasing taken from actual transcripts of classrooms:

> Which is more important in a workout, the warmup or the warmdown?
>
> What is more important in writing a short story, having precise descriptive detail of actions and mannerisms or having abstract generalizations?
>
> If you had the opportunity to do research on defense related projects, would you do it?
>
> Could we think of ourselves being the same without being able to see color?
>
> Does twelve-tone music have any musical value?
>
> Is Rr a heterozygous or homozygous genotype?

Commonly, questions calling for "yes" or "no" answers start with auxiliary verbs such as *do, could, is, are, have, can, should, was,* and *does*. Ambiguous questions quite often start with the words *how* and *why*. Avoid starting any questions with these words. When asking cognitive questions, try to start with the verbs *what, which, when, who*, and *where*. Starting with these words will not insure lack of ambiguous or two-alternative questions, but it will help. Clearly phrased cognitive questions will be precise, have a proper grammatical arrangement, and use easily understood terminology.

Do not think that all questions need to take the form of interrogative statements. Declarative statements indicating that you wish students to say something can be as effective, if not more effective, than interrogative statements (Dillon, 1979; Dillon, 1981). Dillon has found that declarative statements can often elicit longer and more complex student responses.

Do not expect that the cognitive level of the student responses will always correspond to the intended cognitive level of the question. Dillon found that about 13 percent of the responses will occur at a lower level and about 27 percent at a higher level (Dillon, 1982).

When planning questions, consider the answers you are likely to receive. If anticipated answers could go well beyond the topic you wish the students to think about, then rephrase your questions to focus on the intended answers. When planning lessons that involve questions, write out all key questions and include them in your plans. Rarely can a teacher create effective questions extemporaneously, and expecting to possess that skill without considerable experience is unrealistic. Careful planning will prevent false starts, uncertain pauses, poor transitions between questions, and unnecessary and distracting verbal mannerisms to fill in thinking time, all of which reduce the effectiveness of questioning (Land, 1980).

## Eliciting

A question used to evoke a pupil response is called an *eliciting question*. The process of indicating which student you wish to respond to your question is called *eliciting*. One of three patterns can be used to indicate who is to respond:

1. Ask a question and allow any student or group of students to respond spontaneously without indicating who is to respond.
2. Call on a student by name and ask the question that particular student is to answer.
3. Ask a question, pause, call on a student by name to respond, and then have that particular student respond.

The first option usually creates behavioral problems. Such a pattern allows and encourages uncontrolled talking, resulting in disruptive student behavior. Also, interacting with students in this fashion is impersonal, and students quickly feel that they are not being recognized as individuals. As a result, social constraints are removed, thus making disruptive behavior more likely. Allowing students to call out answers indiscriminately will not only create behavioral management problems, but will also make it impossible to conduct questioning in ways likely to encourage student thinking. Effective teacher responses to student answers become difficult if not impossible when students are allowed to answer without being called on to respond. The quality of thought in the classroom is thereby diminished. Such a pattern may not always be undesirable, but is best avoided when you are first learning to interact with groups of students.

The second pattern, calling on a student and then asking a question, is also undesirable. First, as soon as one student is identified to answer the question, other students cease to feel a need to think about the question. Second, the student being asked the question is put in a position of potential embarrassment, making it less likely that the student will respond successfully. The second pattern is often used by teachers as a means of behavior control after using the first pattern with the resultant calling out of answers by students. The second pattern is a poor substitute for good behavioral management and should be avoided.

The third pattern, asking a question, pausing, indicating a student to respond, and then getting a response from that student alone, is preferred for several reasons (Brophy, 1979). First, using this pattern avoids the difficulties presented by the other two patterns. Second, calling on individual students allows you to interact with individuals to the extent you desire.

You may feel that asking students to raise their hands and wait to be called on before responding to questions may stifle their participation. Keep in mind that deliberative bodies all have rules for recognition. While each individual has the right to speak in such a body, each also has an equal right to be heard. The only way to insure that each person's rights to speak and be heard are protected is to insure that not all individuals speak at once. Without rules, a deliberative body could not function. The value in allowing others to speak and be listened to is an important lesson for students to learn.

Until you are able to develop other options, the best means of insuring that you will protect the rights of individual students in your class is to expect students to raise their hands to be called on. The only students talking during a discussion will be those recognized by you and asked to respond by name. At least for the present, you should develop the pattern of asking a question and then calling on a student by name to respond. Do not allow any other students to answer, and if some call out unsolicited answers, do not accept those answers. This may seem rigid, but until your skills in behavioral management are well developed you would be advised to follow such a pattern.

## Use of Silence

Using silence will require effort. The natural tendency on the part of teachers is to fill in any silent periods that arise during questioning with teacher talk. The usual amount of silence can be measured in fractions of seconds (Rowe, 1974). However, using such small amounts of silence will reduce the quality and frequency of student

responses. The use of silence, or wait time, during questioning can have several well-established beneficial effects (Rowe, 1974; Rowe, 1978; Honea, 1982; Tobin, 1984).

1. The use of a brief silent period immediately following your stated question, but before you indicate the student who should respond, will result in students' being more likely to respond and respond correctly or appropriately.
2. When calling on a student to respond and not getting an immediate reply, allow some silence so that the student can think about the question. The student will be more likely to respond with time.

The use of wait time is not a natural behavior for most teachers. Developing this skill will take some practice. Initially, the use of silence will seem strange and artificial, but after you have developed the habit you will not dread the use of silence (Rowe, 1974).

## Teacher Responses

Use questions in the classroom as an instructional aid to find out what students know so that you can help them with their learning. Effective learning is not errorless. Students will make mistakes, and that is to be expected. One of the reasons for asking questions is to discover the difficulties in learning that students may be experiencing. All answers, correct or incorrect, provide valuable information to the teacher about what students are understanding and not understanding and should be viewed as opportunities for you to promote learning. Viewing student responses objectively is essential. Avoid getting your ego involved in the adequacy of student responses. You should not feel elated when students respond correctly, nor should you be upset when they respond incorrectly. Asking good questions is not enough; responding appropriately to student answers, even incorrect ones, is also essential (Good and Brophy, 1978; McKeown, 1977).

## Responses to Correct Answers

If students are going to respond freely to your questions, then they must be encouraged to do so. One form of encouragement is to praise correct replies. This form of reinforcement, however, can be insidious if not used properly. If you constantly tell students that their answers are excellent or good, then students will depend on your response as a measure of the quality of their answers. Constant praise also implies a criticism of students' answers when such praise is not forthcoming because praise tends to be evaluative and judgmental. Praise implies approval, while encouragement conveys acceptance. Forms of encouragement other than praise are sometimes preferred (Grey, 1974).

Encouragement may take the form of pointing out that a student's response was certainly justified on the basis of the evidence the student presented. A student given this kind of feedback may be encouraged to continue to do that kind of thinking. This form of encouragement attempts to point out to the student how his or her response or the thinking leading to the response will benefit him or her. Such encouragement is commonly referred to as *labeled* praise. When using praise, avoid overuse of unthinking praise like "Good!" "Very good!" "I like that answer!" and similar kinds of global praise. Try to encourage student responses and thinking by specifically pointing out examples of effective thinking and why the thinking was effective.

The most effective form of reinforcement is using something a student has said earlier in the lesson. Do this by mentioning the name of the student and what he or she said, and then expanding on that idea or incorporating that idea into the lesson in some fashion. In essence you are telling the student, "I not only heard what you said, but what you said has value to us in this lesson." That idea is powerful reinforcement indeed! While this form of reinforcement is seldom used by teachers, you should learn to incorporate it into your lessons.

If you find yourself constantly saying things like "That's correct!" or "That's right!" then you may be asking too many convergent or factual recall questions. These questions do not encourage student responses or thought and should be avoided except for purposes of drill and practice, for assessing student learning at the conclusion of lessons, or as a preassessment of student learning at the beginning of lessons.

When responding to students' answers with encouragement, try to develop a variety of responses rather than merely repeating the students' answers or adopting some repetitious expression of praise. Repetitious forms of praise and acceptance soon lose their effectiveness. Using students' ideas, and recognizing those ideas by name, is a powerful form of reinforcement. If other forms of encouragement are used, try to indicate the reason the student's contribution would likely help the student, that is, use labeled encouragement or praise. Also guard against giving more encouragement and praise to high achievers than low achievers. Studies have shown that this is a tendency on the part of many teachers (Braun, 1976). Since high achievers are more likely to give correct answers to questions, try to avoid such disparity in your responses.

## Responses to Incorrect Answers

Some teachers have the mistaken notion that students who provide incorrect answers should not be corrected or in any way criticized. No evidence has been found to support the notion that teachers should avoid letting students know when they have replied incorrectly and providing help in correcting the misunderstanding (Soar and Soar, 1979). In fact, available research suggests that correcting students when they are wrong may be more important than praising them when they are correct (Anderson and Faust, 1973). When correcting high ability students, an instructor who gives occasional, justified, mild criticism indicating that they could or should have done better tends to contribute more to their motivation and achievement than does one who only praises (Good and Brophy, 1977; Soar and Soar, 1979).

Many teachers react to incorrect answers by repeating the original question and asking the student to try again (Dunkin and Biddle, 1974). Repeating the question does nothing to correct the student's misconceptions or lack of knowledge. Failure to correct students when they respond incorrectly may indicate to them a teacher's disinterest. Look on your response not as a criticism, but as a response to correct misunderstandings, as corrective feedback that provides information to the student without any evaluation of the person.

When students are unable to respond or respond correctly to knowledge level questions, they should be given the correct answer. Do not encourage them to guess at the answer or call on others for the answer (Good and Brophy, 1977; Anderson and Faust, 1973). When the problem is a lack of specific information, simply furnish the student with the information. Inaccurate factual responses should be corrected; to do otherwise is to show a lack of respect for the truth.

When a student has responded incorrectly to a higher cognitive level question, you have two viable ways of responding. The first kind of response is to deal with the error in a fairly direct manner. This direct corrective feedback will

1. indicate that the student answered incorrectly, with phrases such as

   "Your answer was partially correct, but _____"

"That's not quite right."

"No, that would not usually be considered correct."

2. provide background information that appeared lacking in the student's under-standing including definitions or examples, and
3. provide another opportunity for the student to try again.

The other method of responding is one that some would call a Socratic method. This method involves breaking the original question down into a logical succession of smaller questions. Students are then asked to respond to each of these questions in sequence until they are led to a position of being able to answer the original question. They are then asked the original question, followed by a question similar to the first question. The latter question will then determine if the student can do the kind of thinking required to answer that kind of question (Brophy, 1979).

## Responses to Incomplete Answers

Some student answers to questions will obviously be memorized, textbook responses, others will be unclear or incomplete, while still others may be unsubstantiated assertions. All such answers are opportunities to help the students improve on their understanding (Brophy, 1979) by asking additional questions. These questions are referred to as *probes*. A probe is a question *about a student's response* that requires a student to say more about his or her answer, clarify something that he or she said, or justify his or her response. The teacher, when probing, can also ask another student to do one of these three tasks based on something another student has just said. Kinds of probes are

*Extending.* Asking a student to say more is called *extending*. After a student has responded, the teacher can ask the student to continue to respond. Asking students to extend their replies can be done in many ways, such as

"Say more."

"Say a little more about that."

"Please add to that."

"And then what?"

"What is the next logical step, assuming what you said is true?"

A student should be asked to extend a response if the response is incomplete or if you have some reason to think the student might like to say more about the response. Sometimes students will respond impulsively. If encouraged to continue, they may give their original comments more thought and proceed to expand on an initially limited answer. Asking students to extend their replies will allow them to respond with more deliberation and completeness.

*Clarifying.*   Asking a student to explain more clearly is called *clarifying.* Any word or phrase used by the student that represents memorized answers can be a source for clarification. A teacher could ask

> "Would you please say that in your own words?"
>
> "Please give me an example of what you mean."
>
> "Please rephrase your answer."

If, on the other hand, the student uses ambiguous words or phrases, then a teacher might ask

> "What did you mean by _____?"
>
> "Please give me an example of _____."
>
> "Would you clarify what you meant by _____?"

If a student responds to a question in a way that clearly indicates the answer is merely one memorized, then you should ask for clarification. Asking the student to clarify a response will enable you to find out if a student has any understanding beyond memorized answers. Students using ambiguous terms should be asked to define the terms or give examples. This process will insure clear communication between the student and you as well as between the student and other students. Clarity in communication is a valuable skill all students need to develop. This kind of probe encourages growth in clarity of communication.

*Justifying.*   Asking a student to give the reasons or evidence for an assertion is called a *justifying probe.* When a student responds to a question in a manner indicating lack of thought, or you are uncertain as to the basis for the response, you can ask questions like the following to encourage thought:

> "What reasons do you have for believing that?"
>
> "What evidence suggests that?"
>
> "Is there any evidence to the contrary?"

One important goal of education is to help students think more critically. Students need to learn to recognize the evidence or reasoning that leads them to adopt certain positions, beliefs, or understandings. One of the mechanisms teachers have to encourage this kind of thinking is to ask students to justify responses.

### Redirecting

Times occur when you will want to get as many students as possible to respond during a discussion. One of the ways this can be accomplished, and at the same time encourage the whole class to think about responses, is to redirect some of the students' responses by asking another student to extend, clarify, or justify a student's response. This tactic is called *redirecting*. For example, a teacher may call on a second student following a student response and ask the second student

"What reasons do you have for agreeing or disagreeing with _____?"

"Would you please expand on _____'s answer?"

"What reasons do you think would lead someone to _____'s position?"

"What evidence would support _____'s position?"

"What do you think _____ meant by _____?"

*Silent Probe.* When a student's answer to a higher level question is incomplete, unclear, or an unsubstantiated statement, you can accomplish much the same result as with verbal probing by just remaining silent. During the silence you continue eye contact with the student, nod, or in other nonverbal ways communicate a desire for the student to continue talking. This most important use of silence *following a student's response* is rarely used by teachers (Rowe, 1978). If you can remain silent at the conclusion of a student's response, the student will almost always continue talking. This additional talk will take the form of extending, clarifying, or justifying the initial response, in essence, probing without the necessity of a question. This use of silence will increase length of student responses, increase number of speculative responses, increase number of student questions, decrease failure to respond, increase student involvement, increase student reasoning, increase number of slower students responding, and increase evidence-inference statements (Rowe, 1978). These are powerful reasons for developing this skill.

Some caution in the use of silence, or wait time, is in order. When you are teaching, you need to be alert to the probability that you may have a tendency to vary the amount of silence you allow different students depending on your expectations for those students. This is true of all of the wait times that have been introduced. For example, if you have low expectations for students, you may have the tendency to allow less silence to occur when interacting with them. If you associate ethnicity with certain expectations, then you may allow varying durations of silence depending on the ethnicity of the student. You will need to be aware of such differences in your behavior if you expect not to discriminate against students based on expectations you have for them. The appropriate use of silence is something that you will want to examine carefully in your teaching, and then practice its use in order to utilize it naturally.

## Teacher Directed Discussions

The purpose of a teacher-directed discussion is to allow students, under the direction of the teacher, to examine some topic with which they already have some familiarity in order to develop a deeper understanding of the topic. The teacher's role is to help students remember what they already know and to help them to analyze that knowledge in ways that will allow them to come to a new (for them) understanding. *That students have some knowledge and prior experience with the topic to be discussed is a necessary precondition for any successful discussion.* Some characteristics of effective group discussions are

1. most, if not all of the students, have an opportunity to express their thoughts,
2. most, if not all of the students, have opportunities to talk approximately equal lengths of time,
3. most, if not all of the students, listen to what other students have to say,
4. students are permitted to examine their own and other's views in a nonthreatening environment.

Several kinds of topics are appropriate for discussion. These include

1. possible positions on issues,
2. making predictions or hypothesizing,

3. identification of problems that need further study,
4. interpretation of experiences,
5. exploring beliefs or attitudes.

## Starting a Discussion

The initial question used to start a discussion defines the topic. However, this first question should be an open or divergent question in order to encourage as many responses as possible. Students who respond early in a discussion are more willing to continue to respond. If students have not responded early in a discussion, they will be less likely to want to respond later. Thus, calling on as many students as possible early in a discussion is crucial.

While the initial question should be open or divergent, many teachers tend to begin with an ambiguous question, thinking such a practice is desirable. *Open* is not synonymous with *ambiguous*. While open questions will have many acceptable answers, they should not be ambiguous. For example, if you wish to have a discussion about the effects of discharged sewage on the wildlife in and along a stream, a question like "What do you think are some of the possible effects of pollution on our environment?" opens the subject up to any number of answers which would be totally unrelated to the subject to be discussed. You need, therefore, to phrase the question so that any answer focused on the topic would be acceptable. A properly worded question for the example above would be "What kinds of things do you think might happen to the wildlife in and along a stream when untreated sewage is discharged into the stream?" Notice that this question is open in the sense any answer directly related to the question would be acceptable, but it lets the students know the context of the discussion.

Similarly, divergent questions also need to have clarity even though these questions allow several answers to be correct. For example, when discussing income tax deductions for calamities, you could ask "Why should we have income tax deductions?" Notice that student replies to such a question could range far afield of the intended topic. The question "What hardships on members of our society could result if all income tax deductions dealing with casualty loss and medical expenses were to be discontinued?" would provide for a variety of answers, but would restrict the context to the topic being discussed.

Further, the initial question should not be one beginning with threatening phrases, such as

Can you tell me _____?

Do you know _____?

Who can tell me _____?

The initial question should also not call for a "yes" or "no" answer. One word answers do little to stimulate further discussion. Questions asking students to state their positions on issues also stifle student thought. Students have a tendency, once they have stated a position, to feel a need to defend that position. They will also then have the tendency to remember selectively that data supporting their position and forget that data contradicting their position. When examining issues, teachers need to try to ask questions that will allow a free examination of a multitude of positions without forcing a student to take a position prematurely.

Questions used to initiate a discussion should be stimulating, focus on the topic to be discussed, be in the students' vernacular, and be open or divergent. Kinds of phrases likely to stimulate discussion would include

What kind of things might happen if _____?

In what ways do you think your lives would change if _____?

What kind of things might you do if you were placed in the situation of _____?

In what ways could a change in _____ affect your lives?

What would be some of the problems created and some of the benefits derived from _____?

What possible changes could occur if _____?

When using open or divergent questions to increase the number of students responding during a discussion, attempt to get maximum mileage from such questions. When asking an open or divergent question, keep in mind that many answers will be acceptable in response to the question. After the first student responds to the question, you are encouraged to probe, use silence, and use reinforcement to the extent that these make sense for use with that student. You could utilize a rather extended period of time with that one student if you fully used all of these skills. However, focusing on one student would clearly not be desirable because you will want to include as many students as possible. Therefore, after you think you have interacted with the first student sufficiently, then *using the same question*, or a redirecting probe, move on to another student. Usually you should be able to repeat the initial open question several times before moving on to another question. You will need to sense when dropping a given question is advisable, but do not do so too quickly in an effort to hurry through a lesson. Discussions should not be hurried. Hurrying promotes superficiality and sloppy thinking. Discussions should promote deliberate thought, so do not try to cover too much in a limited time.

## During a Discussion

As you move through the discussion, the sequence of questions should allow an exploration of ideas through the use of divergent questions. Eventually, you will want to begin to narrow the discussion through the use of convergent questions. Do not be too quick in closing down the exploratory phase. You will want as many students as possible to contribute to the exploratory phase. You will also be trying to insure that all participate equally. Eliciting with names and requiring students to wait to be called on to respond will be crucial for accomplishing equal participation.

Probing student answers and using wait time will be very profitable in a discussion situation. Remember, the purpose of discussions is to help students explore ideas they already possess. Students should examine their positions on topics and identify ambiguities and inconsistencies, as well as recognize when positions held are based on incomplete, incorrect, or unsubstantiated information. Probing can insure that this kind of in depth thinking takes place. Look on incorrect and incomplete answers as opportunities for further instruction. Such a perspective will create an atmosphere that makes freedom of expression more likely. Constructive, corrective feedback, however, should be a part of discussion. Do not allow misconceptions to exist at the end of the discussion.

## Closing a Discussion

Any discussion would be incomplete without some form of summary to bring together the ideas presented. If the discussion has been successful, you should be able to use much of what the students said during the discussion in coming to conclusions in the last half of the discussion. Remember, using student ideas, and referring to the name of the person when doing so, is a very powerful form of reinforcement. A summary of a discussion should help students recognize instances of improved logic, corrected or additional information, and revised generalizations that may have been introduced. Through this process, students should have more clearly defined positions, and they should now be better able to recognize the evidence supporting their positions.

Discussions are instructional experiences and should be designed with some objective in mind. Of course, some instances when this may not be the case will occur, but for purposes of most instruction, your discussions will have some instructional objective. The closing of the discussion will then include some partial assessment of students' attainment of the objective. Objectives for discussions should be thought of in terms of the students' ability to think about a topic or justify a position they may hold on an issue, not in terms of the memorization of content. Your objective should therefore be an extension of the actual discussion, that is, students should be asked to apply, analyze, synthesize, or evaluate some aspect of the discussion. While learning some content at the recall level may have occurred, students should be expected to do more than merely recall what they learned as a result of a discussion.

## Improving Discussions

One of the purposes of having discussions, in addition to student learning of content, is to teach students how to interact effectively in group settings. With each successive discussion, students should improve their ability to wait to be called on to respond, to listen to what others have to say, to think about the content, and to contribute about equally.

Occasionally during discussions, students will obviously not be listening to other students but will be concerned with what they wish to say. One method of helping students become more aware of what others are saying is to stop the discussion momentarily and introduce an additional rule that states that before any student can respond he or she must repeat what the preceding student just said. The rule could be made to apply to one or a few students or the entire class. Students should be told beforehand that this will be in force. This will minimize any disruptions during the discussion. Interjecting this rule into discussions when needed will help students learn to listen to what others have to say.

Some students will seldom offer responses during a discussion, while others will tend to dominate. This situation can create barriers to effective discussions. One way of helping students become more aware of their responsibility to contribute and at the same time allow others an equal opportunity to contribute is to do a post-discussion evaluation. Such an evaluation is conducted by giving the students the following criteria for effective discussions prior to the discussion:

1. all students have the right to contribute equally
2. all students have the responsibility to contribute
3. all students have the responsibility to listen to others.

A small group of students can be assigned the task of observing the discussion to see how well the class meets these criteria. Or the class can be told to take notes during the discussion whenever some members of the class do not conform to these criteria. Following the discussion, the observers or the entire class can critique the discussion with these criteria in mind. Those students who have not contributed or those who have dominated the discussion will be identified by the students. As a result, contributions by these students will likely be altered during subsequent discussions. With time, your students will improve in their ability to participate in a group discussion.

## REFERENCES

Anderson, R.C., and G.W. Faust. 1973. *Educational psychology: The science of instruction and learning*. New York: Dodd, Mead.

Andre, T. 1979. Does answering higher-level questions while reading facilitate productive learning? *Review of Educational Research* 49(2): 280–318.

Ausubel, D. 1963. *The psychology of meaningful verbal learning*. New York: Grune and Stratton.

Bloom, B.S., (Ed.) 1956. Taxonomy of educational objectives, handbook I: Cognitive domain. New York: David McKay.

Braun, C. 1976. Teacher expectations: Sociopsychological dynamics. *Review of Educational Research* 46(2): 185–213.

Brophy, J. 1979. Teacher behavior and student learning. *Educational Leadership* 37(1): 33–38.

Centra, J.A., and D.A. Potter. 1980. School and teacher effects: An interrelational model. *Review of Educational Research* 50(2): 273–291.

Clegg, A.A. 1971. Classroom questions. In *The Encyclopedia of Education*, Vol. 2. New York: Macmillan.

Dillon, J.T. 1979. Alternatives to questioning. *High School Journal* 62:217–222.

Dillon, J.T. 1981. Duration of response to teacher questions and statements. *Contemporary Educational Psychology* 6:1–11.

Dillon, J.T. 1982. Cognitive correspondence between question/statement and response. *American Educational Research Journal* 19(4): 540–551.

Dunkin, M., and B. Biddle. 1974. *The study of teaching*. New York: Holt, Rinehart and Winston.

Gall, M.D. 1970. The use of questions in teaching. *Review of Educational Research* 40:707–721.

Gall, M.D., and M. Gillett. 1980. The discussion method in classroom teaching. *Theory into Practice* 19(2): 98–102.

Good, T.L. and J.E. Brophy. 1977. *Educational psychology: A realistic approach*. New York: Holt, Rinehart and Winston.

Good, T.L., and J.E. Brophy. 1978. *Looking in classrooms*. New York: Harper and Row Publishers.

Grey, L. 1974. *Discipline without fear*. New York: Hawthorne Books.

Honea, J.M. 1982. Wait-time as an instructional variable: An influence on teacher and student. *Clearing House* 56:167–170.

Land, M.L. 1980. Teacher clarity and cognitive level of questions: Effects on learning. *Journal of Experimental Education* 49:48–51.

McKeown, R. 1977. Accountability in responding to classroom questions: Impact on student achievement. *Journal of Experimental Education* 45:24–30.

Medley, D.M. 1979. The effectiveness of teachers. In *Research on Teaching*, ed. P.L. Peterson and H.J. Walberg. Berkelely: McCutchan Publishing.

Redfield, D.L., and E.W. Rousseau. 1981. A meta-analysis of experimental research on teaching questioning behavior. *Review of Educational Research* 51(2): 237–245.

Rowe, M.B. 1974. Pausing phenomena: Influence on the quality of instruction. *Journal of Psycholinguistics Research* 3:203–233.

Rowe, M.B. 1978. Wait, wait, wait. *School Science and Mathematics* 78:207–216.

Soar, R.S., and R.M. Soar. 1979. Emotional climate and management. In *Research on teaching: Concepts, findings, and implications,* ed. P.L. Peterson and H.J. Walberg. Berkeley: McCutchan Publishing.

Tobin, K. 1984. Effects of extended wait time on discourse characteristics and achievement in middle school grades. *Journal of Research in Science Teaching* 21(8): 779–791.

Winne, P.H. 1979. Experiments relating teachers' use of higher cognitive questions to student achievement. *Review of Educational Research* 49(1): 13–50.

————————————————— SUMMARY —————————————————

### Purposes of Classroom Questions
1. preassess students' knowledge prior to instruction
2. determine students' current understanding during a lesson
3. assess the attainment of objectives at the end of a lesson
4. determine students' understanding of procedural directions
5. increase student involvement in a lesson
6. provide students with opportunities to think about a topic in more depth

### Openness of Questions
1. Closed question: a question with one correct answer
2. Convergent question: a question with a few correct answers
3. Divergent question: a question with a variety of correct responses
4. Open question: a question with no correct or incorrect answers

### Cognitive Levels of Questions
1. Knowledge: questions that ask students to remember facts about specifics, ways of dealing with specifics, or ways of dealing with facts
2. Comprehension: questions that ask students to translate the message, interpret the message in some fashion, or extrapolate from the message.
3. Application: questions that ask students to identify solutions to problems or demonstrate the ability to use knowledge in a novel or new circumstance.
4. Analysis: questions that ask students to examine a novel or new situation and break it into its component parts, to identify the elements making the whole, to identify the possible relationships that could exist between the parts, and to recognize principles that might govern the operation of the whole.
5. Synthesis: questions that ask students to organize knowledge in order to arrive at unique (for them) solutions to problems or products of thought.
6. Evaluation: questions that ask students to make judgments about the relative values of things and to identify the bases for that judgment.

### Problems in Phrasing Questions
1. Two-alternative Questions: those that begin with auxiliary verbs such as *do, does, should, would, are, can*, etc. and that call for a "yes" or "no" or one of two other responses.
2. Ambiguous Questions: those that begin with the words *why* and *how*, or in other ways are open to overly broad interpretations.

### Properly Phrased Cognitive Questions
1. Many problems with poorly phrased cognitive questions can be avoided by beginning such questions with the words *what, which, when, who*, and *where*.

2. Properly phrased cognitive questions will
   a. be precise
   b. have a proper grammatical arrangement
   c. use easily understood terminology
3. Cognitive questions can take the form of an interrogative or declarative statement.

### Kinds of Eliciting Patterns

1. Teachers should avoid eliciting responses to questions by asking a question and then letting any student or group of students answer. Teachers who follow this pattern have more disruptive behavior in the classroom than teachers who do not.
2. Teachers should avoid calling on a student by name to respond to a question and then asking the student the question. This pattern relieves all students but one from thinking about the question, and places one student in the position of possible embarrassment.
3. When eliciting responses, teachers should ask the question, pause, then indicate the student to respond by name.

### When to Use Silence/Wait Time

1. immediately following a teacher's question, and before identifying the name of the student to reply
2. when having indicated a student to respond to a question and before the student's response
3. following a student's response

### Kinds of Reinforcement for Correct Answers

1. The lowest levels, and ones not be overused, include repeating a student's answer or categorizing an answer with an evaluative statement or phrase.
2. Pointing out to the student how knowledge of his or her response or the thinking that led to the response would be of benefit to the student is an effective form of reinforcement sometimes called encouragement or labeled praise.
3. Identifying something a student has said earlier by mentioning the student's name and what he or she said, and then using the ideas to further develop the lesson, is the highest and most effective form of reinforcement.

### Responses to Incorrect Answers

1. Knowledge Level Questions: provide the student with the correct answer.
2. Higher Cognitive Levels: two possible responses:
   a. Direct corrective feedback: indicate to the student that he or she answered incorrectly, provide needed background information, and then provide another opportunity for the student to answer.

b. Indirect corrective feedback: break the original question down into a sequence of simpler questions that could lead to an answer, and then ask the student to respond to each of these simpler questions. Follow this with a similar question to the same student.

## Responses to Incomplete Answers

1. Probing: a question to a student about his or her response to a question that asks for extension, clarification, or justification of his or her response.
   Kinds of Probes
   a. Extending: asking a student to say more about his or her response.
   b. Clarifying: asking a student to rephrase a reply or to give an example illustrating a response.
   c. Justifying: asking a student to give reasons for a reply or to provide evidence to support a reply.
   d. Redirecting: asking another student to extend, clarify, or justify a student's response.
2. Use of Silence/Wait Time: during this silence, maintain eye contact, and encourage the student nonverbally to continue.

## Teacher Directed Discussions

1. Necessary precondition: students must have had some prior experience or possess knowledge about the topic to be discussed.
2. Kinds of topics for discussion include
   a. possible positions on issues
   b. predictions or hypothesizing
   c. identification of problems that need further study
   d. interpretation of experiences
   e. exploration of beliefs or attitudes
3. Question used to initiate discussion should
   a. be stimulating
   b. focus on the topic to be discussed
   c. be in the students' vernacular
   d. be open or divergent

## Criteria for Effective Discussions

Most, if not all of the students,
1. have an opportunity to respond during the discussion
2. have an opportunity to respond equal lengths of time
3. listen to what other students have to say
4. are allowed to examine their own and others' views in a nonthreatening environment

**Strategies for Improving Discussions**

1. Occasionally interjecting the rule that students need to repeat what the preceding student said before saying what they wish to say improves the ability of students to listen to others.

2. Having the class evaluate a discussion based on the criteria of an effective discussion can help sensitize students to their roles in group discussions.

# EXERCISE 8

## Preassessment Questioning

One of the preconditions for an effective discussion is prior experiences with and knowledge of the topic to be discussed. To assess students' readiness for a discussion, ask a few closed questions just before the discussion to check their understanding of the prerequisite knowledge. This exercise will provide some practice in writing appropriate closed questions for preassessment.

Directions:

1. Write one instructional objective you would attempt to accomplish through a discussion.
2. Write one open or divergent question you would ask to begin the discussion designed to accomplish the instructional objective you wrote for item 1.
3. Write two closed questions you would ask to assess the students' understanding of prerequisite knowledge of the topic.

# EXERCISE 9

## Correctly Phrasing Questions Varying the Degrees of Openness

The purpose of this exercise is to provide some experience in correctly phrasing questions that have varying degrees of openness.

*Directions:* Write two questions of each of the following types: closed, convergent, divergent, and open. Use the suggestions for properly phrasing questions when you develop these questions.

# EXERCISE 10

## Writing Cognitive Questions

The purpose of this exercise is to provide some experience in writing cognitive questions at various levels of complexity. Remember, questions can be phrased at six levels of complexity: knowledge, comprehension, application, analysis, synthesis, and evaluation.

*Directions:* Write one classroom question in the subject in which you are being certified for each of the six levels.

# EXERCISE 11
## Writing Cognitive Questions on a Topic

The purpose of this exercise is to provide some experience in writing cognitive questions at various levels of complexity while confining the questions to a single topic. In Exercise 10 you were free to choose from an unlimited number of topics in your field of certification. In this exercise you are restricted to one topic. Writing questions at all cognitive levels about a single topic is a difficult process, but one that is a closer approximation to the task required when teaching.

*Directions:* Write one classroom question on *one* topic in the subject for which you are being certified at each of the six levels of Bloom's taxonomy: knowledge, comprehension, application, analysis, synthesis, and evaluation.

# EXERCISE 12
## Assessing Instructional Objectives

The purpose of this exercise is to provide some practice in writing higher level instructional objectives that could be accomplished through discussion and in formulating the closed questions that could be used at the end of a discussion to assess the attainment of an instructional objective.

Directions

1. Write one instructional objective at a level other than knowledge that could be achieved through discussion. Choose an objective you have not included in previous exercises.
2. Write one closed question that would be used at the end of the discussion to check students' attainment of the objective listed in item one.

# EXERCISE 13
## Writing Questions for Discussions

The purpose of this exercise is to provide some practice in writing open or divergent questions that could be used when starting a discussion with students. Questions used to initiate a discussion should (1) be stimulating, (2) focus on the topic to be discussed, (3) be in the students' vernacular, and (4) be open or divergent.

1. Write three open or divergent questions that could be used to begin discussion on a topic in your teaching field.

# MICROTEACHING LESSON 5
## Discussion I

In this microteaching lesson you will practice the skills of using open and divergent questions, probing, silence, and reinforcement. Reread Chapter 5, Questioning, before planning this lesson. The basic purpose of this lesson, to encourage student talking rather than your own talking, takes time and should not be rushed. Restrict the complexity of the discussion to the time available and limit the content of the lesson. Trying to discuss too much in a short time invites superficial examination of a topic.

### The Teaching Task
1. During this lesson, you should encourage equal participation of students.
2. Try to reduce the amount of time you talk and increase the amount of time the students talk. Try to insure that the time the students are discussing the questions of the lesson exceeds the time you are talking during the lesson.
3. Try to use each kind of probe about equally. While this introduces some artificiality, with practice you will find more than enough opportunities to use probing so that this attempt at equality can be dropped. Ideally you should use probing whenever a student says something that is incomplete, ambiguous, or lacks justification.
4. Attempt to use an eliciting pattern of asking the question and then calling on a student by name to respond. Do not accept responses from students who have not been called on to respond.
5. Attempt to use approximately three to four seconds of silence following each student's response. Recognize that the actual amount of silence will likely be much less than three to four seconds if students are eager to respond.
6. Try to come back to something a student contributed earlier, refer to the student by name, and then incorporate the student's earlier idea into your lesson. Sometimes this can most easily be done during the process of drawing generalizations from the discussion or in coming to a summary of the discussion. You will need to plan for this if you expect to be able to incorporate this skill into your lesson.
7. During this lesson, try to have some objective in mind, but *do not let this be your primary focus*. The primary focus of this lesson is increased student talk and reduced teacher talk.
8. Review the Self-Analysis, and attempt to incorporate all of the skills and tasks included on the form.
9. Lesson sequence:
   a. Begin the lesson with a set induction that includes at least one open or divergent question to start the discussion. Call on several students using the same question. Probe these students as needed.
   b. Follow this lead question with divergent questions that will cause the students to consider alternatives before you narrow the discussion down to convergent and closed questions.
   c. Attempt to bring closure to the interaction through the use of closed questions or through a summary of important ideas identified during the interaction.

10. The lesson plan to be turned into your instructor on the day of the microteaching lesson should include the following:
    a. List your instructional objective.
    b. Describe the set induction to be used including your verbatim initial question.
    c. List, in order of their use, all of the questions other than probes you intend to ask. To the left of each question, classify it as *open, divergent, convergent,* or *closed*.
    d. List any summarizing statements you intend to make at the end of the discussion.
    e. List the closed questions you will ask at the end of the lesson to assess the attainment of the objective. To the left of each question, classify the cognitive level of the question.
    f. Write notes to yourself throughout the lesson plan to help you incorporate the assigned tasks in your lesson.

## Observing the Lesson

Review the descriptions for making observations from earlier lessons before planning your observations for this lesson. In determining whether questions are open or divergent versus convergent or closed, use a verbatim recording of the questions asked. This will allow you not only to make a judgment about the openness but will also allow you to study the question for possible ambiguity. This process will also make needed changes in questions more apparent.

Tallying the number of times each probe is used is not particularly helpful. A verbatim transcript of each probe asked will allow an analysis of the kind of probe and the sequence and clarity of the probes. Students' verbatim responses to questions will help identify when the teacher used ambiguous language or when student responses needing to be probed were unprobed. Record only those student responses that illustrate some needed change.

At least three patterns of eliciting student responses are possible.

1. The teacher asks a question and students respond without being called on.
2. The teacher calls the student by name and then asks the question.
3. The teacher asks a question and then calls the student by name to respond.

These three patterns can be symbolized for recording purposes as Q-R, N-Q-R and Q-N-R. When recording data regarding eliciting patterns used by the teacher, record each pattern in the order it occurs. Rather than using the symbol "N" for the name of the student, use the actual name of the student. Merely recording the frequency of each pattern used hides useful information. For example, take the following two observations:

| Observation #1 | Observation #2 |
|---|---|
| Q-R | Q-Mary-R |
| Q-R | Q-Bob-R |
| Q-R | Q-Mary-R |
| Bob-Q-R | Q-Bob-R |
| Mary-Q-R | Q-Bob-R |
| Q-R | Q-R |
| Q-R | Q-Al-R |
| Alice-Q-R | Q-Bob-R |

This first sequence demonstrates a teacher's tendency to revert to the N-Q-R pattern when students start calling out answers. This pattern would not be apparent from a tally of frequencies. The second sequence allows a study of the frequency with which patterns are used, and it also shows which students were called on and in what sequence. This second sequence shows that a few students dominated the discussion. This information may help a teacher recognize when he or she is concentrating on only certain parts of the room, common for beginning teachers.

Since not all of the behaviors to be observed for this lesson can be observed simultaneously, a tape recording is absolutely necessary for later analysis. Plan your observation carefully beforehand so that you are clear about those things that need to be observed live and written down and those things that can later be observed from the tape recording.

# Discussion I
# Self-Analysis

Name _____

The items on this Self-Analysis are designed to help you identify those tasks you are doing well and those you may need to improve. Read the section, "Observing Teaching Behavior" in Chapter 2 and "Observing the Lesson" in this and earlier microteaching lessons prior to making observations for this lesson. Observe a videotape or listen to an audiotape of your lesson. Record data that will enable you to make the assessments requested. Circle the number that corresponds to your assessment of your behavior on the tasks of the lesson. *Attach your raw data to your Self- Analysis report.*

**Skills/tasks specific to this lesson**

1. The teacher asked open or divergent questions during the early part of the lesson.

| 1 | 2 | 3 | 4 | 5 |
|---|---|---|---|---|
| Teacher asked only open questions during the first half of the lesson | | Teacher asked few open questions during the first half of the lesson | | Teacher asked no open questions during the first half of the lesson |

2. The teacher used each open or divergent question to increase student participation.

| 1 | 2 | 3 | 4 | 5 |
|---|---|---|---|---|
| Teacher elicited responses from more than one student on each of the open questions asked | | Teacher elicited responses from more than one student for at least two open questions asked | | Teacher elicited responses from only one student for each open question asked |

3. The phrasing of the teacher's questions reflected the intent of the question clearly and was unambiguous.

| 1 | 2 | 3 | 4 | 5 |
|---|---|---|---|---|
| All questions were clear and unambiguous | | About one-half of the questions were clear and unambiguous | | Few questions were clear and unambiguous |

4. The teacher made use of extending, clarifying, and justifying probes equally.

| 1 | 2 | 3 | 4 | 5 |
|---|---|---|---|---|

Teacher made use of all three probes almost equally

Teacher used some probes of some kinds

Teacher used few if any probes

5. The teacher made use of silence following student's responses.

| 1 | 2 | 3 | 4 | 5 |
|---|---|---|---|---|

Three to four seconds on the average

One to two seconds on the average

Less than one second on the average

6. The teacher made proper use of verbal and nonverbal reinforcement.

| 1 | 2 | 3 | 4 | 5 |
|---|---|---|---|---|

Teacher frequently used labeled praise or used student ideas as forms of reinforcement

Teacher used some verbal and nonverbal reinforcement, but it was somewhat repetitious

Teacher rarely used verbal or nonverbal reinforcement

## Skills/tasks applied from previous lessons

7. The set induction of the lesson created an interest in the lesson.

| 1 | 2 | 3 | 4 | 5 |
|---|---|---|---|---|

Attention of the students was effectively gained

Some attempt was made to get the students' attention

There was little or no attempt made to get students' attention

8. The set induction of the lesson gave direction to the rest of the lesson by relating it to students' past knowledge and experiences and the topics to be taught.

| 1 | 2 | 3 | 4 | 5 |
|---|---|---|---|---|

Overall direction or purpose of the lesson was clear

Overall direction or purpose of the lesson was somewhat clear

Direction or purpose of the lesson was unclear

9. The teacher either stated the objectives of the lesson or in some other manner made the objectives clear by the end of the lesson.

| 1 | 2 | 3 | 4 | 5 |
|---|---|---|---|---|
| Objectives were clear to all students | | Objectives were clear to some students | | Objectives were not clear to any students |

10. The content was appropriate in both amount and relevancy.

| 1 | 2 | 3 | 4 | 5 |
|---|---|---|---|---|
| Content was appropriate in both amount and relevancy | | Content was appropriate in one but not the other | | Content was excessive and irrelevant |

Number of open or divergent questions asked during the first half of the lesson _____

Percent of time I talked during the lesson _____

*Record your tallies here.*

Teacher Talking

Students Talking

Silence or Confusion

Number of times I used each of the following eliciting patterns:

Question-Name-Response _____

Name-Question-Response _____

Question-Response _____

Number of times I used each of the following probes:

Extending _____

Clarifying _____

Justifying _____

Number of times I merely repeated a student's response (Avoid excessive use) _____

Complete each of the following tasks on a separate sheet of paper.

1. Record each of your eliciting questions verbatim. Do not include probing questions.
2. If any questions are ambiguous or in any other fashion inadequate, indicate the nature of the inadequacy beneath each question.
3. Rephrase all inadequate questions to remove the inadequacy.
4. Format your analysis for each question as follows:
   a. eliciting question written verbatim
   b. identification of the inadequacy (or write "No inadequacy")
   c. rephrased question (or write "No modifications necessary")

What specific skills practiced during this lesson would you like to improve in your next lesson? Be *specific* about the skill to be changed and the extent to which you will change your *behavior.*

# Discussion I
# Observation Guide

Name _____ Observer _____

Record data during the teaching lesson, listen to an audiotape or watch a videotape of the lesson, and assess the effectiveness of the teacher's behavior for the following items. Read the section, "Observing Teaching Behavior" in Chapter 2 and "Observing the Lesson" in this and earlier microteaching lessons prior to making observations for this lesson. Circle the number that corresponds to your assessment of the teacher's behavior. Ignore any teaching behaviors not listed below. *Attach your observational data to this report.*

### Skills/tasks specific to this lesson

1. The teacher asked open or divergent questions during the early part of the lesson.

| 1 | 2 | 3 | 4 | 5 |
|---|---|---|---|---|
| Teacher asked only open questions during the first half of the lesson | | Teacher asked few open questions during the first half of the lesson | | Teacher asked no open questions during the first half of the lesson |

2. The teacher used each open or divergent question to increase student participation.

| 1 | 2 | 3 | 4 | 5 |
|---|---|---|---|---|
| Teacher elicited responses from more than one student on each of the open questions asked | | Teacher elicited responses from more than one student for at least two open questions asked | | Teacher elicited responses from only one student for each open question asked |

3. The phrasing of the teacher's questions reflected the intent of the question clearly and was unambiguous.

| 1 | 2 | 3 | 4 | 5 |
|---|---|---|---|---|
| All questions were clear and unambiguous | | About one-half of the questions were clear and unambiguous | | Few questions were clear and unambiguous |

4. The teacher made use of extending, clarifying, and justifying probes equally.

| 1 | 2 | 3 | 4 | 5 |
|---|---|---|---|---|

Teacher made use of all three probes almost equally

Teacher used some probes of some kinds

Teacher used few if any probes

5. The teacher made use of silence following student's responses.

| 1 | 2 | 3 | 4 | 5 |
|---|---|---|---|---|

Approximately three to five seconds on the average

Approximately one to two seconds on the average

Approximately less than one second on the average

6. The teacher made proper use of verbal and nonverbal reinforcement.

| 1 | 2 | 3 | 4 | 5 |
|---|---|---|---|---|

Teacher frequently used labeled praise or student ideas as forms of reinforcement

Teacher used some verbal and nonverbal reinforcement, but it was somewhat repetitious

Teacher rarely used verbal or nonverbal reinforcement

## Skills/tasks applied from previous lessons

7. The set induction of the lesson created an interest in the lesson.

| 1 | 2 | 3 | 4 | 5 |
|---|---|---|---|---|

Attention of the students was effectively gained

Some attempt was made to get the students' attention

There was little or no attempt made to get students' attention

8. The set induction of the lesson gave direction to the rest of the lesson by relating it to students' past knowledge and experiences and the topics to be taught.

| 1 | 2 | 3 | 4 | 5 |
|---|---|---|---|---|

Overall direction or purpose of the lesson was clear

Overall direction or purpose of the lesson was somewhat clear

Direction or purpose of the lesson was unclear

9. The teacher either stated the objectives of the lesson or in some other manner made the objectives clear by the end of the lesson.

```
1               2               3               4               5
|_____|_____|_____|_____|
```

| Objectives were clear to all students | Objectives were clear to some students | Objectives were not clear to any students |
|---|---|---|

10. The content was appropriate in both amount and relevancy.

```
1               2               3               4               5
|_____|_____|_____|_____|
```

| Content was appropriate in both amount and relevancy | Content was appropriate in one but not the other | Content was excessive and irrelevant |
|---|---|---|

## Answer the following items in the space provided.

Describe one thing related to the ten criteria above that you thought was particularly effective and that you feel the teacher would be advised to continue.

Offer at least one specific suggestion about what the teacher could have done to improve the lesson. Consider only those tasks directly related to the criteria assessed above.

# MICROTEACHING LESSON 6 _____
## Discussion II

In the last lesson, you had the opportunity to practice the skills involved in a discussion situation: open and divergent questions, set induction, effective eliciting patterns, probing, silence, and reinforcement. In this lesson, you will have the opportunity to continue practicing these skills in a discussion controlled by you, the teacher, in an effort to achieve a specific instructional objective. This is commonly called a teacher-directed discussion. The only difference between this lesson and the Discussion I lesson is the attempt to accomplish a particular objective.

This lesson is a complex series of tasks that will require careful preparation if you are to be effective. Give each question careful consideration, plan on when and how to probe, build reminders in your plans to do certain things at certain times, and study your plans until you are familiar with all aspects of what you want to do. If the discussion is to proceed smoothly, do not be overly dependent on your plans. To insure effectiveness, a few practice runs with friends may be helpful.

### The Teaching Task

Attempt to accomplish the following:

1. Incorporate an effective set induction strategy into the lesson to start the discussion.
2. Use an appropriate pattern (Q-N-R 100%) in eliciting responses from students.
3. Start the discussion with open questions and call on more than one student to respond to each question.
4. Talk less than half the time during the first half of the discussion.
5. Use all forms of probing about equally.
6. Use a variety of cognitive questions that will help you accomplish your objective.
7. Formulate well-phrased questions that are unambiguous and directed toward the topic. Students should have no need to ask for clarification, and you should have no need to rephrase questions because students do not understand what is being asked.
8. Use silence *after* student responses.
9. Use student ideas expressed in the first half of the discussion to arrive at conclusions during the last half of the discussion. Refer to the name of the student when using that student's idea. (Try to do this at least twice.)
10. Use closed questions as part of your summary to assess attainment of objectives. Try to have an objective and a closed question that involve a cognitive level beyond the knowledge level.
11. Since this lesson is an attempt to achieve a particular objective through a discussion method, the objective should become clear to all of the students.
12. The discussion should stay centered on the topic at hand, and, should it stray from the topic, you will respond in ways that will return discussion to the topic without delay.

(NOTE: When you are the student, *do not ask questions* about the lesson *unless* some question asked by the teacher is unclear. Then feel free to ask questions to clarify the question.)

13. Follow the same sequence as the last lesson. Start with open or divergent questions, and, after exploring the topic, begin to use convergent questions in order to focus in on your objective. The end of the lesson may include a brief presentation in order to summarize the discussion. This summary is then followed by closed questions to check for the attainment of the objective.

14. The lesson plan to be turned into your instructor on the day of the microteaching lesson should
    a. list your instructional objective.
    b. describe the set induction to be used, including your verbatim initial question.
    c. list, in order of their use, all of the questions other than probes you intend to ask. To the left of each question classify the question as *open, divergent, convergent,* or *closed.*
    d. list any summarizing statements you intend to make at the end of the discussion.
    e. list the closed questions you will ask at the end of the lesson to assess the attainment of the objective. To the left of each question classify the cognitive level of the question.
    f. make notes to yourself throughout the lesson plan that will help you incorporate the assigned tasks in your lesson.

## Observing the Lesson

Two additional observations will be made in this lesson in addition to those for Lesson 5. First, make a verbatim recording of the teacher using students' ideas. Second, make a verbatim list of the questions asked (other than probes) and categorize each question by cognitive level.

# Discussion II
# Self-Analysis

Name _____

The items on this Self-Analysis are designed to help you identify those things that you are doing well and those that you may need to improve. Read the section, "Observing Teaching Behavior" in Chapter 2 and "Observing the Lesson" in this and earlier microteaching lessons prior to making observations for this lesson. Listen to an audiotape or watch a videotape of your lesson, and record data that will enable you to make the assessments requested. Circle the number that corresponds to your assessment of your behavior on the tasks of the lesson. *Attach your raw observational data to your Self-Analysis report.*

## Skills/tasks specific to this lesson

1. The teacher's eliciting questions during the first half of the lesson were open or divergent.

| 1 | 2 | 3 | 4 | 5 |
|---|---|---|---|---|
| Teacher asked open or divergent questions | | Teacher asked some open or divergent questions | | Teacher asked few open or divergent questions |

2. The phrasing of the teacher's questions reflected the intent of the question clearly and was unambiguous.

| 1 | 2 | 3 | 4 | 5 |
|---|---|---|---|---|
| All questions were clear and unambiguous | | About one-half of the questions were clear and unambiguous | | Few questions were clear and unambiguous |

3. The teacher asked a variety of cognitive questions.

| 1 | 2 | 3 | 4 | 5 |
|---|---|---|---|---|
| Teacher used five categories | | Teacher used three categories | | Teacher used only knowledge questions |

4. The teacher used an appropriate eliciting pattern.

| 1 | 2 | 3 | 4 | 5 |
|---|---|---|---|---|
| Almost all were Q–N–R patterns | | About an equal mix of Q–R, N–Q–R, and Q–N–R | | Almost all were Q–R and N–Q–R |

5. The teacher made use of silence following student's responses to encourage additional thinking.

| 1 | 2 | 3 | 4 | 5 |
|---|---|---|---|---|

Three to five seconds on the average

One to two seconds on the average

Less than one second on the average

6. The teacher made use of extending, clarifying, and justifying probes equally.

| 1 | 2 | 3 | 4 | 5 |
|---|---|---|---|---|

Teacher made use of all three probes almost equally

Teacher used some probes of some kinds

Teacher used few if any probes

7. The teacher made use of student ideas as a form of reinforcement.

| 1 | 2 | 3 | 4 | 5 |
|---|---|---|---|---|

Four or more times

Two times

Not at all

8. The lesson focused directly on the achievement of the objectives.

| 1 | 2 | 3 | 4 | 5 |
|---|---|---|---|---|

All discussion was directed at the objectives

There were a few digressions from the objectives

There was little related to the objectives

9. The teacher used closed questions as part of the summary of the discussion to assess the objectives of the lesson.

| 1 | 2 | 3 | 4 | 5 |
|---|---|---|---|---|

Teacher asked a sufficient number of questions to assess the objectives

Teacher assessed some of the objectives

Teacher asked no closed questions to assess the objectives

10. The teacher made the objective of the lesson clear.

| 1 | 2 | 3 | 4 | 5 |
|---|---|---|---|---|

The objective of the lesson was clear

The objective of the lesson was somewhat clear

The objective of the lesson was unknown

## Skills/tasks applied from previous lessons

11. The set induction of the lesson created an interest in the lesson.

| 1 | 2 | 3 | 4 | 5 |
|---|---|---|---|---|
| Attention of the students was effectively gained | | Some attempt was made to get the students' attention | | There was little or no attempt made to get students' attention |

12. The set induction of the lesson gave direction to the rest of the lesson by relating it to students' past knowledge and experiences and the topics to be taught.

| 1 | 2 | 3 | 4 | 5 |
|---|---|---|---|---|
| Overall direction or purpose of the lesson was clear | | Overall direction or purpose of the lesson was somewhat clear | | Direction or purpose of the lesson was unclear |

13. The content was appropriate in both amount and relevancy.

| 1 | 2 | 3 | 4 | 5 |
|---|---|---|---|---|
| Content was appropriate in both amount and relevancy | | Content was appropriate in one but not the other | | Content was excessive and irrelevant |

## Complete the following tasks on separate sheets of paper.

1. Record verbatim all eliciting questions you asked in the sequence they were asked. Record everything from the time you first started to formulate the question to the time you actively elicited a response from a student including all attempts to rephrase a question until it was in a form that was understandable.
2. Record verbatim the probes you used with each question immediately following the question. Indent the probes so that they will not be confused with the question.
3. Record, in sequence after each eliciting question, the pattern for each eliciting question you made. The three patterns are
   a. Teacher Question—Spontaneous Student Response

      Symbol: Q-R or Q-MR (for multiple responses)

   b. Teacher Question—Name of Student—Student Response

      Symbol: Q-(Name)-R (Use the actual name.)

**131**

c. Student Name—Question—Student Response

   Symbol: (Name)-Q-R (Use the actual name.)

4. To the right of each question, indicate by the words "cut off" the times you cut off a student's response by immediately beginning to talk. Combine the data from the four tasks to look something like this:

- Question: What are some foods that you dislike? Q-(Barb)-R Cut off
- Probe: What do you think might be some of the causes for your dislike of spinach?
- Probe: Bob, what are some reasons other than those Barb has suggested for disliking foods? Cut off

What *specific* improvements on the above tasks will you make in your next microteaching lesson?

# Discussion II
# Observation Guide

Name _____   Observer _____

Record data during the teaching lesson, listen to an audiotape or watch a videotape of the lesson, and record data that will enable you to make the assessments requested. Read the section, "Observing Teaching Behavior" in Chapter 2 and "Observing the Lesson" in this and earlier microteaching lessons prior to making observations for this lesson. Circle the number that corresponds to your assessment of the teacher's behavior on the tasks. Ignore any teaching behaviors not listed below. *Attach your observational data to this report.*

## Skills/tasks specific to this lesson

1. The teacher's eliciting questions during the first half of the lesson were open or divergent.

   | 1 | 2 | 3 | 4 | 5 |
   |---|---|---|---|---|
   | Teacher asked open or divergent questions | | Teacher asked some open or divergent questions | | Teacher asked few open or divergent questions |

2. The phrasing of the teacher's questions reflected the intent of the question clearly and was unambiguous.

   | 1 | 2 | 3 | 4 | 5 |
   |---|---|---|---|---|
   | All questions were clear and unambiguous | | About one-half of the questions were clear and unambiguous | | Few questions were clear and unambiguous |

3. The teacher asked a variety of cognitive questions.

   | 1 | 2 | 3 | 4 | 5 |
   |---|---|---|---|---|
   | Teacher used five categories | | Teacher used three categories of questions | | Teacher used only knowledge questions |

4. The teacher used an appropriate eliciting pattern.

   | 1 | 2 | 3 | 4 | 5 |
   |---|---|---|---|---|
   | Almost all were Q–N–R patterns | | About an equal mix of Q–R, N–Q–R, and Q–N–R | | Almost all were Q–R and N–Q–R |

5. The teacher made use of extending, clarifying, and justifying probing questions equally.

```
1_____2_____3_____4_____5
```

| Teacher made use of all three probes almost equally | Teacher used some probes of some kinds | Teacher used few if any probes |

6. The teacher made use of silence following student's responses to encourage additional thinking.

```
1_____2_____3_____4_____5
```

| Three to five seconds on the average | One to two seconds on the average | Less than one second on the average |

7. The teacher made use of student ideas as a form of reinforcement.

```
1_____2_____3_____4_____5
```

| Four or more times | Two times | Not at all |

8. The lesson focused directly on the achievement of the objectives.

```
1_____2_____3_____4_____5
```

| All discussion was directed at the objectives | There were a few digressions from the objectives | There was little related to the objectives |

9. The teacher used closed questions as part of the summary of the discussion to assess the objectives of the lesson.

```
1_____2_____3_____4_____5
```

| Teacher asked a sufficient number of questions to assess the objectives | Teacher assessed some of the objectives | Teacher asked no closed questions to assess the objectives |

10. The teacher made the objective of the lesson clear.

```
1_____2_____3_____4_____5
```

| The objective of the lesson was clear | The objective of the lesson was somewhat clear | The objective of the lesson was unknown |

Skills/tasks applied from previous lessons

11. The set induction of the lesson created an interest in the lesson.

```
1              2              3              4              5
|_____|_____|_____|_____|
```

| Attention of the students was effectively gained | | Some attempt was made to get the students' attention | | There was little or no attempt made to get students' attention |

12. The set induction of the lesson gave direction to the rest of the lesson by relating it to students' past knowledge and experiences and the topics to be taught.

```
1              2              3              4              5
|_____|_____|_____|_____|
```

| Overall direction or purpose of the lesson was clear | | Overall direction or purpose of the lesson was somewhat clear | | Direction or purpose of the lesson was unclear |

13. The content was appropriate in both amount and relevancy.

```
1              2              3              4              5
|_____|_____|_____|_____|
```

| Content was appropriate in both amount and relevancy | | Content was appropriate in one but not the other | | Content was excessive and irrelevant |

**Answer the following items in the spaces provided.**

Percent of time the teacher was talking during the first ten minutes of the lesson _____

Record your tallies for only the first ten minutes.

Teacher Talking

Students Talking

Silence or Confusion

Describe one thing related to the thirteen criteria above you thought was particularly effective and that you feel the teacher would be advised to continue.

Offer at least one specific suggestion about what the teacher could have done to improve the lesson. Consider only those tasks that are directly related to the criteria assessed above.

# Teaching Concepts and Generalizations  **6**

*I*n earlier chapters you were introduced to some basic teaching skills and how they are applied in presentation and discussion lessons. In this chapter you will be introduced to another teaching strategy using these basic skills. Since you probably have had limited experiences with this new context, some examples may provide needed insights. Study the teaching situations presented carefully. Look for similarities and differences between the two situations being described.

## Lessons

### A Spelling Lesson

One common spelling difficulty is deciding when to double the final letter of a root word when adding a suffix. For example, is the correct spelling *referred* or *refered*, or *occurring* or *occuring*? Several ways of teaching the rules governing the spelling of such words are available. Two examples follow.

### *Teacher A*

Teacher A begins the lesson by explaining to the students that some words are difficult to spell and are therefore commonly misspelled. The teacher goes on to explain that ways exist for students to overcome these difficulties, but first finding out if they have such difficulties is important. The teacher gives the students a short spelling quiz using commonly misspelled words with suffixes (like *ing, ed, al, ate, ary, ence, er*). The students then score their own papers using a transparency with the correct spellings. The students have some difficulty spelling the words correctly.

Teacher A then says, "Let's review some of the basic ideas we will be using in today's lesson. You will remember that we studied these in prior lessons." The teacher then asks the class the following questions, and a discussion of each ensues.

What is the definition of a root word?

What are some examples of root words?

What is the definition of a suffix?

What are some examples of suffixes?

What are some examples of consonants?

What are some examples of vowels?

These questions represent an attempt to assess whether or not the students understand the prerequisite concepts needed to understand the lesson. If necessary, additional instruction may occur on these concepts at this time. If not, the teacher proceeds with the lesson.

Teacher A then tells the students, while recording the rules on the blackboard,

"Today we are going to learn the following spelling rule: Double the final letter of a root word when adding a suffix if the root word ends in a single consonant preceded by a single vowel, and the root word is more than one syllable with the last syllable being accented. Now let's look at some examples."

Then the teacher passes out a worksheet with a list of words and possible suffixes. Students are to add suffixes to each of the words. Students complete the worksheets, and the answers are reviewed with the class. The next day the teacher gives a spelling test on the same words as those practiced in the lesson.

### Teacher B

Teacher B also begins the lesson by explaining to the students that some words are difficult to spell and are therefore commonly misspelled. The teacher goes on to explain that students can overcome these difficulties, but first finding out if they have such difficulties is important. The teacher then gives the students a short spelling quiz using commonly misspelled words involving the use of suffixes, such as *occurring*, and *offered*. The students then score their own papers using a transparency with the correct spellings. The students have some difficulty in correctly spelling the words.

Teacher B then says, "Let's review some of the basic ideas we will be using in today's lesson. You will remember that we studied these in prior lessons." The teacher then asks the class the following questions and a discussion of each ensues.

What is the definition of a root word?

What are some examples of root words?

What is the definition of a suffix?

What are some examples of suffixes?

What are some examples of consonants?

What are some examples of vowels?

As with teacher A's list, this first set of questions represents teacher B's attempt to assess whether or not the students understand prerequisite concepts. If necessary, additional instruction can be provided at this time. If not, the teacher proceeds with the lesson. Teacher B then puts up a list of similar words and asks a series of questions about the words, including

> Notice that all the words are composed of a root word and an attached suffix. What characteristics do those with doubled letters between the word and the suffix have in common?

> What characteristics do those words with single letters between the root word and the suffix have in common?

> How are the two groups of words different?

From this discussion some patterns seem to emerge. The teacher finally says, "Notice that the last letter in the root word is doubled if the word ends in a single consonant preceded by a vowel. This is one of the rules in deciding whether or not to double the final letter."

Teacher B goes on to present another list of words and asks a similar series of questions to help the students analyze similarities and differences among the words. Following the analysis, the teacher says, "Notice in this new set of words, an additional pattern emerges. If the root word is more than one syllable, with the last syllable being accented, then the last letter of the root word is doubled."

Teacher B goes through two more sets of words, each time ending with a clarification of the rule. The teacher then lists the final rule on the blackboard and provides the students with practice followed by corrective feedback using new examples. The next day, the teacher tests the students' ability to apply the rules to another set of new spelling words.

## A Science Lesson

One of the characteristics valued in science (and other fields) is curiosity. Again, let's examine how two different teachers might approach the task of teaching the role of curiosity in science.

### Teacher C

Teacher C begins the lesson by telling the students that today's lesson is going to be on curiosity and the role it plays in science. The teacher then begins the lesson by asking the class, "What is a possible definition of curiosity?"

The teacher then calls on several students who attempt to give their definitions of curiosity. The teacher accepts those definitions that are correct or provides corrective feedback for incorrect answers. The teacher then writes on the blackboard: "Curiosity—the desire to know something."

Teacher C then goes on to explain that curiosity is the motivation behind doing science. Without this motivation, scientists are unlikely to pursue research. Later, one of the items on a test asks the students to complete the following statement: "The desire to know something is called _____."

### Teacher D

Teacher D begins the lesson by telling the students that they are going to be examining a small black box. The teacher then goes on to say that from this experience they will learn something very important about scientists and themselves. Then teacher D starts the activity by passing out to each student a sealed box containing some small objects. All boxes are alike, and all contain the same number of objects. The teacher tells the students to play with their boxes. They can tilt or shake their boxes, but they cannot open them. After about two to three minutes of shaking the boxes, the students are asked to place their boxes on the table. The teacher asks the class, "What questions about the box came to your minds as you played with the box?"

The teacher writes the questions posed by the students on the blackboard. The teacher then says, "Let's take one of the questions and attempt to find an answer. Let's start with the question, 'How many objects are in each of the boxes?' Again take your box and tilt it, shake it and record observations that will allow you to answer this question."

The students then attempt to write down their observations of the boxes. After a time, the teacher has the students stop the activity and asks them for their observations. These observations are written on the blackboard. If any students have misunderstandings about what constitutes an observation, they are corrected. The teacher then asks the class, "What inference about the number of objects in each of the boxes can we make from our observations?"

The students make inferences about how many objects are in each of the boxes and support their inferences with their observations, some of them conflicting. After some discussion, each student votes on how many objects he or she thinks are in each of the boxes. The vote is used to decide the issue. The boxes are then collected without being opened. The students are upset and want to know how many objects are in the boxes. The teacher than asks the class to describe their feelings, and writes their descriptions on the blackboard. Most center around the idea that they are upset because they don't know the answer to the question, and they want to know. The teacher then says something like,

> This feeling you have of wanting to know is called curiosity. This same feeling of curiosity drives scientists to great lengths to find answers to questions. Curiosity is something all of us feel when we feel a need to know something. This feeling is not unique to scientists. Curiosity is the feeling that drives us all to find answers to questions we might have, and this curiosity is necessary if scientific research is to flourish.

Later, the teacher asks the students on a test to define curiosity in their own words.

## Analysis of the Lessons

Lessons taught by teachers A and C are similar to those many of you have experienced as students. The teacher tells you what you are to learn. Some practice may be provided if the learning involves some skill, such as spelling words. This process is then followed by a test of your ability to memorize what you had been told or practiced. This sequence describes an expository strategy that is badly used. When teachers use this pattern of teaching, memorization is often confused with understanding.

An additional example will help to illustrate how an expository strategy, when used improperly, can lead to memorization without understanding. Read the following passage carefully; then, referring to it as necessary, complete the worksheet. After completing the worksheet, take the examination without referring to the passage or worksheet.

_Read the following passage carefully._

_. . .inner retinal disease results in no change of the FRST, but does show an alteration of either the f(s), f(t), or both. In senile macular degeneration, for example, changes occur first in the sustained-_

like function, and secondly in the transient-like function. In the hard exudate stage of early diabetic retinopathy, the f(s) is abnormal in the areas containing hard exudates (Sanderson, 1983).

Now complete the following worksheet.

1. Inner retinal disease results in no change of the _____.
2. What two alterations may occur from inner retinal disease?
3. In the hard exudate stage of early diabetic retinopathy, where is the f(s) abnormal?

Now take the following test.

1. Inner retinal disease results in no change of the _____.
2. List two alterations that may occur from inner retinal disease.
3. In the hard exudate stage of early diabetic retinopathy, where is the f(s) abnormal?

Did you pass the test? If so, you now know something about inner retinal disease. Do you understand what you know? For most of you, obviously not. You have just learned some nonsense words and phrases. Notice the similarities between this lesson and the lessons of teachers A and C. In all cases, the emphasis was on the memorization of facts. Such emphasis confuses memorization with understanding.

Now, let's examine the lessons of teachers B and D. In both cases the students were presented with a situation to analyze. From this analysis, generalizations (rules or definitions) were derived. In the case of teacher B, the students were presented with sets of words which could be used to derive rules about spelling. These rules had meaning in terms of a direct experience with words. In the case of teacher D, the students were provided an experience with sealed boxes. The experience was structured to generate feelings of wanting to know. From this, a definition of curiosity was derived. In both cases, the generalizations had meaning for the students that came from the experiences provided.

Teachers A and C were using what is commonly called an *expository strategy* of teaching (Joyce and Weil, 1980). However, these teachers could have used the strategy more appropriately. Essentially, the process is one of telling followed by showing and/or practicing. Teachers B and D were using what is commonly called an *inductive strategy*. This process provides a direct experience from which meaning is derived. Confusion between memorization and understanding is less likely to occur using an inductive strategy than an expository strategy that emphasizes memorization of facts.

Teaching for understanding beyond memorization is crucial if students are going to be able to use knowledge (Ausubel, 1963). Higher levels of cognitive thinking require that students conceptualize as well as apply rules, principles, and other generalizations in appropriate ways.

## Teaching Concepts

A concept is a category or set of objects, conditions, events, or processes that can be grouped together based on some similarities they have in common (Tennyson and

Park, 1980; Clark, 1971). This category of things can then be represented by a single symbol. For example, if you were asked to draw your concept of a chair, your drawing might be quite different in some respects from one drawn by someone else, but both drawings would have similar elements that we associate with "chairness." Your drawing would be similar to some generalized impression of "chair" based on your experiences with chairs. "Chair," then, would be considered a concept. A chair can be defined in terms of critical characteristics and can be represented by the symbol *chair*. Additional examples of other concepts include adverb, abstract art, primes, classical music, main clause, scale, density, binary numbering system, subject, living organism, animal, or clef.

Concepts can be roughly categorized into two kinds: abstractions derived from concrete objects such as chair, animal, rain, or table, and abstractions derived from conditions or processes such as curiosity, hot, cold, freedom, density, adverb, or music. Object concepts are usually developed through a classification process of finding critical characteristics that define the concept.

A concept is defined by a list of its critical attributes along with some other more general attributes. For example, a definition of the concept "boat" would likely include the general attribute, "a mode of transportation." The definition would also need to include some description of the critical attribute, "a conveyance that is propelled on the surface of the water." Notice that many modes of transportation or conveyances exist, including buses, cars, and airplanes. This general attribute of boats is called a *variable attribute*. A variable attribute is an attribute possessed by an object, but it is not an attribute unique to the object. A *critical attribute*, on the other hand, is one that is used to differentiate the object from other objects that have variable attributes in common. In the case of the boat, the critical attribute is "a conveyance that is propelled on the surface of the water."

When teaching an object concept, you need to decide how sophisticated to make the concept. For example, in developing the concept of a "seat" (chair) with children, introducing all of the kinds of seats at one time would overwhelm them. Chairs or seats may take the form of kitchen chairs, barber chairs, bar stools, thrones, recliners, couches, bleachers, benches, and milking stools. All of these are seats with some characteristics in common, but all differ in some characteristics. An object concept, such as "chair," is one arrived at through the process of classification. Basically, a child sees some object (e.g., kitchen chair) being used, and asks the question, "What is that?" The child is then told the name of the object, "a kitchen chair." On seeing a person sitting on a couch, the child may say, "Look at Uncle Al sitting in the chair!" The child is then corrected and told, "No, that's not a chair, that's a couch." An explanation of the differences may then follow, or the child may be left to determine the differences. Eventually the concept of a seat is developed to a rather sophisticated level. Without direct experiences with a variety of seats, this development would not occur. Also, recognize that after a person has had a wide variety of experiences with seats, reliance on direct experience may no longer be necessary. Pictures, models, or other representations may be used to continue development of the concept (Solomon, 1970).

Regardless of the concept to be introduced, the initial development of concepts is entirely dependent on direct experience. We cannot learn the meaning of hot, cold, music, noise, equilibrium, freedom, density, curiosity, or adverb by being told. Initial direct experience is necessary for understanding. Providing direct experience for students without prior experience is essential for the development of concepts.

Concept learning involves the identification of the critical attributes of a concept along with descriptive variable attributes. Examples are compared to nonexamples, and practice in discriminating examples from nonexamples may be provided. Concept teaching can be accomplished by either of two strategies: an expository strategy or an inductive strategy.

## The Expository Strategy

The expository strategy can be effective in concept development if students have already had prior experiences with the examples and nonexamples used to illustrate and define the concept. Since an expository strategy involves the manipulation of words, symbols, or abstract ideas, this strategy is more effective with older students or students at the formal level of cognitive development as defined by Piaget (Inhelder and Piaget, 1973). If any student, even an older one, has not had certain concrete experiences with examples of the concept, then he or she will be unable to grasp the concept through an expository approach using only verbal interactions (Ausubel, 1963; Lawson, 1983). For example, imagine a teacher teaching the concept of a "radjo." The teacher says that a radjo is a class of "semes" that smell like "quadjo's" and have four "codafs" just like a "tadso." Now, if students have had no experiences with examples of semes, quadjos, codafs, and tadsos, talking about them will do little to develop understanding. Even for those students who have had prior concrete experiences with examples of a concept being taught, presentations using models, photographs, films, or other representations tend to result in greater understanding than instruction using purely abstract language (Solomon, 1970).

Research on concept development using expository strategies suggests what should occur during the process (Clark, 1971; Tennyson and Park, 1980).

1. Select the concept to be taught and identify the critical attributes as well as frequently observed variable attributes of the concept.
2. Analyze the list of attributes, and identify all of the prerequisite concepts that would need to be understood in order to grasp the concept to be taught. Assess the students on their level of understanding of the prerequisite knowledge.
3. Introduce the definition to the students at the beginning of the lesson. Introducing the definition at the start of the lesson can significantly reduce the number of examples that would need to be studied to master the concept (Tennyson and Park, 1980). Terminology used in the definition should be as nontechnical and easily understood as possible.

4. Introduce examples that clearly illustrate the critical attributes of the concept and limit the number of variable attributes. Nonexamples should then be introduced. The nonexamples should differ from the examples in a minimum number of critical attributes at a time. They should also be from the same conceptual class.

5. Examples and nonexamples should then be introduced simultaneously in a random sequence with the examples having variable attributes representing widely different characteristics. Usually four or five examples and nonexamples will be sufficient.

6. Students should then be given some practice in distinguishing examples and nonexamples from additional cases, or in some way be provided opportunities to apply the concept to new situations. This practice may also be used to refine the attributes of an object concept such as the concept of "chair" discussed earlier.

## The Inductive Strategy

An inductive strategy provides a common direct experience to help students understand the rule, concept, or principle being introduced. This strategy involves the well-established psychological principle that the meanings of basic words and symbols are dependent on direct experience with the phenomena that the words and symbols represent (Ausubel, 1963). When students memorize words and symbols in the abstract (that is, with little prior experience with what these represent), they are usually learning meaningless nonsense.

In a teaching/learning context, an inductive strategy provides students with direct experiences that represent specific examples of the concept or generalization to be taught. Following the experience, the teacher helps students analyze the experience through questions, thus leading the students to a statement of the generalization or concept definition (Eggen, Kauchak, and Harder, 1979). Finally, the teacher provides the formal statement or symbols representing the generalization or concept.

A suggested sequence of tasks involved in an inductive strategy is

1. Select the concept to be taught and identify the critical attributes as well as frequently observed variable attributes of the concept.

2. Analyze the list of attributes, and identify all of the prerequisite concepts that would need to be understood in order to grasp the concept to be taught. Assess the student's understanding of the prerequisite knowledge.

3. Provide a hands-on activity, or preferably two or three activities, for students that will provide direct experience with the critical attributes of the concept. The number of variable attributes involved should be kept to a minimum. In the case of object concepts, activities providing experiences with nonexamples should also be provided. The amount of guidance by the teacher may vary. When little guidance is provided, the inductive strategy is commonly referred to as *discovery*

*learning*. When much guidance is provided, the inductive strategy is commonly called *guided inquiry*. Beginning teachers will need to follow more of a guided strategy in order to keep the management of the class within their abilities.

4. Once students have completed the activity, encourage students, through the use of questions, to talk about the experience and to examine and analyze the experience. The use of questions is critical if an inductive strategy is to succeed. Questions used during inductive lessons will not necessarily follow any particular pattern as they do in a discussion lesson. Rather, you need to utilize a sequence of questions that allows you to lead the students from the experience you provided to a point where you will be able to provide the generalization to be taught. The questions may be observational, that is, have the students describe what they saw, felt, smelled, heard, or tasted. Questions may ask students to identify similarities and differences or to draw conclusions from evidence. Most questions will require thought and understanding beyond mere recall.

5. Through the questioning process, the critical attributes of the concept will be identified verbally. Some information giving (presentation or lecture) will be needed at the end of the questioning to summarize the definition of the concept. In rare instances, students will be able to do this without being told, but expecting students to discover the definition of a concept strictly on their own is usually not reasonable. The teacher will then write the definition on the chalkboard or overhead transparency using easily understood vocabulary.

6. Introduce the name symbolizing this definition of the concept.

7. Then give the students some practice in distinguishing examples from nonexamples in other cases, or in some way provide opportunities to apply the concept to new situations. This practice may also be used to refine the attributes of an object concept such as the concept of "chair" discussed earlier.

## Teaching Generalizations

Generalizations can include statements of rules, principles, processes, or other kinds of relationships among concepts. Concepts, then, are the building blocks of rules, principles, or other generalizations (Gagne, 1977).

A rule can be a prescribed set of regulations governing a procedure, or it can be a standard procedure to follow. Rules, important in guiding many of the tasks we do, have applicability in settings beyond those in which they are learned. An example of a rule would be

> If the probability of success in one trial is P1, and the probability of success in a second trial is P2, then the probability of successful outcomes in both trials is P1 × P2.

Principles are established modes of operating or behaving. They make sense out of the behavior of things in our world. Examples of principles would be

Images in advertising have more effect than substance.

The higher the pressure on a gas, the less the volume occupied by the gas.

Principles have wide applicability and represent the most useful and meaningful kind of learning. Principles have more use in the real world than concepts, concepts have more use in the real world than memorized facts, and memorized facts have very little if any use in the real world.

As stated previously, rules and principles involve two or more concepts and their relationships. In teaching any rule or principle, give students an understanding of the prerequisite concepts. Should they lack this understanding, then teaching these concepts before introducing the rule or principle is necessary. Failure to insure understanding of prerequisite concepts will result in incomplete understanding of the rule or principle.

When teaching rules, two contextually similar rules should be taught simultaneously rather than sequentially or randomly (Tennyson and Park, 1980). The comparison of similarities and differences in juxtaposition will improve learning. In most other respects, the teaching of generalizations, either through an expository or inductive strategy, does not significantly differ from teaching concepts.

## Assessment of Inductive Strategies

An inductive strategy is a valuable tool in helping students learn knowledge with understanding. More students enjoy learning in this way than with didactic or expository methods (Renner, Abraham, and Birnie, 1985). Learning abstractions in the context of experiences makes sense to students; they are not merely memorizing symbols, but understanding experiences. When a concept is presented on a concrete level by allowing the students to have direct contact with the object, understanding as measured by student behavior appears to be high (Solomon, 1970).

If properly conducted, an inductive strategy will result in more student involvement, more intrinsic interest in the lesson, better transfer of learning, and higher achievement of more complex cognitive understandings (Hensen, 1980; Hermann, 1969). Evidence also exists that direct attempts to teach thinking skills through inductive strategies have a high probability of success (Anderson, 1983; Sadow, 1983). An inductive strategy, on the other hand, is not an efficient strategy if your intent is to cover large amounts of the subject in short periods of time (Hensen, 1980). The expository strategy, drill-and-practice, and other such strategies are more efficient in exposing students to larger amounts of content.

Using an inductive process requires more planning due to the increased complexity of classroom management. If a teacher's behavioral management skills are less than adequate, more student misbehavior could result from the use of this strategy than with simpler strategies (Emmer, et al., 1984). However, skilled teachers will find this to be a more satisfying strategy for both them and their students. An inductive strategy is one you will want to learn to use with skill.

## REFERENCES

Anderson, R.D. 1983. A consolidation and appraisal of science meta-analyses. *Journal of Research in Science Teaching* 20(5): 497–509.

Ausubel, D. 1963. *The psychology of meaningful verbal learning*. New York: Grune and Stratton.

Clark, C.D. 1971. Teaching concepts in the classroom: A set of teaching prescriptions derived from experimental research. *Journal of Educational Psychology Monograph* 62(3): 253–278.

Eggen, P.D., D.P. Kauchak, and R.J. Harder. 1979. *Strategies for teachers: Information processing in the classroom*. Englewood Cliffs, N.J.: Prentice-Hall.

Emmer, E.T., *et al.* 1984. *Classroom management for secondary teachers*. Englewood Cliffs, N.J.: Prentice-Hall.

Gagne, R. 1977. *The conditions of learning.* 3d Ed. New York: Holt, Rinehart & Winston.

Hensen, K.T. 1980. Discovery learning. *Contemporary Education* 51:101–103.

Hermann, G. 1969. Learning by discovery: A critical review of studies. *The Journal of Experimental Education* 38:58–72.

Inhelder, B., and J. Piaget. 1973. *The growth of logical thinking from childhood to adolescence.* New York: Basic Books.

Joyce, B., and M. Weil. 1980. *Models of teaching.* 2d ed. Englewood Cliffs, N.J.: Prentice-Hall.

Lawson, A.E. 1983. Investigating and applying developmental psychology in the science classroom. In *Learning and motivation in the classroom,* ed. G. Scott, *et al.* Hillsdale, N.J.: Erlbaum.

Renner, J.W., M.R. Abraham, and H.H. Birnie. 1985. Secondary school students' beliefs about the physics laboratory. *Science Education* 69(5): 649–663.

Sadow, S.A. 1983. Creative problem-solving for the foreign language class. *Foreign Language Annals* 16:115–118.

Sanderson, Diana. 1983. Quantitative layer-by-layer perimetry. *Optometry News* Summer, 7–9.

Solomon, G.O. 1970. The analysis of concrete to abstract classroom instruction patterns utilizing the TIP profile. *Journal of Research and Development in Education* 4:52–61.

Tennyson, R.D., and O. Park. 1980. The teaching of concepts: A review of instructional design research literature. *Review of Educational Research* 50(1): 55–70.

## SUMMARY

### Concepts

*Definition*: A concept is a category or set of objects, conditions, events, or processes that can be grouped together based on common similarities and represented by some abstract symbol.

*Kinds of Concepts*:
1. an abstraction derived from concrete objects
2. an abstraction derived from a condition or process

*Concept Statement*: A concept statement is composed of a list of critical attributes along with other more general attributes.

*Concept Learning*: Concept learning involves the identification of the critical attributes of the concept along with some descriptive variable attributes.

### Generalizations

*Rule*: A rule is a prescribed set of regulations that may govern a procedure, or define a standard procedure to follow.

*Principle*: A principle is an established mode of operating or behaving.

## Expository Strategy

*Definition*: An expository strategy provides a definition, followed by the presentation of examples and nonexamples to illustrate the definition.

*Steps in Instruction*
1. Select the concept or generalization and identify the critical attributes.
2. Identify prerequisite knowledge and assess students.
3. Introduce the definition to students.
4. Introduce examples and nonexamples as needed, usually three or four.
5. Introduce examples and nonexamples simultaneously.
6. Provide practice.

## Inductive strategy

*Definition*: An inductive strategy provides students with some kind of direct experience, then, through using questions about the experience, leads students to a statement of the critical attributes followed by the identification of the symbol representing the statement.

*Steps in Instruction*
1. Select the concept or generalization and identify the critical attributes.
2. Identify prerequisite knowledge and assess students.
3. Provide a hands-on activity that provides experience with the critical attributes.
4. Use questioning to analyze the experience.
5. Use a combination of questioning and presentation to identify the critical attributes.
6. Identify the symbol or symbols used to represent the concept or generalization.
7. Provide practice.

## Assessment of an Inductive Strategy

1. Students are more intrinsically interested in lessons.
2. Students achieve more at levels above the knowledge level.
3. Students are better able to transfer the learning.

## Limitations of an Inductive Strategy Compared to Other Strategies

1. not an efficient method for teaching large numbers of facts
2. more misbehavior occurs when used by teachers who lack management skills

# EXERCISE 14
## Concept Analysis

The purpose of this exercise is to identify some concepts that would be taught within your subject field at the secondary level. Once you identify these initial concepts, analyze them and list the other concepts that would be prerequisite to understanding the new ones.

Directions: Complete the following tasks.

1. List two concepts from your subject field that you think would be taught in the secondary classroom. Define each of the concepts and include all of the critical attributes.
2. List all of the prerequisite concepts that a person would need to learn each of these new concepts.

# MICROTEACHING LESSON 7
## Inductive Strategy I

In previous lessons, you have been using questions in the context of presentations and discussions. This lesson will acquaint you with another teaching strategy, an inductive strategy, in which questions play a critical role.

In this lesson, you are going to provide some experience for the students and, through questioning about that experience, lead the students to some understanding of *a concept*. You will encourage students, through the use of questions, to talk about, examine, and analyze the experience. The use of questions is critical to the success of an inductive strategy.

Questions will not necessarily follow any particular pattern as they did in a directed discussion. But you will need to use a sequence of questions that will allow you to lead the students from the experience you provided to the point where you will present the definition and name the concept being taught. The questions may be observational in character; you may have the students describe what they see, feel, smell, hear, or taste. Some questions may ask students to identify similarities and differences or draw conclusions from evidence. Most questions will require thought and understanding beyond mere recall. For guidance, you will want to review the different kinds of cognitive questions and use what you need to achieve your plans.

Some information giving (presentation or lecture) will be needed at the end of the questioning to identify the concept. You will want to derive a definition of the concept, and then introduce the name symbolizing this definition. In rare instances, students will be able to do this without being told, but expecting students to discover the definition and name of the concept strictly on their own is usually not reasonable.

## The Teaching Task

1. Design a lesson that will allow you to use an inductive strategy.
2. Use a combination of cognitive questions to arrive at a point where you can present the definition of a concept.
3. Continue to use and practice the appropriate skills from earlier lessons. Do not feel that you need to conduct a directed discussion, but do practice effective eliciting patterns and use of silence, probing, and student ideas.
4. Use closed questions as part of the conclusion to assess the attainment of your objective.
5. The lesson plan to be turned into your instructor should
   a. state your instructional objectives at the beginning of the plan.
   b. briefly describe your set induction including a verbatim transcript of anything you are going to say.
   c. define the concept to be taught.
   d. describe how the direct experience will be used and include
      1. list of materials
      2. directions (verbatim) to be given
      3. teaching procedures

e. list in proper sequence the questions to be asked during and following the direct experience.

f. list the closed questions to be asked at the conclusion of the lesson to assess attainment of the objectives.

g. integrate items (a) through (f) into a useful and coherent lesson plan.

6. If you have already read and discussed Chapter 7, "Constructing Tests," then, *in addition* to the usual lesson plan, and *on a separate paper,* place your name, list your objective, and write a test question that could be given to the students to assess the attainment of your objective. Use effective testing practices as suggested by readings and class discussions on testing. You will turn this in at the same time as your lesson plan, *but separate from it.*

## Observing the Lesson

Write a description of the direct experience so that deficiencies in the experiences can be identified. A verbatim transcript of the questions (other than probes) in order of sequence will also help you analyze the clarity of the questions, cognitive level of the questions, and the logic of the sequence. The rest of the observations will be the same as earlier lessons.

# Inductive Strategy I
# Self-Analysis

Name _____

The items on this Self-Analysis are designed to help you identify those things that you are doing well and those things you may still need to improve. Listen to an audiotape or watch a videotape of your lesson, and record data that will enable you to make the assessments requested. Review the sections, "Observing Teaching Behavior" in Chapter 2 and "Observing the Lesson" in this and earlier microteaching lessons prior to making observations for this lesson. Circle the number that corresponds to your assessment of your behavior on the tasks of the lesson. *Attach your raw observational data to your Self-Analysis report.*

### Skills/tasks specific to this lesson

1. The direct experience provided was adequate for illustrating the essential characteristics of the concept taught in this lesson.

   1         2         3         4         5

   Direct experience                  Direct experience                  Direct experience
   was adequate                       was adequate                       was inadequate
                                       in part

2. An understanding of the concept was derived from the direct experience before its definition and name were introduced.

   1         2         3         4         5

   Teacher clearly                    Teacher mixed                      Teacher introduced
   waited until                       the sequence of                    symbols before
   understanding was                  observations and                   understanding
   assured to intro-                  introduction of                    occurred
   duce symbols                       symbols

3. The questions leading to the development of the concept were logically sequenced.

   1         2         3         4         5

   Questions led                      There was some con-                There was little or
   directly to the                    fusion in the se-                  no logic in the
   idea                               quence of questions                sequence of questions

**Skills/tasks applied from previous lessons**

4. The set induction of the lesson created an interest in the lesson.

```
1              2              3              4              5
└──────────────┴──────────────┴──────────────┴──────────────┘
```

Attention of                    Some attempt was              There was little
the students was                made to get the               or no attempt made
effectively                     students' attention           to get students'
gained                                                        attention

5. The set induction of the lesson gave direction to the rest of the lesson by relating it to students' past knowledge and experiences and the topics to be taught.

```
1              2              3              4              5
└──────────────┴──────────────┴──────────────┴──────────────┘
```

Overall direction               Overall direction             Direction or pur-
or purpose of the               or purpose of the             pose of the lesson
lesson was clear                lesson was somewhat           was unclear
                                clear

6. The phrasing of the teacher's questions reflected the intent of the question clearly and unambiguously.

```
1              2              3              4              5
└──────────────┴──────────────┴──────────────┴──────────────┘
```

All questions                   About one-half                Few questions
were clear and                  of the questions              were clear and
unambiguous                     were clear and                unambiguous
                                unambiguous

7. The teacher asked a variety of cognitive questions.

```
1              2              3              4              5
└──────────────┴──────────────┴──────────────┴──────────────┘
```

Teacher used all                Teacher used several          Teacher used
categories                      categories                    only knowledge
                                of questions                  questions

8. The teacher used an appropriate eliciting pattern.

```
1              2              3              4              5
└──────────────┴──────────────┴──────────────┴──────────────┘
```

Almost all were                 About an equal                Almost all were
Q–N–R patterns                  mix of Q–R, N–Q–R             Q–R and N–Q–R
                                and Q–N–R

9. The teacher made use of silence following student's responses to encourage additional thinking.

```
1              2              3              4              5
└──────────────┴──────────────┴──────────────┴──────────────┘
```

Three to five seconds           One to two seconds            Less than one
on the average                  on the average                second on the average

10. The teacher made use of student ideas as a form of reinforcement.

| 1 | 2 | 3 | 4 | 5 |

Four or more
times

Two times

Not at all

11. The teacher made use of extending, clarifying, and justifying probes equally.

| 1 | 2 | 3 | 4 | 5 |

Teacher made use
of all three
almost equally

Teacher used some
probes of some
kinds

Teacher used few
if any probes

12. The expression of the teacher's voice was effectively modified during the lesson.

| 1 | 2 | 3 | 4 | 5 |

The teacher varied
his or her voice
to focus and/or
maintain attention

The teacher varied
his or her voice
only occasionally

The teacher rarely
varied his or her voice
during the lesson

13. The teacher used closed questions as part of the summary of the discussion to assess the objectives of the lesson.

| 1 | 2 | 3 | 4 | 5 |

Teacher asked a
sufficient number
of questions to
assess the objectives

Teacher assessed
some of the
objectives

Teacher asked no
closed questions
to assess the
objectives

14. The teacher made the objective of the lesson clear.

| 1 | 2 | 3 | 4 | 5 |

The objective
of the lesson
was clear

The objective
of the lesson
was somewhat clear

The objective
of the lesson
was unknown

15. The content was appropriate in both amount and relevancy.

| 1 | 2 | 3 | 4 | 5 |

Content was
appropriate in
both amount and
relevancy

Content was
appropriate in
one but not
the other

Content was
excessive and
irrelevant

**157**

Complete the following items on separate sheets of paper.

1. Listen to an audiotape or watch a videotape of this teaching lesson. Record verbatim each question you asked in the sequence asked. Record everything from the time you first started to formulate the question to the time you actively elicited a response from a student. Include all attempts at rephrasing in situations where you had to rephrase a question until it was understandable.
2. Record verbatim each probe you used immediately following the question with which it was used. Indent the probe so that it will not be confused with the eliciting question.
3. Study the questions and probes you used. Could the wording of questions be changed to make the intent of the questions clearer? If so, rewrite the particular questions, or indicate the change in phrasing you would make to improve the questions.
4. What specific changes will you make on your Inductive Strategy II Lesson? What specifically will you do prior to the lesson, as well as during the lesson, to insure that you will be successful in making these changes? For example, when analyzing your probing, your reply might look something like this:

Changes in the number and kinds of probes:

From 2 clarifying to 4 clarifying

From 0 extending to 2 extending

From 0 justifying to 4 justifying

From 1 redirecting to 3 redirecting

To accomplish this change, I will write the name of the probe or probes that I intend to use with that question in my lesson plans. I will also record the student replies from this tape and identify those that could have been probed and were not. This process will help me become more sensitive to using probes when I hear students use ambiguous words or phrases (which they need to clarify), make conclusions (which they need to justify), or give answers that seem incomplete (which they need to extend).

Do not restrict your reply to the example given. Include in your reply all behaviors you feel need to be changed.

# Inductive Strategy I
# Observation Guide

Name _____   Observer _____

Record data during the teaching lesson as well as from the audio- and videotape after the lesson that will enable you to make the assessments requested. Reread the section "Observing Teaching Behavior" in Chapter 2 and "Observing the Lesson" in this and earlier microteaching lessons prior to making observations for this lesson. Circle the number that corresponds to your assessment of the teacher's behavior on the tasks of the lesson. *Attach your observational data to this report.*

### Skills/tasks specific to this lesson

1. The direct experience provided was adequate for illustrating the essential characteristics of the concept taught in this lesson.

```
1              2              3              4              5
```

| Direct experience was completely adequate | Direct experience was adequate in part | Direct experience was inadequate |

2. An understanding of the concept was derived from the direct experience before its definition and name were introduced.

```
1              2              3              4              5
```

| Teacher clearly waited until understanding was assured to introduce symbols | Teacher mixed the sequence of observations and introduction of symbols | Teacher introduced symbols before understanding occurred |

3. The questions leading to the development of the concept, rule, or principle were logically sequenced.

```
1              2              3              4              5
```

| Questions led directly to the idea | There was some confusion in the sequence of questions | There was little or no logic in the sequence of questions |

**Skills/tasks applied from previous lessons**

4. The set induction of the lesson created an interest in the lesson.

```
1               2               3               4               5
├───────────────┼───────────────┼───────────────┼───────────────┤
```

| | | |
|---|---|---|
| Attention of the students was effectively gained | Some attempt was made to get the students' attention | There was little or no attempt made to get students' attention |

5. The set induction of the lesson gave direction to the rest of the lesson by relating it to students' past knowledge and experiences and the topics to be taught.

```
1               2               3               4               5
├───────────────┼───────────────┼───────────────┼───────────────┤
```

| | | |
|---|---|---|
| Overall direction or purpose of the lesson was clear | Overall direction or purpose of the lesson was somewhat clear | Direction or purpose of the lesson was unclear |

6. The phrasing of the teacher's questions reflected the intent of the question clearly and unambiguously.

```
1               2               3               4               5
├───────────────┼───────────────┼───────────────┼───────────────┤
```

| | | |
|---|---|---|
| All questions were clear and unambiguous | About one-half of the questions were clear and unambiguous | Few questions were clear and unambiguous |

7. The teacher asked a variety of cognitive questions.

```
1               2               3               4               5
├───────────────┼───────────────┼───────────────┼───────────────┤
```

| | | |
|---|---|---|
| Teacher used five categories of questions | Teacher used three categories of questions | Teacher used only knowledge questions |

8. The teacher used an appropriate eliciting pattern.

```
1               2               3               4               5
├───────────────┼───────────────┼───────────────┼───────────────┤
```

| | | |
|---|---|---|
| Almost all were Q–N–R patterns | About an equal mix of Q–R, N–Q–R, and Q–N–R | Almost all were Q–R and N–Q–R |

9. The teacher made use of silence following student's responses to encourage additional thinking.

```
1               2               3               4               5
├───────────────┼───────────────┼───────────────┼───────────────┤
```

| | | |
|---|---|---|
| Three to five seconds on the average | One to two seconds on the average | Less than one second on the average |

10. The teacher made use of student ideas as a form of reinforcement.

| 1 | 2 | 3 | 4 | 5 |
|---|---|---|---|---|
| Four or more times | | Two times | | Not at all |

11. The teacher made use of extending, clarifying, and justifying probes equally.

| 1 | 2 | 3 | 4 | 5 |
|---|---|---|---|---|
| Teacher made use of all three kinds of probes almost equally | | Teacher used some probes of some kinds | | Teacher used few if any probes |

12. The expression of the teacher's voice was effectively modified during the lesson.

| 1 | 2 | 3 | 4 | 5 |
|---|---|---|---|---|
| The teacher varied his or her voice to focus and/or maintain attention | | The teacher varied his or her voice only occasionally | | The teacher rarely varied his or her voice during the lesson |

13. The teacher used closed questions as part of the summary of the discussion to assess the objectives of the lesson.

| 1 | 2 | 3 | 4 | 5 |
|---|---|---|---|---|
| Teacher asked a sufficient number of questions to assess the objectives | | Teacher assessed some of the objectives | | Teacher asked no closed questions to assess the objectives |

14. The teacher made the objective of the lesson clear.

| 1 | 2 | 3 | 4 | 5 |
|---|---|---|---|---|
| The objective of the lesson was clear | | The objective of the lesson was somewhat clear | | The objective of the lesson was unknown |

15. The content was appropriate in both amount and relevancy.

| 1 | 2 | 3 | 4 | 5 |
|---|---|---|---|---|
| Content was appropriate in both amount and relevancy | | Content was appropriate in one but not the other | | Content was excessive and irrelevant |

Complete the following items in the spaces provided.

Percent of time the teacher was talking
(Show the data used to determine this in the space provided.)                    _____

Teacher Talk

Student Talk

Silence or Confusion

Describe one thing related to the criteria listed under "Skills/tasks specific to this lesson" that you thought was particularly effective and that the teacher would be advised to continue. Describe why you believe this behavior was effective.

Offer at least one specific suggestion about what the teacher could have done differently to improve the lesson. Consider only those tasks directly related to the tasks of this lesson.

# MICROTEACHING LESSON 8 ———————————————
## Inductive Strategy II

This lesson will provide further practice in the use of an inductive teaching strategy. An inductive strategy is a valuable tool in helping students learn knowledge with comprehension. More students enjoy learning this way than with expository or didactic methods. Examining your own and other students' reactions to the inductive strategy used in these microteaching lessons should verify this assertion.

### The Teaching Task

1. Design a lesson that will allow you to use an inductive strategy.
2. Use a combination of cognitive questions to arrive at a point where you can define a concept.
3. Continue to use and practice the appropriate skills from prior lessons. Do not feel that you need to conduct a directed discussion, but do practice effective eliciting patterns, use of silence, probing, and student ideas.
4. Use closed questions as part of the conclusion to assess the attainment of your objective.
5. The lesson plan to be turned into your instructor should
   a. state your instructional objectives at the beginning of the plan.
   b. briefly describe your set induction including verbatim anything you are going to say.
   c. describe how the direct experience will be used, including
      1. list of materials
      2. directions (verbatim) to be given
      3. teaching procedures
   d. list in proper sequence the questions to be asked during and following the direct experience.
   e. write out the definition of the concept to be taught.
   f. list the closed questions to be asked at the conclusion of the lesson to assess attainment of the objectives.
   g. integrate items (a) through (f) into a useful and coherent lesson plan.
6. *In addition* to the usual lesson plan, but *on a separate paper,* place your name, list your objective, and write a test question that could be given to the students to assess the attainment of your objective. Use effective testing practices as suggested by readings and class discussions on testing. You will turn this in at the same time as your lesson plan *but separate from it.*

### Observing the Lesson

Write a description of the direct experience so that deficiencies in the experiences can be identified. A verbatim transcript of the questions (other than probes) in order of sequence will also be help you analyze the clarity of the questions, cognitive level of the questions, and the logic of the sequence. The rest of the observations will be the same as earlier lessons.

# Inductive Strategy II
# Self-Analysis

Name _____

The items on this Self-Analysis are designed to help you identify those things that you are doing well and those things you may need to improve. Reread the section "Observing Teaching Behavior," in Chapter 2 and "Observing the Lesson" in this and earlier microteaching lessons prior to making observations for this lesson. Listen to an audiotape or watch a videotape of your lesson, and record data that will enable you to make the assessments requested. Circle the number that corresponds to your assessment of your behavior on the tasks of the lesson. *Attach your raw data to your "Self-Analysis" report.*

## Skills/tasks specific to this lesson

1. The direct experience provided was adequate for illustrating the essential characteristics of the concept taught in this lesson.

| 1 | 2 | 3 | 4 | 5 |
|---|---|---|---|---|
| Direct experience was adequate | | Direct experience was adequate in part | | Direct experience was inadequate |

2. An understanding of the concept was derived from the direct experience before its definition and name were introduced.

| 1 | 2 | 3 | 4 | 5 |
|---|---|---|---|---|
| Teacher clearly waited until understanding was assured to introduce symbols | | Teacher mixed the sequence of observations and introduction of symbols | | Teacher introduced symbols before understanding occurred |

3. The questions leading to the development of the concept were logically sequenced.

| 1 | 2 | 3 | 4 | 5 |
|---|---|---|---|---|
| Questions led directly to the idea | | There was some confusion in the sequence of questions | | There was little or no logic in the sequence of questions |

**Skills/tasks applied from previous lessons**

4. The set induction of the lesson created an interest in the lesson.

```
1                2                3                4                5
|_____|_____|_____|_____|
```

| Attention of | Some attempt was | There was little |
| the students was | made to get the | or no attempt made |
| effectively | students' attention | to get students' |
| gained | | attention |

5. The set induction of the lesson gave direction to the rest of the lesson by relating it to students' past knowledge and experiences and the topics to be taught.

```
1                2                3                4                5
|_____|_____|_____|_____|
```

| Overall direction | Overall direction | Direction or pur- |
| or purpose of the | or purpose of the | pose of the lesson |
| lesson was clear | lesson was somewhat | was unclear |
| | clear | |

6. The phrasing of the teacher's questions reflected the intent of the question clearly and unambiguously.

```
1                2                3                4                5
|_____|_____|_____|_____|
```

| All questions | About one-half | Few questions |
| were clear and | of the questions | were clear and |
| unambiguous | were clear and | unambiguous |
| | unambiguous | |

7. The teacher asked a variety of cognitive questions.

```
1                2                3                4                5
|_____|_____|_____|_____|
```

| Teacher used | Teacher used three | Teacher used |
| five categories | categories | only knowledge |
| | of questions | questions |

8. The teacher used an appropriate eliciting pattern.

```
1                2                3                4                5
|_____|_____|_____|_____|
```

| Almost all were | About an equal | Almost all were |
| Q–N–R patterns | mix of Q–R, N–Q–R, | Q–R and N–Q–R |
| | and Q–N–R | |

9. The teacher made use of silence following student's responses to encourage additional thinking.

```
1                2                3                4                5
|_____|_____|_____|_____|
```

| Three to five seconds | One to two seconds | Less than one second |
| on the average | on the average | on the average |

166

10. The teacher made use of student ideas as a form of reinforcement.

| 1 | 2 | 3 | 4 | 5 |
|---|---|---|---|---|
| Four or more times | | Two times | | Not at all |

11. The teacher made use of extending, clarifying, and justifying probes equally.

| 1 | 2 | 3 | 4 | 5 |
|---|---|---|---|---|
| Teacher made use of all three probes almost equally | | Teacher used some probes of some kinds | | Teacher used few if any probes |

12. The expression of the teacher's voice was effectively modified during the lesson.

| 1 | 2 | 3 | 4 | 5 |
|---|---|---|---|---|
| The teacher varied his or her voice to focus and/or maintain attention | | The teacher varied his or her voice only occasionally | | The teacher rarely varied his or her voice during the lesson |

13. The teacher used closed questions as part of the summary of the discussion to assess the objectives of the lesson.

| 1 | 2 | 3 | 4 | 5 |
|---|---|---|---|---|
| Teacher asked a sufficient number of questions to assess the objectives | | Teacher assessed some of the objectives | | Teacher asked no closed questions to assess the objectives |

14. The teacher made the objective of the lesson clear.

| 1 | 2 | 3 | 4 | 5 |
|---|---|---|---|---|
| The objective of the lesson was clear | | The objective of the lesson was somewhat clear | | The objective of the lesson was unknown |

15. The content was appropriate in both amount and relevancy.

| 1 | 2 | 3 | 4 | 5 |
|---|---|---|---|---|
| Content was appropriate in both amount and relevancy | | Content was appropriate in one but not the other | | Content was excessive and irrelevant |

Complete the following items on separate sheets of paper.

1. Listen to an audiotape or watch a videotape of this teaching lesson. Record verbatim all eliciting questions in the sequence in which they were asked. Record everything from the time you first started to formulate the question to the time you actively elicited a response from a student. Include all attempts at rephrasing the question in situations where you had to rephrase a question until it was understandable.
2. Record verbatim each probe that you used immediately following the question. Indent the probe so that it will not be confused with the eliciting question.
3. Could the phrasing of some questions or probes be improved to make their intent clearer? If so, rewrite the particular questions or probes to improve the phrasing.

# Inductive Strategy II
# Observation Guide

Name _____     Observer _____

Record data during the teaching lesson, listen to an audiotape or watch a videotape of the lesson, and record needed additional data that will enable you to make the assessments requested. Reread the section "Observing Teaching Behavior" in Chapter 2 and "Observing the Lesson" in this and earlier microteaching lessons prior to making observations for this lesson. Circle the number that corresponds to your assessment of the teacher's behavior on the tasks of the lesson. *Attach your observational data to this report.*

## Skills/tasks specific to this lesson

1. The direct experience provided was adequate for illustrating the essential characteristics of the concept taught in this lesson.

   | 1 | 2 | 3 | 4 | 5 |
   |---|---|---|---|---|
   | Direct experience was adequate | | Direct experience was adequate in part | | Direct experience was inadequate |

2. An understanding of the concept was derived from the direct experience before its definition and name were introduced.

   | 1 | 2 | 3 | 4 | 5 |
   |---|---|---|---|---|
   | Teacher clearly waited until understanding was assured to introduce symbols | | Teacher mixed the sequence of observations and introduction of symbols | | Teacher introduced symbols before understanding occurred |

3. The questions leading to the development of the concept were logically sequenced.

   | 1 | 2 | 3 | 4 | 5 |
   |---|---|---|---|---|
   | Questions led directly to the idea | | There was some confusion in the sequence of questions | | There was little or no logic in the sequence of questions |

Skills/tasks applied from previous lessons

4. The set induction of the lesson created an interest in the lesson.

```
1              2              3              4              5
|_____|_____|_____|_____|
```

Attention of                  Some attempt was              There was little
the students was              made to get the               or no attempt made
effectively                   students' attention           to get students'
gained                                                       attention

5. The set induction of the lesson gave direction to the rest of the lesson by relating it to students' past knowledge and experiences and the topics to be taught.

```
1              2              3              4              5
|_____|_____|_____|_____|
```

Overall direction             Overall direction             Direction or pur-
or purpose of the             or purpose of the             pose of the lesson
lesson was clear              lesson was somewhat           was unclear
                              clear

6. The phrasing of the teacher's questions reflected the intent of the question clearly and unambiguously.

```
1              2              3              4              5
|_____|_____|_____|_____|
```

All questions                 About one-half                Few questions
were clear and                of the questions              were clear and
unambiguous                   were clear and                unambiguous
                              unambiguous

7. The teacher asked a variety of cognitive questions.

```
1              2              3              4              5
|_____|_____|_____|_____|
```

Teacher used                  Teacher used three            Teacher used
five categories               categories                    only knowledge
of questions                  of questions                  questions

8. The teacher used an appropriate eliciting pattern.

```
1              2              3              4              5
|_____|_____|_____|_____|
```

Almost all were               About an equal                Almost all were
Q–N–R patterns                mix of Q–R, N–Q–R,            Q–R and N–Q–R
                              and Q–N–R

9. The teacher made use of silence following student's responses to encourage additional thinking.

```
1              2              3              4              5
|_____|_____|_____|_____|
```

Three to five seconds         One to two seconds            Less than one second
on the average                on the average                on the average

10. The teacher made use of student ideas as a form of reinforcement.

| 1 | 2 | 3 | 4 | 5 |
|---|---|---|---|---|

Four or more
times

Two times

Not at all

11. The teacher made use of extending, clarifying, and justifying probes equally.

| 1 | 2 | 3 | 4 | 5 |
|---|---|---|---|---|

Teacher made use
of all three
probes almost
equally

Teacher used some
probes of some
kinds

Teacher used few
if any probes

12. The expression of the teacher's voice was effectively modified during the lesson.

| 1 | 2 | 3 | 4 | 5 |
|---|---|---|---|---|

The teacher varied
his or her voice
to focus and/or
maintain attention

The teacher varied
his or her voice
only occasionally

The teacher rarely
varied his or her voice
during the lesson

13. The teacher used closed questions as part of the summary of the discussion to assess the objectives of the lesson.

| 1 | 2 | 3 | 4 | 5 |
|---|---|---|---|---|

Teacher asked a
sufficient number
of questions to
assess the objectives

Teacher assessed
some of the
objectives

Teacher asked no
closed questions
to assess the
objectives

14. The teacher made the objective of the lesson clear.

| 1 | 2 | 3 | 4 | 5 |
|---|---|---|---|---|

The objective
of the lesson
was clear

The objective
of the lesson
was somewhat clear

The objective
of the lesson
was unknown

15. The content was appropriate in both amount and relevancy.

| 1 | 2 | 3 | 4 | 5 |
|---|---|---|---|---|

Content was
appropriate in
both amount and
relevancy

Content was
appropriate in
one but not
the other

Content was
excessive and
irrelevant

Answer the following items in the space provided.

Percent of time the teacher was talking
(Show the data used to determine this in the space provided.)                    _____

Teacher Talk

Student Talk

Silence or Confusion

Describe one thing related to the criteria listed under "Skills/tasks specific to this lesson" that you thought was particularly effective and that you feel the teacher would be advised to continue. Describe why you believe this behavior was effective.

Offer at least one specific suggestion about what the teacher could have done differently to improve the lesson. Consider only those tasks that are directly related to the tasks of this lesson.

# EXERCISE 15
## Final Appraisal of Teaching

While you have learned many skills during the microteaching lessons, much is yet to be learned. Taking the time to identify those skills you have learned and those yet to be learned can be productive. In this exercise, you will examine both these aspects in detail. Listening to the first and last tapes of your microteaching lessons may assist you in this task.

Directions:

On a separate sheet of paper, titled Final Appraisal, do a self-appraisal on the teaching tasks listed here. *Use complete sentences only, and use behavioral language.* (Avoid the use of vague expressions like "I am doing well in this area"; "I need to improve on phrasing questions"; or "I'm satisfied (or dissatisfied) with ".) In your appraisal of each task, include

1. a specific assessment of your competence in doing the task, titled "Competence"
2. specific improvements you feel you still need to make, titled "Needed Improvements"

Teaching Tasks

1. Teaching for an instructional objective with clarity
2. Asking closed questions at the end of lessons to assess attainment of objectives
3. Creating a set induction that creates interest
4. Creating a set induction that gives direction to a lesson
5. Creating a set induction that relates the current lesson to past knowledge and experiences
6. Organizing the content of presentations in logical sequence
7. Choosing a reasonable amount of content to include in lessons
8. Choosing content relevant to a general group of students
9. Maintaining adequate volume in voice
10. Interjecting changes of expression in voice
11. Using gestures and other refocusing tactics to maintain student interest
12. Closing lessons in ways likely to reinforce and clarify the lesson
13. Asking interesting and effective open or divergent questions at the start of discussions
14. Using all four kinds of probes about equally
15. Asking clear and unambiguous questions
16. Using silence following student responses
17. Using student ideas by mentioning the name of the student and the idea and incorporating the idea into the lesson
18. Using labeled praise effectively
19. Using only the eliciting pattern of asking the question and then calling on a student by name to respond

20. Incorporating questions of various cognitive levels into lessons
21. Providing sufficient direct experiences to allow the development of concepts when using an inductive strategy
22. Ordering questions in a sequence that will allow the development of concepts when using an inductive strategy

*Constructing* **7**
*Tests*

*T*ests serve many purposes. This chapter will focus on tests constructed and used by teachers to measure students' cognitive understandings. Tests of cognitive understanding play an important role in the school classroom and are routinely administered by teachers. Fundamentally, tests are instruments used to gather information to help us make decisions about students (Kubiszyn and Borich, 1984). Specifically, tests are commonly used to

1. measure the achievement of students for grading purposes
2. measure achievement of students for purposes of informing parents and institutions of higher education making admissions decisions

Tests are less commonly used to

3. assess students' prerequisite understandings prior to instruction
4. check the effectiveness of instruction
5. measure student mastery of material to decide if remedial instruction is needed
6. measure student mastery of material in self-paced instruction to make instructional decisions
7. evaluate the curriculum and/or school organization
8. measure student achievement for placement purposes

Some of the uses of tests in an educational setting are perceived as significant by students as well as by those using the results. Therefore, learning to develop and use tests effectively is an essential skill for all teachers.

## Constructing a Test

Central to the teaching process is the formulation of objectives of instruction. Objectives are formulated to 1. provide guidance in the choice of instructional experiences, 2. improve the clarity of instruction, and 3. increase the effectiveness of evaluation. Part of most student evaluations will be the administration of teacher-made tests to assess student learning.

The initial task in test construction is choosing or writing the test items that will measure the instructional objectives. At times, developing the objectives and the test items concurrently is advisable. Regardless of whether the objectives are determined prior to or concurrent with the test items, once the objectives are identified, the nature of the items on a test is specified. It is to be hoped that both the objectives and the resultant test items will also be concerned with significant learning because many students perceive tests as measuring the objectives of your course. This perception dictates what students attempt to learn (Medley, 1979).

The next task in constructing the test will be to group together like kinds of items: short essay questions, for example, or multiple-choice questions. Do not mix different kinds of test items within one section, even though you will usually use several different kind of items on a test, including essay and multiple-choice. Avoid constructing a test composed solely of true-false, matching, or completion items. Such tests place a premium on low level understanding and encourage students to do that kind of learning (Medley, 1979).

Once items are grouped, provide directions for students to follow in answering each kind of question. For example, students need to be told either to confine their answer to an essay question to the space provided or to write their answer on a separate answer sheet. In the case of multiple- choice questions, they need to be told that there is only one best answer. They need to be told to circle their choice, place an "x" through the answer, or respond on an answer sheet in some fashion. They need to be told what to do, how to do it, and where to do it. Nothing is left for their interpretation.

If different kinds of test items have different values, then students should be told the value of the various items. For example, if a test is composed of true-false and essay items, and the essay items have twice the value of the true-false items, then the teacher should indicate those relative values either in the directions at the beginning of the test or in the directions for each type of item. If different essay questions will be assigned different values, then the value of each essay question could be indicated at the left of the number for each item.

Ease of scoring should also be a consideration when designing the format for a test. Many schools now have computer scoring available for teachers. The answer sheets provided with the computer system will dictate the nature of your answer sheets. If such a system is not available, you will need to design your own answer sheets. If most or all of your test is composed of objective test items, or if you are going to be scoring a large number of very lengthy tests, you should consider using a separate answer sheet. For most objective items, scoring a separate answer sheet is easier than scoring answers spread all over the test itself. Finally, the test should have overall directions listed at the beginning of the test. For example, a place for the student's name should be provided, and the student should be directed to place his or her name in that space before proceeding to answer questions on the examination. If the test has a time limit, then this should also be stated.

## Sample Format for Tests

The formats of tests can vary depending on several factors, including

1. Will a separate answer sheet be used?
2. Will students need to confine answers for essay questions to the space provided, or will they respond on a separate sheet of paper?
3. Will different kinds of items be scored differently?

Figures 7.1 and 7.2 illustrate a commonly used arrangement that involves the use of a separate answer sheet.

When an answer sheet is first used with a group of students, explain to students the care needed in recording answers. Students may be provided some practice using answer sheets on short examinations before using answer sheets on major tests. Students in late elementary or early secondary classes may make many errors in recording answers on a separate answer sheet even with practice. To minimize these errors use the same format for all examinations so that the examination procedures become routine. Routine formats, learned through practice, may help reduce the errors students make when recording answers on a separate answer sheet.

Much variation in scores on examinations may result because some students are "test wise" and others are not. Students need to be taught how to take examinations. They should be told to go through the examination and answer only questions for which they know the answers before proceeding to answer others for which they are uncertain. Sometimes they will pick up clues for answering questions they initially did not know. If taking a multiple-choice examination, they should answer all questions for which there is a strong likelihood they will be correct. For the questions that would require guessing, students should choose the same alternative, usually (c) or (3), for each question. Before responding to essay questions students should underline key words. If there is doubt about the meaning intended for these key words, they should ask the teacher to clarify meanings. Such guidance, with time, will enable students to improve their test scores.

## Cognitive Levels of Questions

A test should measure a variety of understandings. Some teachers tend to write test items measuring only simple memorization. Focusing on simple memorization is not a recommended practice because students perceive tests as indicators of the important things to remember (Medley, 1979). The kinds of items on tests will ultimately determine the kinds of learning on which students will focus. Therefore, testing for outcomes beyond memory is advisable. Students must understand the content beyond the knowledge level if the content is to be of any use to them in situations other than merely responding to items on tests. Benjamin Bloom's taxonomy of educational objectives (Bloom, 1956) is a useful guide, not only for determining instruc-

NAME _____

Read these directions before starting.

1. Place your name in the space provided above and also on the answer sheet before continuing with this examination.
2. All answers should be placed on the answer sheet.
3. You have fifty minutes to complete this examination.
4. Should you complete the examination before others, quietly turn it over and be silent until all examinations are collected.

I.   Multiple-choice (1 point each.)
Each question has only one best answer. Place an "X" through the letter on the answer sheet to indicate your answer.

1. The stem of the question will go here
   a. the alternatives from which to choose go here
   b. alternative
   c. alternative
   d. alternative

2. The next item stem
   a. alternative
   b. alternative
   c. alternative
   d. alternative

II.   True-False (1 point each).
Place an "X" through the T (true) or F (false) on the answer sheet to indicate your answer.

3. First statement

4. Second statement

III. Essay (5 points each).
Write your answers on the answer sheet in the space provided for each question. Do not exceed that space.

5. First essay question

6. Second essay question

FIGURE 7–1
**Sample Examination
(Using an Answer Sheet)**

Name _____

I.   Multiple-choice Answers (Place an "X" Through your answer.)

  1. a  b  c  d

  2. a  b  c  d

                              (etc.)

II.   True-False Answers (Place an "X" Through your answer)

  3. T  F

  4. T  F

                              (etc.)

III. Essay Answers (Confine your answers to the space provided.)

  1.




  2.

**FIGURE 7–2**
**Sample Examination Answer Sheet**

tional objectives and classroom questions, but also for determining the nature of test questions. Questions can be classified by degree of complexity as follows:

1. Knowledge: questions asking the student to remember specific
   a. facts
   b. definitions
   c. rules
   d. past trends
   e. sequences
   f. criteria
   g. classifications
   h. generalizations
   i. methodologies
   j. theories
   k. structures
   l. principles
2. Comprehension: questions asking the student to
   a. translate a message
   b. interpret a message
   c. extrapolate from a message
3. Application: questions asking the student to use knowledge in particular situations. The problem situation should be new or in some way different from the situations used in the instruction. These questions might ask students to
   a. determine which principles or generalizations are relevant in dealing with a new problem situation
   b. restate a problem to determine which principles are necessary for a solution
   c. specify the limits within which a particular principle or generalization is true
   d. recognize the exceptions to a particular generalization or rule, and be able to identify the reasons for the exceptions
   e. explain new phenomena or situations in terms of known principles, generalizations or rules
   f. predict what would happen in new situations
   g. determine a particular course of action in a new situation
4. Analysis: questions asking the student to examine a novel problem situation and break it into component parts, identify the elements, identify the relationships that exist between the parts, and/or recognize organizational principles that might govern the whole. The situation to be analyzed should be different from any used in the instruction. A description of the situation should be provided to the student, and it should be available for reference as the student answers the question. These questions might ask students to
   a. classify words, phrases, and statements according to given criteria
   b. infer particular qualities not directly stated from clues available in the description
   c. infer from data or information what underlying qualities, assumptions, or conditions must be implicit or necessary

    d. use criteria such as relevance or causation to determine an order in data or in a document

    e. recognize organizational principles or patterns on which an experiment or work is based

    f. infer the framework, purpose, or point of view on which a position or experiment is based

5. Synthesis: questions asking a student to respond to a problem, task, or situation that is new or different from those experienced during instruction. When scoring synthesis questions, judge either the adequacy with which the task was accomplished or the adequacy of the process used in accomplishing the task. Synthesis questions may ask students to

    a. develop a new communication

    b. produce a plan or organization

    c. invent a set of relations

    d. produce a solution to a problem

6. Evaluation: questions asking a student to make judgments about the relative value or worth of things and recognize the evidence and criteria used in those judgments. The material to be evaluated must be new or unfamiliar, but available to the student in the testing situation. These questions may ask students to

    a. judge the accuracy or precision used in conducting an experiment, writing a document, or creating a work of art

    b. judge the internal consistency of the arguments used in a document or experiment

    c. list the reasons supporting or refuting a position on an issue

    d. make judgments of a created work by comparing it with other relevant works

Using this classification merely to classify existing questions is of little value to a teacher constructing a testing instrument. As with any classification, actual items do not fall easily into distinct categories. This scheme is useful, however, in helping you identify possible instructional objectives that might otherwise be overlooked. Also, using this classification scheme to generate test items will help you write items that will test beyond mere memorization. If you seldom ask questions on tests from all of these categories, then you need to put more emphasis on your planning in order to increase the frequency with which you teach and test for more complex levels of understanding.

## Kinds of Test Items

### Essay questions

Essay questions are meant to allow a student to answer questions in his or her own words. The student is asked to recall from memory that knowledge referred to in the question, and then to structure or use that knowledge in a response.

1. Suggestions
   a. For the sake of efficiency, essay questions should generally be used to measure more complex understandings that require students to synthesize, organize, or solve unusual or novel problems. Objective items can usually be used to test for other understandings.
   b. The question should be phrased in a way to delimit the area being covered.
   c. The question should usually require short answers. Questions calling for lengthy responses are prone to scoring errors as well as to the introduction of additional criteria unrelated to the understandings being tested (Chase, 1968; Klein and Hart, 1968). If the teacher wishes to provide opportunities for students to write essays on a topic, then these opportunities usually should be provided outside a testing situation. If longer responses are needed to assess an objective, then the criteria for the students' responses to the item must be listed as part of the question. The absence of these criteria for longer answers will significantly reduce the reliability and validity of the item. Essay questions calling for lengthy responses have the added disadvantage of limiting the number of kinds of learning that can be sampled. This results in an advantage to some students and a disadvantage to others depending on whether or not they guessed the topics to be examined. Broader sampling of learnings reduces the probability of this disparity occurring on an examination.

d. The reliability of an essay test can be improved by using a relatively large number of questions requiring short answers rather than a few questions with long answers.

e. Measure only one kind of understanding within one question. Do not try to measure two quite different kinds of understanding with the same question. Making two separate questions from a question with two parts is better for purposes of reliability than keeping the parts together in the same question.

f. The criteria used to score the question should be implied in the question itself. Avoid the use of words or phrases such as "Tell how"; "Describe"; "Explain"; "What would happen"; or "Discuss." It is preferable to use phrases such as "List three reasons"; "Record two factors"; "What are three products"; "What two things could happen if"; "List three similarities"; or "What are two differences."

g. Use time and care in writing essay questions. Teachers sometimes think that essay tests take less time to prepare than other kinds of tests. This misconception can lead to poorly constructed essay tests. Removing ambiguity from essay questions can be a difficult and time-consuming task. While less time may be needed to write an essay question than to construct a multiple-choice question, the time differential is not large.

h. The reliability of scoring an essay test can be improved by scoring the same item for all students before going to the next item to be scored. The scores will more likely be the same or similar for comparable answers.

i. Prepare a key for scoring the test before it is administered. Using a key will insure that you do not introduce additional criteria after having read some of the students' replies. The key will also insure more consistency in your scoring. If you cannot prepare a key before you see student replies, then the item is undoubtedly too ambiguous to use on an examination.

2. Some faulty items. An analysis of some essay items may provide some insights into common errors found in essay questions and help you avoid some of these undesirable practices.

   a. Ambiguous items: items that poorly define the task the student is asked to perform. The student is left to guess the criteria to be used in grading or scoring the item.

   Item A: Discuss what is needed for good health.

   Item B: What is Abraham Lincoln noted for?

   Item C: Describe some of the differences between classical and popular musical compositions.

   Item D: Briefly discuss some of the major differences between democratic and socialistic forms of government.

   b. Testing for details: items that involve fragments of information that, if important, would be better tested through the use of objective items.

   Item A: Who was the "father" of our country, when was he born, and when did he serve as President of our country?

   Item B: When and where did the first battle of the Civil War occur?

   Item C: What is the difference between a pentagon and an octagon?

c. Unreasonable: items that ask for extensive discussions of topics are usually both ambiguous and unreasonable. Efforts to find out the extent to which students understand a topic may lead to questions that a well-informed person could write on for days.

Item A: What is the role of trigonometry in engineering?

Item B: What developments led to the cubistic school of art?

Item C: What kind of actions could be taken to insure the civil rights of minorities in our society?

3. Understandings tested. Essay questions can be used to test for all levels of understanding. These questions might include

   a. stating and defending positions on issues
   b. identifying and listing similarities and differences
   c. identifying processes
   d. listing examples illustrating some principle or rule
   e. analyzing deficiencies in arguments
   f. making predictions
   g. relating causes and effects

4. Some examples of essay questions

   a. Evaluations

      Item A: The use of nuclear power plants for the generation of electricity is presently controversial. List two factors that advocates cite in support of these plants, and two factors that critics cite in opposition to these plants.

      Item B: List two advantages and two disadvantages in the use of diets to control body weight.

   b. Comparisons

      Item A: What are two similarities and two differences in body structures between insects and spiders?

      Item B: List two differences between popular and classical music.

   c. Applications

      Item A: List two changes that could be made to reduce friction in an automobile and thereby reduce fuel consumption.

      Item B: Describe a process that could be used to separate salt from sea water.

5. Advantages of essay questions

   a. Essay questions can measure students' organizational skills better than other kinds of items.
   b. Essay questions allow the testing of all cognitive levels of understanding.
   c. Somewhat less time is required to write essay questions than multiple-choice and other kinds of objective test items.

6. Disadvantages of essay questions

   a. Scoring is more unreliable than with objective items.
   b. Writing unambiguous questions is extremely difficult, and teachers in haste tend not to do this task well.
   c. Essay tests are burdensome to score.
   d. Communication skills, in addition to the knowledge being tested, can affect the scoring of essay items. To the extent that this bias is allowed to occur, the

scores on tests may not indicate the students' understanding of the content as much as their ability to communicate. Some teachers would argue that this is acceptable because students should learn how to communicate, and therefore the assessment of communication skills on tests should motivate students to learn these skills. A contrary view holds that if the objectives of learning to communicate are important, then specific tests on these skills should be given. From a testing point of view, measuring two distinctly different abilities within one item should be avoided when possible because this practice lowers the validity and reliability of items.

e. Since answers to essay questions need to be written out, students will be spending more time responding to questions than thinking about answers. This means that the amount of student learning that can be sampled will be more limited with essay questions than with other kinds of questions.

## Multiple-choice Questions

Multiple-choice items are designed to ask a student to examine a question and recognize a correct choice by matching the alternatives to a correct answer that already exists in memory, generating a correct answer and comparing the alternatives to it, or evaluating each alternative as a potential answer and trying to reason from the question to that answer.

1. Suggestions
   a. The number of alternatives usually should be the same for all multiple-choice questions on a particular test. The usual number of alternatives will be four or five. If the number of alternatives needs to vary between four and five, then those with the same number of alternatives should be grouped together. Students should then be cautioned on the test when they reach the point where the number of alternatives per item changes. This caution will help reduce errors students make when inadvertently checking an unintended alternative.
   b. The item stem should be in the form of a question or an incomplete statement. If the stem is an incomplete statement to be completed by the choice of one of the alternatives, then the alternatives listed should
      (1) be grammatically consistent with the stem
      (2) complete the statement so as to make a complete sentence
      (3) be short phrases or sentences rather than one or two words
   c. Item stems should be stated positively. The use of "not" and "least" should be avoided. The use of negatives in the stem will lower the reliability of the responses because such stems create confusion. If using "not" is unavoidable, then use capital letters for the word "NOT" so that it will be clearly visible.
   d. Avoid ambiguity in the stem. While ambiguity may be less a problem in multiple-choice questions than in essay questions, using words that may have different meanings to different individuals should be avoided.
   e. Avoid giving clues to the correct answer in the stem.

f. The alternatives listed should be approximately the same length. Different length alternatives can give clues to the correct answer. Usually longer alternatives indicate the correct response.

g. The alternatives should be presented in a single column. Presenting the alternatives in linear sequence, in a paragraph form, or in multiple columns will cause students to make more errors by inadvertently checking an unintended alternative.

h. Using the alternative "all of the above" should generally be avoided. "None of the above" can be used if it is a plausible *distractor* and if used occasionally as the correct answer.

i. If the understanding of a definition is being tested, it is better to place the word to be defined in the stem, and then list possible alternative definitions. Avoid stating the definition in the stem, and then listing alternative words representing the definition. Such a practice encourages guessing, but more importantly, it encourages a trivial form of learning.

j. All distractors should be plausible. Avoid using any nonfunctioning distractors, that is, distractors that all students know are incorrect. Avoid distractors that are the opposite of the correct response. Such a practice eliminates all other distractors as possible alternatives. Avoid having two distractors with the same meaning. This eliminates them as possible correct answers. The use of nonfunctioning distractors will lower the reliability of the test.

k. Avoid using the same words and phrases for the correct alternative as those used in the textbook. Such a practice encourages trivial learning.

l. All alternatives should be logically related to the stem and should be similar in character. The alternatives should not be an unrelated collection of true and false statements.

m. Since multiple-choice questions involve more reading than other forms of test items, reasonable vocabulary should be used. To do otherwise is to test both reading ability and the content being tested. The validity of a test is then suspect. Wordiness should also be avoided. Extraneous words increase the time needed to answer questions and can also introduce confusion.

n. Avoid placing part of a question at the end of one page and continuing it on the next page. Dividing questions in this fashion is an especially poor practice.

2. Some faulty items

Item A: The Frenchman who developed a vaccine for rabies was

1. Fleming
2. Salk
3. Pasteur
4. Schroedinger
5. Whiting

Explanation: The stem gives a clue to the answer. Pasteur is the only French name.

Improvement: A Frenchman by the name of Pasteur is noted for the development of

1.  a vaccine for rabies
2.  a cure for tuberculosis
3.  a disinfectant against bacteria
4.  a new strain of virus

Item B: The battle of Chattanooga ended

1.  December 12, 1945
2.  December 25, 1960
3.  November 25, 1863
4.  July 4, 1920
5.  August 10, 1492

Explanation: Inconsequential subject matter and nonfunctioning distractors are being used. The only date related to time of the event is 1863.

Improvement: Testing for this kind of knowledge is not recommended. Therefore, this item cannot be improved and should not be included in a test.

Item C: An eight-sided polygon is an

1.  octagon
2.  pentagon
3.  triangle
4.  parallelogram
5.  decagon

Explanation: The stem leads grammatically to the answer. Using a list of names also promotes guessing and tends to lower reliability.

Improvement: Move the article down with the responses, and use the correct article with each, for example, "an octagon." Or better, start with a stem like "Which one of the following figures is an octagon?" Then list five drawings of figures.

Item D: An amount of surface is called

1.  volume
2.  area
3.  space
4.  length times width
5.  distance

Explanation: Using a list of names promotes guessing and tends to promote trivial kinds of learning.

Improvement: Reverse the stem and responses to read

Area can best be defined as

1.  length times width
2.  the space occupied by matter
3.  an amount of surface
4.  displacement times displacement
5.  an interval between two lines

Item E: If the radius of the earth were increased three feet, the circumference of the earth at the equator would be increased approximately (1) 28 feet, (2) 16 feet, (3) 9 feet, (4) 12 feet, (5) 3 feet.

Explanation: The alternatives are arranged so as to create confusion.

Improvement: Arrange the responses vertically and in descending or ascending order.

If the radius of the earth were increased three feet, the circumference of the earth at the equator would be increased approximately

1. 3 feet
2. 9 feet
3. 12 feet
4. 16 feet
5. 28 feet

3. Advantages of multiple-choice questions
   a. The amount of testing time spent on thinking about the question will be considerably greater than the amount of time spent on responding to the question.
   b. Since little time is needed to respond to multiple-choice questions, the reliability of tests can be improved by including a larger number of questions on an examination than would be possible with an essay examination.
   c. Multiple-choice questions lend themselves to statistical analysis for purposes of improvement. The ability to apply a statistical analysis allows the teacher constructing a test to improve the items on subsequent tests both by revising existing items and by developing his or her ability to write such items. The revision of items can lead to better reliabilities and more appropriate levels of difficulty.
   d. The scoring of multiple-choice items is simple and fast.
   e. Multiple-choice items can measure a wide variety of cognitive levels, that is, most of the same levels measured by essay questions, with the exception of synthesis.

4. Disadvantages of Multiple-choice Questions
   a. The construction of multiple-choice tests is very time-consuming.
   b. Without some training, teachers will usually test for trivial content and focus on memory/recognition items. The ability to construct items measuring for higher cognitive levels of understanding takes some training and practice.
   c. More paper and typing are required to prepare the testing instruments.
   d. Scores are likely to be distorted by reading and test-taking ability.

Because multiple-choice questions have so many advantages, some authorities suggest that teachers should try to construct multiple-choice questions first. They should switch to other forms only if the type of objective makes an alternate form more desirable (Gronlund, 1977). For most teachers, however, such a practice may not be practical due to the inordinate amount of time required.

## True-False Questions

True-false questions require a student to judge the accuracy of a statement. The student essentially compares the statement as written with his or her recollection of facts.

1. Suggestions
   a. Avoid the use of "all", "no", "always", "never", or other absolutes. Writing a valid true statement using absolutes is difficult, and their use usually indicates a false answer.
   b. Check each item carefully for ambiguity in words or phrases.
   c. Students should be told to circle or place an "x" through the words "true" and "false" on an answer sheet rather than write out the words or write the first letter. Since the first letters of the two words when capitalized can look similar, errors in scoring can be introduced.
   d. Use an approximately equal number of true and false items.
   e. Do not mix a true statement and a false statement within the same item.
   f. Avoid negative statements if possible. They will tend to have rather low reliability.
   g. Avoid very long statements. They will also tend to have low reliability.
   h. Avoid using phrases taken directly from the textbook.
2. Some faulty items
   Item A: The battle of the Alamo was fought in 1836 B.C.
   Explanation: This is a trick question. The choice of B.C. makes the question false.

   Item B: The value of pi is 3.14.
   Explanation: This is not the exact value of pi but one commonly used. The question could be either true or false depending on one's interpretation. This problem is common whenever measured quantities are involved in a true/false question.
   Item C: All dogs have a sharp sense of smell.
   Explanation: Use of "all" makes the question false because obviously at least one dog exists, if not more, that has lost its sense of smell by accident or disease.
3. Advantages of true-false items
   a. Testing a broad range of topics in a fairly short period of time is possible.
   b. Answer sheets are very easily scored.
4. Disadvantages of true-false items
   a. Many of the understandings measured with this kind of item are trivial.
   b. Writing a statement that is either clearly true or clearly false without giving the answer away is very difficult.
   c. Students have an even chance of guessing the correct answer. This reduces the range of scores and increases the amount of random error, making tests composed of these items unreliable.
   d. Those students who actually know more tend to score lower because they are able to read more into the statements. Those with superficial understandings are more likely to take the statement at face value and respond correctly.

## Matching Questions

Matching questions are designed to allow a student to identify pairs of matching statements, words, phrases, or other facts from separate lists of each.

1. Suggestions
   a. Place a list of numbered stems to the left. The stems can be incomplete sentences, statements, words, or phrases. Place the choices to the right, each identified with a letter.
   b. The stems and the choices should deal with similar content and similar kinds of content. Items should not be highly heterogeneous.
   c. The number of choices should exceed the number of stems to reduce the effect of guessing.
   d. The total number of items in the stems should be limited to no more than ten to twelve items.
   e. The items composing the stems should be longer than the items composing the choices if any differential in length occurs. People tend to read from left to right, so such a placement reduces the reading time needed to complete the item.
   f. If names of people are used in either the stem or the choices, then complete names should be used to avoid confusion.
   g. Stems or choices composed of one or two words should be alphabetized to reduce reading time.
   h. The directions for the item should include descriptions of the columns to be matched and tell the students where to place the answers.

2. A Faulty Item

   |   |   |   |   |
   |---|---|---|---|
   | a. Carter | 1. First astronaut on the moon |
   | b. King | 2. Long-time president of the coal miners |
   | c. Nixon | 3. Inventor |
   | d. Armstrong | 4. President at the time of the Watergate affair |
   | e. Bell | 5. Civil rights leader |
   | f. Lewis | 6. President in the last fifty years |

   Explanation: This item violates almost every one of the suggestions made. Also, the names "Carter" and "Nixon" both match choice (6).

   Improvement: Longer stems need to be arranged on the left, the choices need to be alphabetized, directions need to be complete, and the choices need to be homogeneous.

   Improved Item:

   Directions: Column A lists some processes that occur in the human body during digestion, and Column B lists parts of the digestive system. Match the process on the left with the part on the right by placing the appropriate letter for the part in the space to the left of the numbers in Column A. The name of each part can be used only once.

|  | *Column A* | *Column B* |
|---|---|---|
| _____ 1. | Most digestive absorption occurs in the | a. bile duct |
| _____ 2. | Hydrochloric acid dissolves food primarily in the | b. colon |
|  |  | c. esophagus |
| _____ 3. | Food passes directly from the stomach into the | d. gall bladder |
|  |  | e. mouth |
| _____ 4. | Mechanical digestion occurs primarily in the | f. small intestine |
|  |  | g. stomach |

3. Advantages of matching questions
   a. A large number of specific understandings can be tested in a short period of time.
   b. These items are easy to score, and score reliably.
4. Disadvantages of matching questions
   a. The level of learning tested is restricted to the recognition of simple relationships. Matching questions are unable to measure understandings beyond this rather low level of understanding.
   b. Giving clues within the items is difficult to avoid. This lowers the reliability of the items.

## Completion Questions

Completion questions require the student to associate some incomplete statement with some word or words recalled from memory.

1. Suggestions
   a. Avoid varying the length of spaces to be filled in. This practice will give clues to the answers and will promote guessing.
   b. Avoid statements to be completed by inserting measured quantities. Students would usually not know the degree of accuracy that would be required for a correct answer.
   c. Study each question carefully for ambiguity.
   d. Avoid more than one blank for each question, and place the blank toward the end of the sentence.
2. Faulty Items
   Item A: The capital city of Ohio is _____
   Explanation: Possible answers include "large," "clean," "in the middle of the state," and "Columbus."
   Improved Item:
   The name of the capital city of Ohio is _____
   Explanation: Even here, the purist could insist that the answer, "composed of eight letters" would also be correct, which merely illustrates the difficulty of writing completion items without ambiguity.
   Item B: _____ was the first President of _____.

Explanation: So many parts of the sentence have been omitted that numerous answers are possible. In addition, the lengths of the blanks vary and may encourage students to guess.

Improved Item

The name of the first President of the Confederacy was ———.

3. Advantages of completion questions
   a. Items can usually be constructed rather easily.
   b. Many different memorized words can be tested in a short period of time.
4. Disadvantages of completion questions
   a. Completion items can test only for the ability to associate memorized words or phrases with incomplete statements.
   b. The items must be scored by reading the responses; therefore, scoring takes more time and may involve more error than other types of objective questions.
   c. Writing unambiguous items is difficult, and the questions will probably test for specific wording in a textbook.
   d. Testing for recall of specific words trivializes the content being tested to the point that these questions are almost better left unasked.

## Test Administration

When administering tests to whole classes, you should make procedures as simple and routine as possible. The more predictable the procedures, the less thought students need to give them and the more they can concentrate on the task at hand. Several things need to be considered to reduce the amount of confusion:

1. The copies of the tests to be administered should be readily available and arranged in a way to minimize the time needed to distribute them.
2. All students should be silent before the tests are distributed, while they are being distributed, and while the tests are being completed.
3. The teacher should insure that all students have the needed materials before the tests are distributed. All pencils should be sharpened and the needed paper on hand.
4. All materials, except those needed to take the test, should be removed from the surface of the desk or table being used by the students.
5. All tests should remain face down when distributed, and should remain face down until the teacher gives the students a signal to turn them over.
6. Before students begin the test, they should read the directions, and the teacher should check for understanding by asking the students to repeat the directions.
7. Students should be told what to do when they finish the test so as not to disturb those still completing the test.
8. When tests are completed, they should be collected in a way that reduces confusion.

## Evaluating Tests

### Validity

Determining if a test measures what you want it to measure is difficult. Students must accomplish a particular task to answer a test question correctly. Correctly perceiving the nature of this task is difficult at best. We are easily deceived when we analyze questions that we write. Asking another person to examine our objectives and to compare them with the test items measuring the objective can help identify some obvious incongruities. Such an examination will give you an indication of the content validity, that is, the extent to which the items match your objectives.

Another form of validity is the degree to which your test might correspond to a test designed by someone else (i.e., a standardized test) to measure the same thing. This kind of validity is called *concurrent validity*. To establish concurrent validity, you would need to administer your test and the test with which it will be compared, then calculate a correlation coefficient between the two.

Another indication of validity available to most teachers is *construct validity*. This form of validity indicates the degree to which your test conforms to some theoretical model that you might develop. For example, assuming an honors class would score higher on a particular instrument than a regular class studying the same subject, a test with construct validity would distinguish between these two groups. To test for construct validity, you would administer your test to these two groups, then determine if the averages of the two groups were significantly different. If such a difference were found, your test would have construct validity. You might also predict, in the case of a science test, that it would have a low correlation with a reading test, since the intent of the science test is not to test for reading ability but for understanding of science. To check this assumption, you would administer both tests and calculate a correlation between the two sets of scores. If a correlation exists, then your science test would lack construct validity, since it obviously was measuring reading ability as well as science understanding.

Most teachers lack the time to do extensive tests of validity. However, checking for content validity by comparing items with objectives is the least teachers should do for each of their tests.

### Item Quality

The level of difficulty of test items, as well as the ability of test items to discriminate between students, are measures that are easily calculated and quite useful. If you are going to improve your skills in test writing, then learning and using these two kinds of analyses will be helpful.

#### *Level of Difficulty*

Tests designed to measure the cognitive understandings of students are usually administered for two quite different purposes. First, tests are used to measure mastery learning when evaluating the effectiveness of instruction or when diagnosing students during individualized instruction. Second, tests are given to rank students in relation to one another for purposes of assigning grades or placement. These two different purposes require tests with different characteristics.

For example, if a test is going to be used to decide whether or not students are ready for the next instructional experience, the test would be composed of items measuring minimal prerequisite understandings required for the next instructional experience. Most, if not all, of the students who were successful in completing the instructional lesson would answer the questions successfully. The same could be said for a test used to evaluate the effectiveness of some curriculum materials or method of instruction. If the materials or method of instruction were successful, most students should be able to answer the items on the test. Tests designed to measure minimum understanding are referred to as *criterion-referenced tests*. Such tests would be expected to produce very high scores. Ideally, most students would get all of the items correct. Criterion-referenced tests, or diagnostic tests, are designed so that the average scores will be approximately 80–100 percent.

Tests designed to assess student achievement for purposes of ranking students and then assigning grades are called *norm-referenced tests*. Such tests need to be reliable; they need to measure accurately and consistently. If an achievement test has a low reliability, then students could have positions in the ranking higher or lower than other students not because of some real difference in their knowledge but because of errors in the measurement. Such measurement error differences would result in inaccurate grades; therefore, the scores for achievement tests should extend over a wide range in order to maximize their reliability. The range of scores on achievement tests will be from 30 percent to 95 percent, with an average of approximately 50–60 percent.

Trying to measure mastery and achievement with the same instrument will lower the reliability of the instrument and insure that neither task is done well. Including mastery items on an achievement test, for example, would be counterproductive for reliably measuring achievement. These different objectives demand different tests.

Each item on a test will present its own challenge to students attempting to respond. If an item is too easy, almost all students will answer correctly. If an item is too difficult, almost all students will answer incorrectly. On mastery or criterion-referenced tests, students should answer most, if not all, items correctly. On the other hand, each item on an achievement test should be answered correctly by 50–60 percent of the students. Studies have shown that the precision of a test is highest when all of the items composing an achievement test possess approximately the same level of difficulty, with the average level between 60–70 percent correct responses (Diederich, 1969). Such an unvarying level of difficulty for all items is almost impossible for most teachers to achieve, but teachers should at least try to avoid the usual practice of deliberately varying the item difficulty from easy to difficult.

The calculation of level of difficulty for a test item is commonly calculated in one of two ways. The simpler is to take the number of students answering a question correctly and divide it by the total number of students responding to the question. For example, if all of the students out of a sample of twenty students answered a question correctly, then the difficulty level would be 20/20 = 1.0. If all of the students answered the question incorrectly, the level of difficulty would be 0/20 = 0. If one-half of the students answered the question correctly, the level of difficulty would be 10/20 = .5.

A second method of calculating level of difficulty is to arrange all of the test papers from highest to lowest score. Then take the top 27 percent of the tests and the bottom 27 percent of the tests, and follow the same procedure with this reduced sample as described in the preceding paragraph. This second method is preferred when one is also analyzing for *discrimination,* which will be explained in the next section. You will understand why the second method is preferred when you see the method of determining the discrimination of items.

### *Item Discrimination*

If a test is to be reliable, then items on the test must discriminate between those students who know the material well and those who know the material poorly. You would not want a student who knows the material better than other students to score lower than someone who knows it less well. To test the ability of an item to discriminate, a discrimination coefficient is calculated.

To calculate a discrimination coefficient, arrange the test papers from highest to lowest scores. If the test is valid, the total score will represent a student's total understanding of the content being tested. The student who knows the most content overall should have the highest score, the one who knows the least should have the lowest score, and the other students should fall someplace between.

Take the papers representing the top 27 percent of the scores and the papers representing the bottom 27 percent of the scores. Be sure that the size of both samples is the same. Then take the number of students in the top group that answered the first item correctly and subtract from this number the number of students in the bottom group who answered the item correctly. Take the difference and divide by the number of students in the top group (or bottom group). For example, let's assume that on the first item on the test, five of eight students in the top group answered the item correctly, and that three of eight students in the bottom group answered the item correctly. Your calculation would look like this:

$$\frac{5 - 3}{8} = .25$$

Don't be surprised, when you do this calculation on your test items, to find that some items have a negative coefficient. For example, imagine that four out of eight students in the top group got an item correct, while six out of eight in the bottom group got the same item correct. The discrimination coefficient would be:

$$\frac{4 - 6}{8} = -.25$$

A negative coefficient indicates that students who score lower on the test as a whole are more likely than are those who scored higher on the test to get the answer to that question correct. Having items on a test with negative discriminations is obviously undesirable. Such items should be removed from a test because they lower the reliability of the test.

A slight variation of this process is necessary when calculating the difficulty and discrimination coefficients for essay and matching test items. Imagine you gave a matching or essay question with a maximum of four possible points. The maximum number of points that a high group composed of eight students could receive would be thirty-two points ($4 \times 8 = 32$). A discrimination of 1.0 would occur if all of the high group received the maximum points possible, and the low group received no points:

$$\frac{\text{Points by High Group} - \text{Points by Low Group}}{\text{Maximum Points Possible/Group}} = \frac{32 - 0}{32} = 1.0$$

To determine the number of points received by each group, set up a simple table. Record in the table the number of students in each group receiving each of the possible points. Then take the number of students in each cell and multiply that times the points each received. Then add up the points received by each group. For example,

| | *High* | | | *Low* | |
|---|---|---|---|---|---|
| 4. | 6 | ($6 \times 4 = 24$) | 3 | ($3 \times 4 = 12$) |
| 3. | 1 | ($1 \times 3 = 3$) | 2 | ($2 \times 3 = 6$) |
| 2. | 1 | ($1 \times 2 = 2$) | 1 | ($1 \times 2 = 2$) |
| 1. | | | 1 | ($1 \times 1 = 1$) |
| 0. | | | 1 | ($1 \times 0 = 0$) |

Points for High = 29    Points for Low = 21

Maximum possible points for both groups combined = 64

$$\text{Difficulty} = \frac{29 + 21}{64} = .78$$

$$\text{Discrimination} = \frac{29 - 21}{32} = .25$$

Items on a test should have discriminations of at least .30 or higher (Kubiszyn and Borich, 1984). One word of caution, however. Questions that test simple knowledge level are easier to write and will tend to have higher discriminations than will items measuring more complex levels of understanding. If the sole criterion for appropriate items on a test was a high discrimination coefficient, then one should test for knowledge level understandings in an attempt to make the discrimination coefficient as high as possible. *This practice should be avoided.* Obviously, the sole criterion should not be discrimination. You want a sample of items representing all of the objectives. When using the discrimination coefficient for purposes of evaluating the item compare only those questions that measure approximately the same level of complexity on Bloom's taxonomy. The only items for which this comparison is not necessary are those with negative discriminations. Always eliminate from future tests any items with negative discriminations regardless of level unless the item can be improved so that it is no longer negatively discriminating.

If items have low discrimination, look for practices you should have avoided in designing that kind of item. The reason to avoid those practices listed is that some deficiencies lower the discrimination. Then too, items that are too easy or too difficult will also tend to have low discriminations, so check the level of difficulty first when you find an item with low discrimination. The calculation of discrimination coefficients as described will not tell you the nature of the deficiency, but it will help you avoid obviously deficient items.

Calculating discrimination coefficients for multiple-choice items can be slightly altered to provide additional information about the quality of the question. Divide the test papers into the top and bottom 27 percent as described previously, and then do as follows:

*Step 1:*   Make a small table. (Assume five responses listed after the stem.)

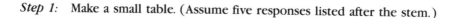

|   | Top | Bottom |
|---|-----|--------|
| a |  |  |
| b |  |  |
| c |  |  |
| d |  |  |
| e |  |  |

*Step 2:*   Count the number of students in the top group that answered the item by marking the first choice, and place this number in the top left box. Count the number of students in the top group that answered the item by marking the second choice, and place this number in the next lower box. Continue to record the responses made by each student in each group in the appropriate spaces. When finished your table will look like this:

| | Top | Bottom |
|---|---|---|
| a | | |
| b | | |
| c | 1 | 1 |
| d | 4 | |
| e | 3 | 7 |

If item e were the correct answer, then the discrimination coefficient would be

$$\frac{3 - 7}{8} = -.50$$

With a negative discrimination, this question is unsuitable as written. First, review the suggestions for constructing multiple-choice items. If you violated any of these suggestions, make changes to correct these errors. Now examine the data. Notice that the first two responses are not acting as distractors for either group. These would need to be changed to become more plausible so that some students would begin to choose them. Since the third response does not discriminate between the groups, it needs to be replaced. Since the fourth response is obviously misleading those students who know more about the content (as evidenced by their higher scores), this response would need to be revised or eliminated. The last response is one to which students knowing less are guided. Since this is the correct answer, it will need to be retained. Some revision of the correct response might be considered, however. The stem of the question could also be examined for possible revision. Usually if an item is this poor, elimination without revision is necessary.

Notice that once you have the data table for determining the discrimination coefficient, you also have the necessary data to calculate the level of difficulty. For example, ten of sixteen students whose responses are being assessed answered the question correctly. The level of difficulty is therefore $10/16 = .62$. Now you know why the second method for determining level of difficulty is used.

Let's examine another example taken from an actual test administered by the author. The test item administered read as follows:

Which one of the following is the most common reason for student misbehavior in the high school classroom?

a. There may be a past history of failing grades on the part of the student misbehaving.
b. The student misbehaving usually does not realize he or she is misbehaving.
c. The student misbehaving does not feel a need to be involved in the class activity.
d. The student misbehaving wants the teacher's attention.
e. The teacher may not have demonstrated an interest in the concerns of the student misbehaving.

The correct answer is "c." The item analysis showed the following results.

|   | Top | Bottom |
|---|---|---|
| a |   | 1 |
| b | 1 | 3 |
| c | 4 | 1 |
| d |   | 2 |
| e | 2 |   |

The difficulty level of the item is .36 (5/14), and the discrimination coefficient is .43 (3/7). Notice that the alternative "e" seems to be discriminating against those students with the highest score; therefore, this item needs to be changed. Also the difficulty level is fairly high. (Remember, a small percent indicates a difficult item.) Some of the difficulty may stem from the wordiness of the test item. Based on this analysis, a revised item might look like this:

---

The most common reason for misbehavior in a high school classroom would be that the misbehaving student

a. has a past history of failure
b. does not realize he or she is misbehaving
c. does not feel a need to be involved in the activity
d. wants the teacher's attention
e. is emotionally disturbed

---

We have little way of knowing if this item will actually discriminate better until we actually administer the item and do an analysis. This inability to predict the quality of an item is reason enough for suggesting that all items should be analyzed if you are serious about improving the tests you administer. To fail to do such an analysis is to insure continued mediocrity in the quality of your tests.

## Reliability

Tests are measuring instruments that provide us useful data for making decisions. One such decision is that of assigning grades. In this context, tests are used to measure cognitive understandings in order to rank students. The testing process, however, involves error, as does any measuring process. Sources of possible error affecting test scores include, but are not confined to

1. errors introduced during the administration of the test by providing poorly worded directions, being unconcerned about the physical discomfort of students, placing unrealistic time limits on the examination, and/or creating anxiety by tell-

ing the students that the test is very difficult or very important for determining grades
2. errors introduced through scoring, such as errors in keys, counting, or calculations
3. inadvertent errors by the student taking the test, such as distractions in his or her personal life, inability to concentrate due to poor health, test anxiety, timidness and the resulting reluctance to even guess at answers, lack of knowledge about how to take tests, and/or lack of experience in taking a test using the format of the current test
4. errors introduced by the nature of the test itself, such as trick questions, items too easy or too difficult, poorly phrased questions, items that are too wordy, ambiguous items, items too difficult to read, technically deficient items, and /or items that discriminate poorly

To help you recognize the effect of the errors due to the nature of the test itself, some understanding of reliability is needed. A test is considered *reliable* when it yields nearly the same ranks over repeated administrations. That is, students ranked in a sequence on one administration of the test would be ranked nearly the same if the test could be administered again, with no learning occurring from the first administration. If the rankings determined by a test varied significantly from one administration to the next for the same group, then such a test would not be an accurate measuring instrument. We would not want to use the scores from such an instrument to assign grades; much injustice would result.

### Test-Retest Reliability
The definition of reliability gives some clue as to what you might do to check the reliability of your tests, namely, give the same test to the same group after a lapse of time. Then a correlation between the two sets of scores is calculated. This is called *test-retest reliability*. Such a reliability calculation may have a lower correlation not only because the test may be unreliable but also because students will have learned something from the first test and will score differently. This can be partially overcome by allowing a long interval between the two administrations.

### Calculating a Correlation Coefficient
To calculate a correlation coefficient, use a minimum of twenty-five to thirty scores. Take the two sets of scores and arrange them into two columns, one titled "X" and the other "Y." Then set up three columns to the right of these columns. The third column will list the product obtained by multiplying the score in column "X" by the score in column "Y." Title the third column "XY." The fourth column will list the values for the square of the scores in column "X," calculated by multiplying the score in "X" by itself. Title the fourth column "XX." The fifth column will list the values for the square of the scores in column "Y," calculated by multiplying the score in "Y" by itself. Title this column "YY." Now add up each of the five columns. Your table should look something like this.

| Student | X | Y | XY | XX | YY |
|---------|-----|-----|------|------|------|
| A | 24 | 26 | 624 | 576 | 676 |
| B | 19 | 22 | 418 | 361 | 484 |
| C | 26 | 25 | 650 | 676 | 625 |
| Sum | 69 | 73 | 1692 | 1613 | 1785 |

Now do the calculation of the correlation coefficient following the steps listed. $N$ is equal to the number of pairs of scores used. For example, in the illustration above, N would be equal to 3.

*Step 1:*

$$\frac{\text{Sum of X}}{N} = \#1$$

*Step 2:*

$$\frac{\text{Sum of Y}}{N} = \#2$$

*Step 3:*

$$\frac{\text{Sum of XY}}{N} = \#3$$

*Step 4:*

$$\#1 \times \#2 = \#4$$

*Step 5:*

$$\#3 \times \#4 = \#5 \text{ (\#5 will be used later.)}$$

*Step 6:*

$$\frac{\text{Sum of XX}}{N} = \#6$$

*Step 7:*

$$\#1 \times \#1 = \#7$$

*Step 8:*

$$\#6 - \#7 = \#8$$

*Step 9:*

Square root of #8 = #9 (#9 will be used later.)

*Step 10:*

$$\frac{\text{Sum of YY}}{\text{N}} = \#10$$

*Step 11:*

$$\#2 \times \#2 = \#11$$

*Step 12:*

$$\#10 - \#11 = \#12$$

*Step 13:*

Square root of $\#12 = \#13$ ( $\#13$ will be used later.)

*Step 14:*

$$\#9 \times \#13 = \#14$$

*Step 15:*

$$\frac{\#5}{\#14} = \text{Correlation Coefficient}$$

(Note: This particular correlation coefficient is called a *product-moment correlation coefficient.*)

### Internal Consistency Reliability

Another way of looking at reliability is to assume that tests that measure homogeneous learnings, that is, very similar learnings, should be composed of items that will correlate with each other and the total score on the test. Students who get one item correct should more probably get other items correct. Such a reliability is called a measure of *internal consistency.*

One mathematical formula used to calculate a ratio representing internal consistency is the Kuder Richardson Formula 20. The process of calculating this ratio is not simple but is well within the abilities of teachers. This calculation is not something you would likely do for all tests, but the calculation of a test-retest correlation coefficient or reliability coefficient of internal consistency for major tests is recommended. These coefficients can give you some indication of your skills in test construction. To fail to analyze your tests statistically is to insure that your skills in test development will not likely improve. This analysis is also valuable in providing insight into the uncertainty of the grades you assign test scores.

### Calculating a Reliability Coefficient

*Step 1:*  Record all of the scores for one or two classes of students in a vertical column and add the scores.

*Scores*

10
9
8
6
7
10
6
5
——
61

*Step 2:* Take the sum of the scores and divide by the number of scores listed. This will give you the *average* score (also called the *mean*).

$$\frac{61}{8} = 7.6 \text{ (average score)}$$

*Step 3:* Next take each score in your column of scores and subtract the average score from each score listed. If the average score is larger than the score listed, then the resulting number will be negative. Record this difference between the score and the average score in Column 2.

| *Scores* | *Column 2* | |
|---|---|---|
| 10 | 10 − 7.6 = | 3.4 |
| 9 | 9 − 7.6 = | 1.4 |
| 8 | 8 − 7.6 = | .4 |
| 6 | 6 − 7.6 = | − 1.6 |
| 7 | 7 − 7.6 = | − .6 |
| 10 | 10 − 7.6 = | 3.4 |
| 6 | 6 − 7.6 = | − 1.6 |
| 5 | 5 − 7.6 = | − 2.6 |

*Step 4:* Take each of the numbers in column 2 and multiply it by itself, and record the product in column 3.

| *Scores* | *Column 2* | | *Column 3* |
|---|---|---|---|
| 10 | 10 − 7.6 = | 3.4 | 11.56 |
| 9 | 9 − 7.6 = | 1.4 | 1.96 |
| 8 | 8 − 7.6 = | .4 | .16 |
| 6 | 6 − 7.6 = | − 1.6 | 2.56 |
| 7 | 7 − 7.6 = | − .6 | .36 |
| 10 | 10 − 7.6 = | 3.4 | 11.56 |
| 6 | 6 − 7.6 = | − 1.6 | 2.56 |
| 5 | 5 − 7.6 = | − 2.6 | 6.76 |

*Step 5:* Add the resultant numbers in Column 3 and divide by the number of scores. This number is called the *variance.*

| Scores | Column 2 | | Column 3 |
|---|---|---|---|
| 10 | 10 − 7.6 = | 3.4 | 11.56 |
| 9 | 9 − 7.6 = | 1.4 | 1.96 |
| 8 | 8 − 7.6 = | .4 | .16 |
| 6 | 6 − 7.6 = | −1.6 | 2.56 |
| 7 | 7 − 7.6 = | − .6 | .36 |
| 10 | 10 − 7.6 = | 3.4 | 11.56 |
| 6 | 6 − 7.6 = | −1.6 | 2.56 |
| 5 | 5 − 7.6 = | −2.6 | 6.76 |
| | | | 37.48 |

$$\text{variance} = \frac{37.48}{8} = 4.685$$

(Note: The square root of the variance is called the *standard deviation.* The standard deviation will not be used directly in this calculation, but it will be referred to later.)

*Step 6:* Make another table of four columns. In the first column, merely place numbers from 1 through the number of items on the test. For example, if you had ten items on the test, the first column would have the numbers 1 through 10.

*Step 7:* In the second column, record the decimal fraction of students who answered each item correctly, and in the third column record the decimal fraction of students who answered each item incorrectly. Multiply the number in column 2 by the number in column 3 for each item, and place the product in column 4.

| Item | Column 2 | Column 3 | Column 4 |
|---|---|---|---|
| 1 | .35 | .65 | .228 |
| 2 | .85 | .15 | .128 |
| 3 | .20 | .80 | .160 |
| 4 | .90 | .10 | .090 |
| 5 | 1.00 | .00 | .000 |
| 6 | .50 | .50 | .250 |
| 7 | .75 | .25 | .188 |
| 8 | .00 | 1.00 | .000 |
| 9 | .45 | .55 | .248 |
| 10 | .60 | .40 | .240 |
| | | Sum = | 1.532 |

*Step 8:*   Add column 4. The sum in this example would be 1.532.

*Step 9:*   Take the number of items on the test and subtract 1 from it. Divide the number of items on the test by the resultant number.

$$\frac{10}{(10 - 1)} = 1.11$$

*Step 10:*   Take the variance found in Step 5 and subtract the number found in Step 8 from it.

$$4.685 - 1.532 = 3.153$$

*Step 11:*   Take the number from Step 10 and divide it by the variance from Step 5.

$$\frac{3.153}{4.685} = .673$$

*Step 12:*   Multiply the number found in Step 11 by the number found in Step 9.

$$.673 \times 1.11 = .75 = \text{reliability coefficient}$$

The resultant number from Step 12 is the *RELIABILITY coefficient*. This coefficient is an indication of how well the items on the test correlate with each other. This number will be less than 1.00. The higher this decimal fraction, the more reliable the instrument is in measuring what it purports to measure. A well-made teacher test will usually have a reliability between .60 and .80 (Diederich, 1969).

### Interpreting a Reliability Coefficient

To get a feeling for what a reliability coefficient is saying about your tests, an examination of some of the numbers calculated in the previous example may help. These numbers include:

Average = 7.6

Standard Deviation = 2.16

Reliability = .75

If scores are distributed normally, approximately 68 percent of the scores will fall within one standard deviation from the average, 95 percent of the scores will fall within two standard deviations from the average, and 99 percent of the scores will fall within three standard deviations from the average.

In this example then, approximately 68 percent of the scores fall within one standard deviation above and below the average, that is, from 5.44 to 9.76. Approximately 95 percent of the students will have scores that fall between 3.28 and 11.92, and 99.8 percent of students will have scores that fall between 1.12 and 14.08. This information can be useful when combined with a value called a *standard error of measurement*. The standard error of measurement is an estimation of the standard deviation that would be obtained if the same individual repeatedly took the examination.

### Calculating the standard error of measurement

*Step 1:*   Subtract the reliability coefficient from 1.

$$1 - .75 = .25$$

*Step 2:*   Calculate the square root of the number from Step 1. In this case the square root of .25 = .50

*Step 3:*   To find the standard error of measurement, multiply the number found in Step 2 by the standard deviation.

$$.50 \times 2.16 = 1.08 = \text{standard error of measurement}$$

In this example, an individual with a score of 7 who retook the test (assuming total lapse of memory about the test) would have a 32 percent chance of achieving a score higher than 8.08 or lower than 5.92. Obviously, fractional scores have no meaning, but they give some notion of the uncertainty inherent in scores. Using the same example, the same student would have only a 4.6 percent chance of receiving a score higher than 9.16 and lower than 5.44 (that is, 2 standard error measurements).

Another way of viewing information using the same numbers is to examine the probability that two students could exchange places in their ranking if, theoretically, the test could be administered again with no learning having occurred from taking the test. For an example, let's compare a student at the 50th percentile with a student at the 75th percentile. The probability of these students reversing the direction of difference between their scores per one hundred administrations of tests with different reliabilities would be

| Reliability | % Reversal |
|:-----------:|:----------:|
| .00 | 50 |
| .40 | 40 |
| .50 | 37 |
| .60 | 32 |
| .70 | 27 |
| .80 | 20 |
| .90 | 9 |
| .95 | 2 |

In the example of a test with a reliability of .75, the odds that a student at the 50th percentile will have a score higher than a student at the current 75th percentile on a readministration of the test would be approximately twenty-four in one hundred, or about one in four.

### *Factors that affect reliability*

Several factors can affect the reliability of tests. Scoring errors will lower the reliability. Tests that are too easy or too difficult will tend to have low reliabilities. The more heterogeneous the students being tested, the higher the reliability. Finally, as the number of items on a test increases, the reliability of the test will tend to increase. If you have given a test which has a reliability lower than you wish, you can increase the reliability of that test the next time you administer it by increasing the number of items. A simple formula will allow you to calculate the size of the test you would need to write to achieve the reliability you wish to have, assuming the additional items you would add would be of comparable quality to the items on the test being modified (Diederich, 1969, p. 153).

$$\text{Number of items on revised test} = N \times \frac{(\text{desired R}) \times (1 - R)}{R \times (1 - \text{desired R})}$$

Where: N  = number of items on original test

R  = reliability of original test

## Characteristics of Effective Tests

If a test is to measure significant learnings well, it should possess certain essential characteristics:

1. The test should measure what is intended to be measured, that is, it should be *valid.* The sum total of the items on the test should be a complete, or at least a representative, sample of the objectives to be tested. Further, the actual task to be completed by the student in answering the item should correspond to the task that the test maker intended. Therefore, each item needs to be carefully analyzed to determine the kind of thinking the student will use to answer the question successfully and to compare that thinking with the kind of thinking that is intended to be measured.

2. An achievement test should be *reliable;* each individual should receive the same ranking with repeated administrations of the same instrument. Just as you would not want to measure some critical distance with an inaccurate ruler, so too you should not want to measure a student's understanding with an inaccurate or inconsistent test.

3. The items on a test should be *reasonably difficult.* If a test is designed to measure achievement for the purpose of ranking students, then it would not be reasonable to have items on the test that all students could answer. The difficulty level of items should be chosen so that the range of scores will be the range desired.

4. The cognitive levels of the questions should vary from those requiring memory to those requiring more complex understanding. Any one test will not necessarily include questions from all categories of Bloom's taxonomy, but at least some variety, consistent with the objectives, should be present.

5. Questions should be devoid of ambiguity. High inference vocabulary should be avoided. Descriptive vocabulary and nontechnical vocabulary should be used wherever possible.

6. Trick questions should be avoided. Questions with hidden exceptions or questions testing two different things within the same question should be avoided.

7. Optional items on achievement tests should be avoided. To include optional items means that students may be taking different tests with different levels of difficulty and reliability.

## REFERENCES

Bloom, B.S., ed. 1956. *Taxonomy of educational objectives, handbook I: Cognitive domain*. New York: David McKay.

Blumberg, P., M.D. Alschuler, and V. Rezmovic. 1982. Should taxonomic levels be considered in developing examinations? *Educational and Psychological Measurement* 42:1–7.

Chase, C.I. 1968. The impact of some obvious variables on essay test scores. *Journal of Educational Measurement* 5(4): 315–318.

Diederich, P.B. 1969. Short-cut statistics for teacher-made tests. In *Statistics and measurement in the classroom*. ed. C.F. Hereford, L. Natalicio, and S.J. Farland. Dubuque, Iowa: Kendall/Hunt Publishing.

Gronlund, N.E. 1977. *Constructing achievement tests*. 2d ed. Englewood Cliffs, N.J.: Prentice-Hall, Inc.

Klein, S.P., and F.M. Hart. 1968. Chance and systematic factors affecting essay grades. *Journal of Educational Measurement* 5(3): 197–206.

Kubiszyn, T., and G. Borich. 1984. *Educational testing and measurement*. Glenview, Illinois: Scott, Foresman.

Medley, D.M. 1979. The effectiveness of teachers. In *Research on teaching*, ed. P.L. Peterson and H.J. Walberg. Berkeley, Calif.: McCutchan Publishing.

## SUMMARY

**Roles of Tests**
1. measure achievement of students
2. preassess student knowledge and skills
3. diagnose student mastery
4. evaluate the instruction or the curriculum

### Constructing a Test
1. Identify the instructional objectives.
2. Write items congruent with the instructional objectives.
3. Group like kinds of items together.
4. Decide on the use of a separate answer sheet.
5. Write directions for the test as well as each kind of item.
6. Indicate the value placed on each item of the test.

### Cognitive Levels of Questions
1. Knowledge: questions asking the student to remember specific facts, definitions, rules, past trends, sequences, criteria, classifications, generalizations, methodologies, theories, structures, or principles.
2. Comprehension: questions asking the student to translate a message, interpret a message, or extrapolate from a message.
3. Application: questions asking the student to
   a. determine which principles are relevant in dealing with a new problem situation
   b. restate a problem so as to determine which principles are necessary for solution
   c. specify the limits within which a particular principle or generalization is true
   d. recognize the exceptions to a particular generalization and be able to identify the reasons for the exceptions
4. Analysis: questions asking the student to examine a novel problem situation from a description provided and break it into component parts, identify the elements, identify the relationships that exist between the parts, and/or recognize organizational principles that might govern the whole.
5. Synthesis: questions asking students to respond to a novel problem, task, or situation and develop a new communication, produce a plan or organization, invent a set of relations, or produce a solution to a problem.
6. Evaluation: questions asking students to make judgments about the relative value or worth of something novel and recognize the evidence and criteria used in those judgments.

### Essay Questions
1. Essay questions should
   a. usually require answers of short duration
   b. measure one kind of understanding within one question
   c. include the criteria for scoring
   d. be unambiguous
   e. be scored one question at a time for all respondents.
2. Advantages of essay questions
   a. can measure students' organizational skills
   b. can measure all cognitive levels of understanding
   c. take less time to prepare than some other kinds

3. Disadvantages of essay questions
    a. scoring can be less reliable than with other kinds
    b. difficult to write unambiguous questions
    c. takes more time for students to respond
    d. cumbersome to score

## Multiple-Choice Questions
1. Multiple-choice questions should
    a. be composed of the same number of alternatives
    b. be composed of alternatives of about the same length
    c. have the alternatives listed in a column
    d. be stated positively
    e. be composed of equally plausible distractors
    f. use reasonable vocabulary
    g. have alternatives logically related to the stem

2. Advantages of Multiple-Choice Questions
    a. little response time is needed for each question
    b. questions can be improved through statistical analysis
    c. can measure a wide variety of cognitive levels
    d. scoring is simple and accurate

3. Disadvantages of Multiple-Choice Questions
    a. time consuming to construct
    b. usually takes training in order to write items beyond memory/recognition
    c. more paper and typing are required to prepare the test
    d. test-wise students can score higher than others

## True-False Questions
1. True-false questions should
    a. not be statements of absolutes
    b. not be ambiguous
    c. be evenly distributed between those that are true and those that are false
    d. be stated positively
    e. be relatively short sentences
    f. not be composed of phrases taken directly from the textbook

2. Advantages of true-false items
    a. short response time
    b. easily scored

3. Disadvantages of true-false items
    a. writing items that test for significant understanding that are either true or false
       is difficult
    b. guessing can play a significant role in individual scores

## Matching Questions

1. Matching questions should
   a. be composed of numbered items to the left and lettered choices to the right
   b. be composed of stems and choices dealing with similar content
   c. have a larger number of choices than stems
   d. have longer statements composing the stems and shorter statements composing the choices
   e. have the directions for responding at the beginning of the item
2. Advantages of matching questions
   a. response time is short
   b. items are easy and accurate to score
3. Disadvantages of matching questions
   a. level of understanding tested is limited to the simple recognition of related items
   b. difficult not to give clues

## Completion Questions

1. Completion questions should
   a. have the same length of blank space for each item
   b. not include questions about measured quantities
   c. not have more than one blank per question
   d. not be composed of statements taken directly from the textbook
2. Advantages of completion questions
   a. items can be constructed easily
   b. many words for definitions can be tested in a short time
3. Disadvantages of completion questions
   a. test only for association of words with phrases
   b. scoring takes longer than for other objective questions
   c. writing unambiguous items is very difficult

## Administering of Tests to Whole Classes

1. Copies should be distributed with a minimum of confusion.
2. All students should be silent before they begin the examination.
3. Only examination materials should be on the students' desks.
4. Directions should be made clear to students before they begin the examination.
5. Students finishing early should have an assigned task to accomplish.

## Evaluating Tests

1. Validity: degree to which a test measures what it is purported to measure.
   a. Content validity: degree to which the test items conform to the instructional objectives
   b. Concurrent validity: degree to which the test corresponds to other tests purported to measure the same thing
   c. Construct validity: degree to which a test conforms to some theoretical model

2. Item quality
   a. Level of difficulty: the fraction of the students answering the question correctly
      (1) Mastery tests should be composed of items having difficulties of approximately .8 to 1.0.
      (2) Achievement tests should be composed of items having difficulties of approximately .50 to .60.
   b. Item Discrimination: the degree to which an item distinguishes those students with higher scores from those with lower scores
3. Possible testing errors
   a. errors introduced through administration of the test, such as poor directions, physical discomfort, or unnecessary anxiety
   b. scoring errors
   c. student errors due to distractions, poor health, or anxiety
   d. errors introduced by the test itself, such as trick questions, poorly phrased questions, ambiguous items, or items that discriminate poorly
4. Reliability: degree to which a test measures consistently
   a. Test-retest reliability: the correlation between two administrations of the same test to the same students
   b. Internal consistency reliability: degree to which items correlate with each other and the total score for the test
   c. Standard error of measurement: an estimation of the standard deviation that would be obtained if the same individual repeatedly took the test
   d. Factors that affect reliability
      (1) Tests that are too easy or too difficult tend to have lower reliabilities.
      (2) The more heterogeneous the group being tested, the higher the reliabilities will tend to be.
      (3) As the number of items on a test increases, the higher the reliabilities will tend to be.

## Characteristics of effective tests
1. The test is valid if it measures what it is intended to measure.
2. The test is reliable if it measures consistently.
3. The test is of reasonable difficulty.
4. The cognitive levels of the questions vary.
5. Questions on the test are not ambiguous.
6. The test is composed of a variety of kinds of items.
7. Optional items are not used.

# EXERCISE 16
## Evaluating Test Items

Name _____

This exercise is designed to provide you experience in recognizing deficiencies in test items and correcting those deficiencies.

### Directions
1. Read each of the test questions, and in the space below the test item titled "Deficiency," identify the deficiency exhibited by the item.
2. Then in the space provided for the "Improved Item," rewrite the item to reflect recommended practices.

A. Essay items
   1. Discuss the different kinds of question types introduced in this chapter.

      Deficiency

      Improved item:

   2. List the disadvantages of essay test questions.

      Deficiency

      Improved item

B. Multiple-choice questions
   1. Multiple choice questions should (a) make frequent use of "all of the above" as a response; (b) have alternative responses of approximately the same length; (c) have some implausible alternatives; (d) never use questions in the stem; (e) all of the above.

   Deficiency



   Improved item






   2. Effective multiple-choice questions
      a. are answered correctly by most students
      b. can measure student understanding at a variety of cognitive levels
      c. these questions should not be used

   Deficiency




   Improved item

C. Matching question
   a. Longer stems              _____ items in the right column
   b. Shorter stems             _____ homogeneous
   c. Relationship of items     _____ items in the left column
   d. Number of items           _____ same in both columns

   Deficiency




   Improved item








D. True-False Questions
   1. True-False questions should never use "not," "always," etc.

   Deficiency




   Improved item

2. Negatively worded statements and ambiguity are anathemas.

   Deficiency




   Improved item

# EXERCISE 17
## Assessing Test Items

This exercise is designed to provide you experience in writing a test item and determining the level of difficulty and the discrimination of the item.

### Directions

1. Write one multiple-choice test item
   a. measuring some level of understanding beyond recall
   b. dealing with the content of this course studied to date
   c. appropriate for measuring the achievement of students in your class
   d. composed of four responses, and with letters from "a" through "d" to the left of each response.
2. Directly below the item, and separate from it, indicate the answer to the item by recording "Answer: _____" and placing the letter for the answer in the blank.
3. Turn in your question when requested by your instructor.
4. During a subsequent class period your instructor will administer a test composed of the items submitted, and these will be scored.
5. The class, or a small group of volunteers, will be organized in a way allowing you to analyze each item for discrimination and level of difficulty.
6. Some recommendations for revision of items may then be discussed by the class.

# EXERCISE 18
## Content Validity

This exercise is designed to provide you experience in constructing test items that are congruent with your instructional objectives, that is, that have *content validity.*

### Directions

1. Choose a topic or sequence of topics from your teaching field that could be appropriately taught in approximately one week. Write four instructional objectives for the topics of potential lessons that will allow you to write the test items requested below. Follow the criteria established in Chapter 1, "Planning Instruction," dealing with writing instructional objectives. List and number each instructional objective.
2. Concurrent with writing the objectives above, also write the corresponding test item(s) that would be used on an achievement test to measure attainment of these objectives.

3. Write one test item of each of the following:
   a. essay question
   b. multiple-choice item
   c. matching question composed of 5 item stems
   d. true/false item
4. To the left of the number for each test item, in parentheses, indicate the number of the objective being tested by inserting the number corresponding to the objective on your list of objectives.


# EXERCISE 19
## Test Construction


This exercise is designed to provide you experience in constructing a test using the suggestions provided in this chapter on test construction.

### Directions

1. Construct a complete test. The test should be neatly printed or typed and in a *form ready to administer* to a class of students.
2. The test should be composed of the following number and kind of items:
   a. Two essay questions (one at a cognitive level above knowledge)
   b. three multiple-choice items (two at cognitive levels above knowledge)
   c. one matching question composed of five item stems
   d. three true/false items
3. Include a separate answer sheet also correctly formatted, and indicate the answer to each question and any criteria to be used in scoring the essay questions.

## Assigning **8** Grades

*A*ssigning grades or marks is one of the most unpleasant, least comfortable, and least understood tasks teachers face. The process is fraught with pitfalls to lead the unwary teacher to unfairness in grading. The mistaken notion that students earn grades is one of the major pitfalls because it prevents many teachers from examining the actual process they use in arriving at grades. In this chapter, the processes used by teachers to determine grades will be examined, some of the mistaken assumptions made in using these processes will be identified, and alternatives will be provided. Grading practices should minimize the trauma experienced by students and result in more reliable and fairer estimates of grades.

## Reasons for Using Grades

People are concerned about grades. Parents expect their children to receive grades in schools and, thinking they understand what a grade represents, they are comfortable with them. Parents seem to need grades as indicators of their children's achievement. Some school systems have successfully replaced grades with alternative systems but only by using a process in which parents were informed and involved. Since you will not likely be working in such a district, alternative systems will not be dealt with here.

Students also expect to receive grades and think they understand them. Some students have been conditioned into relying on grades for motivation. Teachers' constant reminders of the importance of grades eventually convince some students that they are important. Some students would feel quite uncomfortable if grades were removed as a source of motivation and achievement could suffer.

Many businesses, colleges, and universities rely on grades as indicators of a student's potential success. Since grades are moderate predictors of success in institutions of higher education, such use is not without foundation. While the reliability of predictions based on grades alone is not high, when grades are coupled with standardized test scores and other student data, teachers can make useful predictions.

Teachers are usually the people most concerned about grades. Imagine what you would face if you taught in a school that did not assign grades to students. How would you motivate students who were not interested in what you were trying to teach? What would you use to inform parents of students' progress? How would you maintain student records? What mechanisms for quality control would be used?

Teachers have come to depend on grades. Many teachers have the mistaken notion that grades are a desirable extrinsic motivation to get students to want to learn. They constantly remind students that they need to learn to "get a good grade." Actually, students who are likely to respond favorably to this form of motivation are already interested in learning. They have probably been achieving success and want to maintain that level. These students are also likely to respond favorably to other forms of motivation. Unhappily, using grades as a form of motivation with these students actually causes them to depend on grades for motivation.

The students that teachers most want to motivate by using low grades as a threat are the very students least likely to be affected. Disinterested students with histories of failure or low grades know that they will not experience success in most classrooms even if they try. Past failures cause some of them to create situations that will allow them to rationalize their anticipated failure when they enter a new classroom. If they withdraw and don't try, they can always say, "I could have learned it if I tried, but I just couldn't see trying to learn that dumb stuff." Or, if they misbehave and are disruptive, they can say, "She was always picking on me. She gave me a bad grade because she just didn't like me." The threat of a bad grade will not modify this behavior. If anything, such threats make it more likely that these students will adopt one of these coping mechanisms.

Some teachers depend on the threat of low grades as a behavior management tool. If teachers depend on grades for this purpose, their behavioral management skills are deficient and they need help in developing their behavioral management skills. Using threats of poor grades to compensate for inadequate behavioral management does a disservice to students. Grades should be indicators of achievement. When other factors, such as disruptive behavior, are allowed to influence grades, they become useless as indicators of achievement, and the threat of lower grades seldom motivates students to behave. Students most likely to misbehave, those with histories of little success, are students who are least concerned about grades and least likely to modify their misbehavior as a result of such threats.

In spite of their deficiencies, grades do serve the function of being rough indicators of student achievement on which parents, institutions of higher education, and students have come to rely. Beyond this, grades have little to recommend them. However, because they continue to be used and are a necessary obligation of teachers, you must learn to apply the process of assigning grades in ways that will be equitable and will cause the least harm to students.

## Characteristics of Grades

Teachers tend to think of grades as something students earn. They fail to see the role that teacher subjectivity plays in determining grades. Let's examine a set of data taken from an actual school situation. The set of data compares the grade distributions of six different classes in the same subject and in the same school for each of three teachers. The students in the six classes were randomly assigned, and no reason exists for believing the students in different classes possessed different abilities.

|  | *Percentage of Grades* | | | | |
|  | A | B | C | D | F |
| *Teacher A* | | | | | |
| Class 1 | 8 | 15 | 19 | 31 | 27 |
| Class 2 | 8 | 13 | 26 | 33 | 19 |
| *Teacher B* | | | | | |
| Class 1 | 16 | 25 | 27 | 23 | 9 |
| Class 2 | 11 | 27 | 30 | 23 | 8 |
| *Teacher C* | | | | | |
| Class 1 | 13 | 32 | 37 | 18 | 0 |
| Class 2 | 26 | 31 | 32 | 10 | 1 |

How can the differences among these three teachers be explained? There are several possible explanations. Teacher A might not be as successful as Teachers B and C in getting students to learn (assuming comparable material is being taught, and comparable tests are being administered). If this were the case, should the students in Teacher A's classes be penalized for the teacher's inadequacy?

Another explanation might be that Teacher A has higher expectations for his or her students than do Teachers B and C. If 58 percent and 52 percent of the students in the classes receive D's or F's, how reasonable are Teacher A's expectations? Any teacher can try to teach material that the majority of students cannot learn or teach the material in such an obscure way that students cannot learn. Is this really setting a higher standard than the teacher who chooses material most students *can* learn or who teaches with clarity so most students *do* learn?

A third explanation might be that the teachers are teaching the same material and students are achieving equally, but the three teachers have different grading philosophies. Teacher A may feel that giving lower grades will motivate students. Teacher C may feel that giving higher grades will motivate students. Teacher C may feel that student failure is the result of poor teaching, and that an effective teacher is one who insures the success of students. Teacher C might be very uncomfortable with large numbers of D's and F's, while teacher A may be quite comfortable, and even pleased, with large numbers of D's and F's. Variation in grading philosophies is the most likely explanation for most of the differences in grade distributions among different teachers (Terwilliger, 1968). Since teachers have a preconceived notion about the distribution of grades with which they are comfortable, they manipulate the system consciously or subconsciously to achieve that distribution. This process is essentially a subjective one, not objective as many believe.

## Indicators of Learning

Indicators of learning, other than tests, include homework, written assignments, projects, library research papers, skill performances, oral reports, laboratory reports,

term papers, book reports, drawings, student-made visual materials, journals, notebooks of classroom notes, and teachers' records of students' ability to respond during discussions.

To base grades only on test scores is to measure student achievement too narrowly. Introducing other achievement measures, however, introduces even more variability into the process of grading, and so some care must be taken to reduce errors as much as possible.

For example, when grading written assignments or projects, teachers have the tendency to give higher grades for the same quality of work to students who are considered disadvantaged, slow, or who have better penmanship, even when penmanship is not one of the stated criteria (Chase, 1968; Klein and Hart, 1968). Knowing these tendencies may help you be more fair in assigning grades to written work.

Some simple procedures may help you avoid introducing extraneous criteria into the grading process. First, *establish the criteria to be used in grading the task before the task is assigned*. Define the criteria with enough specificity that the task can be scored objectively. For example, saying that students "will write a term paper" or "create a musical composition" is too vague. You will need to list all of the factors that will be judged to decide which term papers or musical compositions will be given an A, which will be given a B, and so on. Will you be concerned about the length? The format? Applications of certain principles or rules? You need to decide these matters in detail before giving the assignment.

Second, *announce the criteria to the students at the time the task is assigned*. Students need to know how they will be evaluated. This will not only make the evaluation system more fair to students but will make the introduction of extraneous variables more unlikely. If such variables are introduced, students will let you know in a hurry!

Third, *when scoring the task, refer to your criteria*. Score the task for all the students on the first variable, then for all of the students on the second variable, etc. Extraneous variables will less likely be introduced by this process. Essentially, this is the same process proposed for grading essay questions on tests.

When measuring student classroom participation, the process should be as systematic as possible. Keeping careful anecdotal records on each student introduces consistency and reduces error. Three-by-five-inch cards are useful for this purpose. As with all such measures, state the criteria, and only record data related to those criteria. When evaluating participation, try to focus on the quality of thinking involved in students' questions and responses. Since frequency of questions or responses quite often depends on students' personalities or needs, avoid emphasizing frequency. Through the continual use of anecdotal records, you will gain a more accurate perception of the actual participation of students. Without such records, grades on participation would be based on long-term impressions that are usually highly inaccurate.

## Assigning Grades to Test Scores

Teachers, when faced with the task of assigning grades to a set of test scores, will tend to use one of two options. First, some teachers score the test and then assign grades on the basis of predetermined percentages of correct responses based on two common distributions of percentages.

| 90–100 | A | | 90–100 | A |
|--------|---|-----|--------|---|
| 80–89 | B | | 80–89 | B |
| 70–79 | C | or | 70–79 | C |
| 60–69 | D | | 0–69 | F |
| 0–59 | F | | | |

(D's may be assigned to students with scores below 69, if the students tried "their best".)

At first these seem to be objective methods for determining grades; students' receive whatever grade they "earn." However, such thinking is fallacious. When teachers write an examination, they choose the content to test and then put the content to be tested into questions. Will they try to anticipate the level of difficulty of questions? Will they choose levels of difficulty for questions that will likely result in a distribution of scores they are comfortable with? The answer is usually yes to both questions. If on the preceding examination students had particularly high scores, the teacher would be likely to increase the difficulty level of the questions on the next test so that the scores (and hence the grades) average out to a distribution with which he or she is more comfortable. On the other hand, if the scores on the preceding examination were very low, the same teacher would be likely to choose easier questions for the next test in order to try to attain a more acceptable distribution of score. If this seems like a subjective process to you, your perception is correct. Teachers will consciously or subconsciously manipulate the system to achieve an approximate grade distribution with which they are comfortable.

Relying on set percentage distributions to determine grades also involves some questionable assumptions, that the instruction provided is always of equal effectiveness and that the level of difficulty for different examinations does not vary. To assume otherwise is to grade students not only on their achievement but also on the teacher's teaching effectiveness and the variation in difficulty of tests. Both practices would be unfair. Unfortunately, teaching effectiveness is seldom without variation, and tests rarely have the same level of difficulty. While the practice of using a set distribution of scores to determine grades seems objective and fair, it turns out to be neither.

The second option for assigning grades to a set of test scores is to "curve" the scores so that a preset percentage of students receives each grade. A common example of curving is based on the normal curve.

| | |
|---|---|
| Top 10% | A |
| Next 20% | B |
| Next 40% | C |
| Next 20% | D |
| Next 10% | F |

This method obviously avoids some of the problems inherent in using fixed scores to determine grades. The assumptions of equal levels of difficulty for tests and unvarying effectiveness of instruction are unnecessary. However, curving grades is not without problems. The choice of percentages of students to receive each grade is subjective. The ability levels of the students in a class are assumed to be normally distributed, but normal distributions seldom occur for small groups. No matter how hard students try to succeed, some students will always fail. Since the distribution of scores on most tests will correlate highly with the ability levels of the students, the same students will usually be the ones to fail. These students will quickly realize the trap they are in and will either withdraw from the competition or become disruptive. The process of insuring the failure of some students is inherently destructive to students.

Any system you adopt for assigning grades to test scores will be subjective. If your test is reliable (not always a safe assumption), students will earn a rank in a group of students by the score they receive on a test. The assignment of a grade to that ranking is going to be subjective. Recognizing this, you who decide to assign grades to test scores, may want to use the following procedure:

1. Make out a key for an examination before the examination is administered. Then examine each item on the test and decide which items are measuring basic understandings. Estimate the number of questions measuring basic understandings you feel a student with a "passing" knowledge should be able to answer. (Note: Realize that any student will miss approximately 10 percent of the items on an achievement test by misreading them, misplacing the intended answer, or in some way accidentally missing the items.) Now determine the minimum score you feel a student should make to pass, as well as the maximum score that is likely to be attained. Then arrange, at approximately equal intervals, the cut-off scores (those scores that indicate the breaking point between grades) for other grades between these two scores. With this process, you are establishing some standard to compare scores based on your professional judgment.

2. After the test is administered and scored, arrange the test papers from the highest score to the lowest score. Calculate the average or mean for the test. (At this point, assume that from test to test, unless there is strong reason to believe that some outside event significantly affected the students' performance, students as a group will exert about the same amount of effort to learn and to succeed on tests.) If the mean varies greatly from what you anticipated, either the test varied in difficulty or the instruction varied in effectiveness. Since neither factor should influence the grades of students, adjust your cut-off scores to reflect these variations.

3. Again examine the passing cut-off score. If the number of students failing to achieve this score is greater than you are comfortable with, then you may wish to adjust the cut-off score downward. If some of the students attempted to complete *all* of the learning activities provided and were still not able to score well on the examination, then it is probable that the learning activities provided were ineffective or the test was too difficult. You may wish to adjust the cut-off scores downward to include these students.

4. In situations requiring percentage scores to coincide with grades, translate the grades assigned into the required standard scores. Record these adjusted scores along with the assigned grade rather than the raw scores and assigned grades.

When deciding on cut-off scores for grades, recognize that the cut-off score should allow for errors in measurement, that is, the standard error of measurement. For example, if 70 percent is chosen as a passing score, recognize that a student with a score of 69 may know just as much or more than the student who received a 70 or 71 or even higher. Allowing for this error in measurement when deciding on grades to be assigned to scores is recommended (Drayer, 1979).

Some experts feel that no grades should be assigned to individual test scores but should only be assigned at the end of a grading period (Terwilliger, 1971). This practice may have the advantage of reducing the emphasis on grades, but students will still need to be informed about their performance on individual tests to give them some indication of the test score's ultimate effect on their grades. Failure to inform students of their performance on tests could create anxiety and uncertainty that would be counterproductive to good performance.

**Determining Grades for a Grading Period**

Some experts like to refer to the symbols used to indicate achievement on individual tasks as "grades," and the symbols used to indicate achievement for a grading period as "marks" (Kubiszyn and Borich, 1984). Such a distinction is not made here.

Determining a student's grade for a grading period involves comparing the student's performance to criteria. The following comparisons are possible:

1. student's achievement compared to the student's ability
2. student's achievement compared to the student's effort
3. student's achievement compared to other students' achievements
4. student's achievement compared to a standard
5. the change in the student's achievement (improvement) compared to the student's effort or ability, other students' improvement, or a standard.

## Achievement vs. Ability

Grades based on ability are assigned depending on how well a student achieved compared to how he or she could be expected to achieve. A student with average ability who achieves at an above average level would be given a high grade; a student with poor ability who achieves at an average level would also be given a high grade. On the surface this appears to be a reasonable system; however, some problems do arise. If a student with high ability achieves at an average level, the student should be given a low grade because he or she is not achieving to potential. Let's say that this student is given a grade of D. Suppose another student with low ability has an achievement equivalent to that of the high ability student that is well beyond that which would be expected. This student would then be given a grade of A. These two grades indicate that the low ability student has achieved more than the high ability student, when in fact, the two have approximately the same level of achievement in absolute terms. How are others to interpret grades from such a system? What measures will be used to determine ability? What system of calculations will be used to assure objectivity? What weight will reading ability play in judging achievement in mathematics, music, etc.? Will all students need to be given ability or aptitude measures in all areas each year? Would comparing a student's ability to his or her achievement be fair if such measures were not used? Such a system is not without rather severe difficulties.

## Achievement vs. Effort

Grades based on effort require a teacher to adjust the achievement of each student by some factor dependent on the amount of effort exerted. A low ability student who exerted a great deal of effort and achieved at the expected low level would be given a high grade, possibly an A. A student with high ability who achieved at the expected high level who exhibited average effort would be given a grade of C. The teacher who uses such a system has the intention of rewarding students for effort exerted.

This is a noble goal; however, it creates serious problems. As in the case of comparing ability with achievement, what does a grade mean in such a system? If a teacher wishes to evaluate effort, then establishing a system calling for separate achievement and effort grades would better serve the purpose. Such a system has many advantages and should be given serious consideration.

If such a separate effort grade is to be assigned, then do not attempt to grade effort strictly on incidental things students say to you. Since some students are more willing than others to mention the effort they put into school work, to depend solely on incidental student comments as indicators of effort is to insure that some students' efforts are overlooked. If you intend to estimate a grade based on effort, keep systematic anecdotal records on each student, using predetermined and announced criteria.

## Achievement vs. Other Students

Assigning a grade based on the relationship of the achievement of a student to other students in the class is commonly referred to as grading on a "curve." This system is based on some assumptions that may inherently be unfair to students, that in every class some students will get high grades and some will get low grades or will not pass. When two classes have quite dissimilar populations, the students in a high ability class who achieve at an average level compared to students in a low ability class who achieve at an average level may have very different absolute achievements but receive the same grade. This system suffers from an inherent unfairness unless classes are all equal and similar distributions of grades are adopted. Such a system will also assure the failure of a certain segment of the student population. No matter how much a teacher is willing to work with these low ability students and no matter how much they achieve, if they are still at the bottom of their class in absolute achievement, they will fail. This would be demoralizing to both teacher and student. Students under such a system will quickly lose their self-esteem and become alienated from the school, and they will either become disruptive or withdraw.

## Achievement vs. a Standard

The teacher who measures a student's achievement against a standard establishes criteria for each grade. Students meeting the criteria for a certain grade are assigned that grade. In theory, no preconceived distribution of grades is used. All students who meet the criteria for a grade of A would be given As, all students who meet the criteria for a B would be assigned a B, and so on. No inherent reason exists for limiting the number of A's or any other grades students in a class are assigned.

However, some problems arise. Teachers who have a preconceived notion about the distribution of grades with which they are comfortable will modify the criteria used as a standard so that with time, the distribution of grades for their classes will be that with which they are comfortable. Establishing a standard then becomes anything but an objective process. A teacher can make the standards anything he or she wishes. Achievement that would be considered an A by one teacher may be a B for another teacher. And how long would an administrator allow a teacher to assign all A's or some other distorted (in their minds) distribution of grades?

## Improvement as a Criterion

Teachers sometimes determine grades by attempting to measure the change in achievement from the beginning of the grading period to the end of the period. This measurement is then compared to a measure of the student's ability or effort, the improvement of other students, or some predetermined standard. This system has little to recommend it. Pretests and posttests used to measure achievement will both measure with error. To use the difference between the scores merely magnifies the error. In addition, students who score high on the pretest have fewer items on which to demonstrate improvement. Those who score low on the pretest can increase their posttest scores more easily because many more items are available for them to answer correctly on the posttest. The phenomenon called *regression toward the mean* operates in such a situation. Those who scored high on the pretest in part scored high because they were on the positive side of the random errors being made. Those who scored low were on the negative side of random errors. On subsequent tests, those who scored high on the pretest will, by chance, score lower on the posttest, while those who scored lower on the pretest will score higher on the posttest—scores for both groups will move toward the mean. This phenomenon makes demonstrating improvement for those who initially scored high very difficult. Accounting for regression toward the mean is difficult at best. Due to these and other factors, the use of improvement as a basis for assigning grades should be avoided.

## Combining Scores to Determine Grades

Before recommending a system for determining grades at the end of the grading period, examining some other factors involved in the process will be helpful. One factor is combining scores from tests or other measures of achievement.

If percentage scores on tests or other measures are recorded in a grade book, merely averaging the percentages will result in some measures affecting the grade more than other measures. For example, assume two tests were being averaged, one test composed of four items and the second test composed of twenty items. If one student received a score of 50 percent on the first test and 100 percent on the second test, that student would have an average score of 75 percent. If a second student received a score of 100 percent on the first test and a 50 percent on the second test, that student too would have an average of 75 percent. The first student would have answered twenty-two out of twenty-four items correctly on the two tests, while the second student would have answered fourteen out of twenty-four. Obviously, the two students did not achieve equally.

Another option is to record the raw score for each test, and then add up the raw scores and determine the final percent by dividing this sum of raw scores by the sum of the maximum possible points from each test and multiplying by 100. For example, assume a student on one test received a score of 15, which was the highest score in the class on a test composed of twenty items. On a second test the same student received a score of 10, which was an average score on a twenty-item test. A second student on the first test received a score of 10, which was the average score. On the second test, this same student received a score of 20, which was the highest score on the test. The average of the first student would be 25 divided by 40 or 62.5 percent. The average for the second student would be 30 divided by 40 or 75 percent. Both received the highest score on one of the two tests, and both scored at the average level on the other. When compared with the performance of the whole class the two performed equally, but because one test had more range between the highest and lowest scores than the other test, the two tests turn out not to have equal weightings. Given the fact that the two tests had equal numbers of items, equal weighting for the two tests was probably the teacher's intention. So averaging scores in this fashion will introduce different weightings for tests that have the same number of items but different ranges.

When combining scores for measures, avoid simply adding raw scores or averaging percentage scores. The second process of adding raw scores can be used, but only if the range (actually the variance) between tests is taken into account. When a test has a greater variance, then the scores may need to be modified so that the effect of different variances between tests is removed. The difference in variance can be removed by calculating and using T-scores when combining scores.

## Calculating T-Scores

When raw scores are converted to T-scores, the resulting set of scores will have a mean (average) of 50, and a standard deviation of 10. This process eliminates any differences in the variances for a set of scores. T-scores can then be added or averaged, and differences in variances between the tests will not be a factor.

When calculating T-scores from raw scores, you will need to determine the mean and the standard deviation. To determine the average or mean, add all of the scores and divide by the number of scores. A simple way to calculate the standard deviation when the set of scores is not too different from a normal curve is to take the difference between the highest and lowest score and divide that difference by four. If either the highest or lowest score is far removed from the next score, then drop the highest and/or lowest score, and use the next score in finding the difference between highest and lowest. For example, imagine you had the following set of scores with which you were working (you undoubtedly will have more scores):

$$
\begin{array}{ll}
\text{Score 1} & 20 \\
\text{Score 2} & 50 \\
\text{Score 3} & 70 \\
\text{Score 4} & 80 \\
\text{Score 5} & 90 \\
\text{Score 6} & 70 \\
\text{Score 7} & 80 \\
\text{Score 8} & 60 \\
\text{Score 9} & 70 \\
\text{Score 10} & 60 \\
\text{Sum} = & 650 \\
\text{Mean} = & \dfrac{650}{10} = 65
\end{array}
$$

Removing the score of 20, which is very far removed from the other scores, and using the next lowest score of 50, the mean would be 70. So a mean of 70 should be used for subsequent calculations.

$$
\text{Mean} = \frac{630}{9} = 70
$$

Also, the next lowest score of 50 should be used when determining the range. A rough approximation of the standard deviation is calculated by dividing the difference between the highest and lowest score by 4.

$$\text{Standard Deviation} = \frac{90 - 50}{4} = \frac{40}{4} = 10$$

To calculate the T-score for each of the nine remaining scores, follow these steps.

*Step 1:*  Subtract the mean from each score. You will get some negative numbers. That's all right. Record the negative numbers.

    e.g.    Score 2 − Mean = 50 − 70 = −20

*Step 2:*  Divide the number you obtained in Step 1 by the standard deviation.

    e.g.    $\dfrac{-20}{\text{S.D.}} = \dfrac{-20}{10} = -2$

*Step 3:*  Multiply the number you obtained in Step 2 by 10.

    e.g.    −2 × 10 = −20

*Step 4:*  Add 50 to the number you obtained in Step 3. This number is the T-score for that score.

    e.g.    −20 + 50 = 30 = T-score

Calculating T-scores, reliability coefficients, and correlations may appear to be a great deal of work. However, many schools now have test scoring programs for personal computers that will do all of these calculations for you at the time your tests are scored. You need only learn how to use the information provided in appropriate fashion. Even when the school does not have a computer already programmed to make these calculations, any computer spreadsheet program can be quickly programmed to do them. The steps for the calculations in this textbook should make such programming easy.

## Weighting Measures

When combining the scores and/or grades for a variety of performance measures, determine the weighting for each measure beforehand. The weighting assigned to each measure should be a reflection of the importance placed on the particular learnings being measured. Any grade determined by this process will reflect the student's achievement of your goals and objectives.

    For example, if you wish one test composed of twice as many items as another test to count twice as much toward a grade, then the T- score for this measure would need to be multiplied by 2 before it was added or averaged with the other score. This test would have twice the effect on the grade as the test with half as many items.

To the extent possible, scores for all achievement measures should be converted to T-scores and then combined to form a ranking for the weighted average of all of the measures. To determine the cut-off scores for the final averages, merely calculate the T-scores for the cut-off scores of each measure. These individual scores are then multiplied by the weighting factor, added together, and averaged by dividing the sum by the number of scores being added.

In situations where you are required to record numerical grades (i.e. 90–100 as equivalent to an A, 80–89 as equivalent to a B, etc.), then the average T-scores will need to be converted into equivalent numbers. For example, if a T-score of 70 is to be the cut-off score between A's and B's, then change T-scores of 70 to 90. If a T-score of 60 is to be the cut-off score between a B and a C, and a B on the numerical scale is to be 85, then add 25 to the T-score of 60 to convert to the numerical grade. To calculate the numerical grade for a student with a T-score of 64, determine the fraction above a B this score represents on the T-score scale.

$$\frac{\text{Student's Score (64)} - \text{Score for B (60)}}{\text{Number of T-score points from B to A (10)}} = .4$$

Then determine the number of points between an A and a B on the numerical scale.

Numerical score for A (90) − Numerical score for B (85) = 5

Multiplying these two numbers will give you the number of points you will need to add to 85 to get the student's numerical score.

$$(.4 \times 5) + 85 = 87$$

## A Recommended Philosophy of Grading

Working effectively with students requires that each student be provided an opportunity to succeed. One way to provide that opportunity is to structure grading so that it does not insure failure. If tests are the only measure of achievement for grading purposes, then some students may be doomed to failure.

A question often raised is, "But, how do I insure against failure for students and still assign grades in some legitimate way acceptable to the school administration?" The answer to this question is not easy for many teachers to accept because it involves a rather significant change in both basic philosophy and practice.

## Basic Assumptions

Two basic assumptions need to be made about students and teaching in order to put this grading philosophy into proper perspective:

1. Students are capable of learning if provided learning experiences using effective methodology of adequate duration and presenting content within the ability levels of the students.
2. Students are capable of demonstrating this learning if assessed with appropriate measures.

Too often when a student's score falls below the chosen cut-off score, the student is assumed at fault. The student, not the instruction or the test, is called into question. In reality, if a student has made an honest attempt to complete *all* classroom activities and homework assignments and does not demonstrate "passing" achievement, then the teacher can safely assume that

1. ineffective methodology was used
2. the instruction was of too short a duration
3. the student lacked the prerequisite knowledge, skills, or intellectual development to learn the content being taught
4. the test was too difficult or did not measure that which was taught

Should a student be failed through no fault of his or her own? Such a practice is intuitively and actually unfair. When faced with that situation, you should examine the four possible causes of failure listed *before* you decide something is wrong with the student. The factors causing the lack of success for the student should then be adjusted. Any student who conscientiously does *all* you ask him or her to do should be able to demonstrate acceptable learning. If he or she cannot, then the placement process used may be faulty, and he or she may be inappropriately placed in your course.

If you cannot accept the fact that all students are capable of learning when appropriate learning experiences are provided, then you will be unable to accept this philosophy of grading, and the practices it implies. To accept the grading philosophy being proposed requires that you have confidence in the quality of the learning experiences you provide students. You must believe that students who complete all of the activities provided in your classroom have learned the minimum expected of all students. Teachers with this kind of confidence will have little difficulty in accepting this grading philosophy. They also will have little difficulty in being able to justify their grading practices to parents and school administrators.

## Recommended Procedures

In using this philosophy of grading, all students must have the assurance of at least a grade of C, or satisfactory, if they attend class on a regular basis and *if, and only if,* they make *an honest attempt to complete all of the activities*, including tests, that are expected of all students. Students need to have an absolute assurance that if they meet these two criteria they cannot fail, and if their test grades warrant, they are eligible to receive higher grades. Students must recognize that they are not being "given" anything. They must do the activities to receive any credit. They must attend class if they are going to do the activities. Students should never be given anything they have not earned. Neither should they be denied credit they earn simply to satisfy someone's arbitrarily imposed grading standards. Choosing to do or not to do things is *the student's* option. All you as a teacher can do is assure them that if they attend class and make an honest effort to do the activities, credit will not be denied. If they fail to do the activities reasonably, then they will not earn credit for those activities. To earn credit, they must demonstrate acceptable knowledge of the subject through test scores, assignments, projects, and other evaluated activities.

Some will say that this will result in grade inflation. It will not. Grade inflation results when teachers raise the average grades of students while achievement is not raised. In this case we are allowing students to achieve at higher levels and recognizing that achievement in our grade structure.

To accept this grading scheme, and to make it work successfully, you must have confidence that if you provide learning experiences appropriate for all students, they will learn. You must also have the ability to provide learning experiences that insure that students who make an honest effort to learn will learn the minimum required of all students for passing.

## Guidelines for Grading

Grades are symbols conveying the teacher's evaluation of a student's performance. As symbols, they have serious limitations in communicating the various factors that go into determining the grade. In essence, very little is communicated other than a simple categorization of a student's achievement. Grades, when used improperly, can be dehumanizing and destructive. The grading process is neither pleasant nor easy. Trying to build in as much accuracy and humaneness into the process as possible is something on which teachers should place high priority. To accomplish this goal, the following guidelines are suggested:

1. Establish reasonable standards consistent with the prerequisite knowledge and skills students bring to your classroom. Base your grades on these standards and avoid trying to compare achievement of a student with other students or with the student's effort or ability. Choose content consistent with the intellectual development of students. If you choose to teach abstract content beyond the intellectual development of students, then you insure their failure (Deutsch, 1979; Lawson and Renner, 1975; Sayre and Ball, 1975).
2. Explain your grading policies early in the year and remind students of those policies periodically (Drayer, 1979). Prior to each task to be evaluated, inform students of the criteria to be used in the evaluation.

3. Base grades for a grading period on a variety of objective evidence, systematically obtained on each student. To use incidentally obtained subjective evidence does a disservice to many students due to the unfairness of such a practice. Such a practice also makes the influence of subconscious biases more likely.

4. Tie grades to important objectives, not merely trivial memorization of facts. Avoid assigning high grades only to those students who conform to your views in situations where other views could reasonably be held (Bostrum, Vlandis and Rosenbaum, 1961). Remember, students will tend to try to accept and/or learn those things for which they are rewarded.

5. Provide credit and/or recognition for students for those parts of work successfully completed. Students will be encouraged to sustain effort as a result.

6. Remember that all measurement involves error. Try to allow for this error when making distinctions between the grades assigned to different students.

7. Grades assigned to students should be indicators of achievement only. If other factors, such as effort or behavior, are to be evaluated, then separate grades for these factors should be used. Do not allow extraneous factors to influence grades meant to communicate achievement.

## REFERENCES

Bostrum, R.N., J.W. Vlandis, and M.E. Rosenbaum. 1961. Grades as reinforcing contingencies and attitude change. *Journal of Educational Psychology* 52:112–115.

Chase, C.I. 1968. The impact of some obvious variables on essay test scores. *Journal of Educational Measurement* 5(4): 315–318.

Deutsch, M. 1979. Education and distribution justice: Some reflections on grading systems. *American Psychologist* 39:391–401.

Drayer, A.M. 1979. *Problems in middle and high school teaching: A handbook for student teachers and beginning teachers.* Boston: Allyn & Bacon.

Klein, S.P. and F.M. Hart. 1968. Chance and systematic factors affecting essay grades. *Journal of Educational Measurement* 5(3): 197–206.

Kubiszyn, T. and G. B. Borich. 1984. *Educational testing and measurement.* Glenview, Ill.: Scott, Foresman.

Lawson, A.E., and J.W. Renner. 1975. Relationships of science subject matter and developmental levels of learners. *Journal of Research in Science Teaching* 12(4): 347–358.

Sayre, S. and D.W. Ball. 1975. Piagetian cognitive development and achievement in science. *Journal of Research in Science Teaching* 12(2): 165–174.

Terwilliger, J.S. 1968. Individual differences in the marking practices of secondary teachers. *Journal of Educational Measurement* 5(1): 9–15.

———. 1971. *Assigning grades to students.* Glenview, Ill.: Scott, Foresman.

———————————————— SUMMARY ————————————————

## Functions of grades

1. communicate students' academic achievement to parents, institutions of higher education, businesses, and others
2. serve as crude predictors of future academic success

## Characteristics of grades

1. are based on teacher's subjective process
2. are not directly earned by students, but are assigned by teachers
3. as single symbols, have serious limitations in communicating factors determining the grade

## Assigning grades to tasks and assignments

1. Establish the criteria to be used for grading before the task is assigned.
2. Announce the criteria to the students at the time the task is assigned.
3. When scoring the task, score all students for the first criterion before going on to the next.

## Assigning grades to achievement tests

1. Make a key to be used in scoring the examination prior to the administration of the examination.
2. Determine a passing cut-off score based on an analysis of the number of questions measuring basic understanding.
3. Determine other cut-off scores.
4. After the test is administered, adjust cut-off scores based on the distribution of scores and standard error of measurement.

## Combining test scores

1. Avoid simply averaging raw scores.
2. Avoid adding raw scores and then determining the percentage of the total possible score.
3. Convert raw scores to T-scores before combining if you have reason to believe that differences in variance exist between tests.
4. Determine the weighting to be given to each test and then adjust the T-scores by multiplying the score by the weighting factor before adding the T-scores.

## Determining grades for a grading period

1. Evaluate a variety of performances, not just tests.
2. Collect objective data on all measures systematically so that the same kinds of data are collected for each student.

3. Determine the relative weightings to be given to each measure and insure that the final grade reflects these weightings.
4. The basic criteria, or standards chosen for passing a course, should allow all students the opportunity to achieve success.
5. Avoid comparing the achievement of a student with other students or with the student's effort or ability.
6. Tie grades to important objectives, not merely trivial memorization of facts.
7. Provide credit and/or recognition for students for those parts of work successfully completed.
8. Remember that all measurement involves error. Try to allow for this error when making distinctions among the grades assigned different students.
9. Grades assigned students should be indicators of achievement only. If other factors, such as effort or behavior, are to be evaluated, then separate grades for these factors should be used.

# EXERCISE 20
## Combining Test Scores

Combining test scores is a task to be done with care. How scores are combined can affect the rank a student receives and the grade assigned. This exercise will give you some practice in doing some of the calculations that are involved in the process of combining grades. Through the process of determining ranks by three different methods, you will come to see the importance of using T-scores.

*Directions:* Record the following calculations in the spaces provided on the following pages.

1. Calculate the average raw score for each of two sets of scores listed.
2. Calculate the standard deviation for the two sets of scores by finding the difference between the highest and lowest scores and dividing by four.
3. Calculate the T-score for each of the two sets of scores.
4. Calculate the average of the two raw scores for each student. Recognize that the raw scores in this case will be the same as the percentage scores since each test is composed of one hundred items.
5. Calculate the average of the two T-scores for each student.
6. Determine the rank of each student for the average of the raw scores and the average of the T-scores. The highest score is ranked 1, the second highest is ranked 2, and so on. Identical scores are all given the same rank.
7. For how many students do the rankings differ?

Name _____

|  | Number of Items | Average | Standard Deviation |
|---|---|---|---|
| Test 1 | 100 | _____ | _____ |
| Test 2 | 100 | _____ | _____ |

| Student | Raw Scores Test 1 | Test 2 | T-Scores Test 1 | Test 2 |
|---|---|---|---|---|
| 1 | 88 | 70 | _____ | _____ |
| 2 | 84 | 75 | _____ | _____ |
| 3 | 87 | 65 | _____ | _____ |
| 4 | 81 | 62 | _____ | _____ |
| 5 | 87 | 67 | _____ | _____ |
| 6 | 80 | 65 | _____ | _____ |
| 7 | 77 | 62 | _____ | _____ |
| 8 | 75 | 47 | _____ | _____ |
| 9 | 85 | 61 | _____ | _____ |
| 10 | 80 | 39 | _____ | _____ |
| 11 | 90 | 73 | _____ | _____ |
| 12 | 78 | 42 | _____ | _____ |
| 13 | 82 | 47 | _____ | _____ |
| 14 | 82 | 60 | _____ | _____ |
| 15 | 83 | 52 | _____ | _____ |
| 16 | 85 | 59 | _____ | _____ |
| 17 | 84 | 56 | _____ | _____ |
| 18 | 83 | 58 | _____ | _____ |
| 19 | 86 | 52 | _____ | _____ |
| 20 | 83 | 59 | _____ | _____ |

| Student | Average of Raw Scores | Average of T-Scores | Rank by Raw Scores | Rank by T-Scores |
|---|---|---|---|---|
| 1 | | | | |
| 2 | | | | |
| 3 | | | | |
| 4 | | | | |
| 5 | | | | |
| 6 | | | | |
| 7 | | | | |
| 8 | | | | |
| 9 | | | | |
| 10 | | | | |
| 11 | | | | |
| 12 | | | | |
| 13 | | | | |
| 14 | | | | |
| 15 | | | | |
| 16 | | | | |
| 17 | | | | |
| 18 | | | | |
| 19 | | | | |
| 20 | | | | |

Number of students for whom the rankings differ _____

# EXERCISE 21
## Assigning Grades to Test Scores

One of the tasks you may face as a teacher is assigning grades to test scores. In this exercise you will be given descriptions of students taking a test and their test scores. You will then assign grades to each student for this examination.

*Directions:* Record the results of the following tasks on the answer sheets provided.

1. Using any criteria, process and/or procedures you wish, assign a grade to each of the scores recorded for each student on the examination.
2. Also indicate how many of each grade you assigned the class.
3. After you have completed giving each student a grade, and you have arrived at a distribution of grades, answer the following questions in the spaces provided on the answer sheet.
   a. What are the cut-off scores between the grades A and B and between D and F? Give one reason for arriving at each of the cutoff scores listed.
   b. Did you make any exceptions to the cutoff scores chosen between any of the grades? If so, list the name of each exception and give the reason for each exception made.
4. During the next class period, your instructor will have you discuss the following questions either as a small group or as a whole class.
   a. What set of decisions were used in arriving at the cut-off scores?
   b. How did your assigned grades for selected students differ? What were some of the reasons for these differences? Were all of the reasons equally valid?
   c. How did your grade distributions vary? What were some of the reasons for the differences? Were all of the reasons equally valid?

*Student Descriptions:* Use these descriptions for both Exercises 21 and 22.

1. Aleck, Smart. Has an easy time in school. IQ about 140. Comes from a broken Anglo family. Doesn't seem to work hard at school but turns everything in.
2. Black, Bart. Constantly disrupts class and puts little effort into his work. IQ about 130. Upper-middle class Anglo family. Drives a fancy sports car.
3. Bell, Dumb. Has consistently been assigned to slow groups. IQ about 85. Comes from a broken Anglo home and lives with grandmother. Makes an attempt to do all activities, but she says she is not able to do homework because her grandmother makes her work.
4. Guy, Nice. A fairly friendly Black boy. IQ about 90. Lives with his widowed mother. Says he tries hard and really wants to do well.
5. Glass, Looking. Consistently good student in all of her classes. IQ about 120. Both parents are professional people. Looking is a very popular Black girl and seems to enjoy school.
6. Heavy, Very. A well-behaved girl who is not popular with her peers. A good student who tries hard. IQ about 110. Comes from a middle class Anglo family.
7. Jones, Davey. A typical "goof-off." Makes little attempt to do assignments. IQ about 100. Comes from a middle class Anglo family. Likes cars and doing mechanical things.
8. Juice, Orange. Says she really tries hard, but has trouble learning. IQ about 90. Lives with her divorced mother. She is Hispanic and has some problems with English.

9. Makit, Willie. Has consistently been assigned to slow groups. IQ about 90. Comes from a middle class Anglo family. Turns in all homework and says he tries his best on everything.
10. Nutt, Ima. Very friendly and well behaved Black girl. IQ about 110. Lives with her divorced mother. Seems well-intentioned and is always willing to answer questions.
11. Ray, Violet. Average Anglo student. IQ about 110. Very quiet and seldom talks in class. Lives with her divorced father.
12. Seedy, Pretty. Just doesn't seem able to grasp the subject. IQ about 95. Comes from a poor Anglo family. Has given up trying to do class assignments.
13. Sharp, Kinda. Seems to do well in most classes. IQ about 120. Comes from a middle class Hispanic family. Says her cheerleading keeps her from spending needed time on her homework.
14. Sore, Cold. A dirty, smelly little girl. IQ about 95. From a poor Anglo family. Very quiet and shy. Seldom says anything in class.
15. Vendor, Street. An average student. IQ about 100. Lower-middle class Anglo family. Occasionally misbehaves, but tries to do most classroom activities.
16. Welk, Larry. An Anglo who talks with an accent. IQ about 140. Likes to get up in front of the class and show off. Tends toward the artistic.
17. Won't, Betty. Rarely comes to class. IQ about 120. Lower-middle class Hispanic family. Seems more interested in things other than school.

# Chapter Examination Scores

Name _____

Maximum score possible is 50.

| Student | Score | Grade |
|---|---|---|
| Aleck, Smart | 50 | |
| Black, Bart | 45 | |
| Bell, Dumb | 29 | |
| Glass, Looking | 44 | |
| Guy, Nice | 39 | |
| Heavy, Very | 41 | |
| Jones, Davey | 25 | |
| Juice, Orange | 38 | |
| Makeit, Willie | 39 | |
| Nutt, Ima | 44 | |
| Ray, Violet | 40 | |
| Seedy, Pretty | 27 | |
| Sharp, Kinda | 42 | |
| Sore, Cold | 34 | |
| Vendor, Street | 36 | |
| Welk, Larry | 42 | |
| Won't, Betty | 29 | |

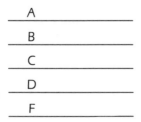

*Grade Distribution:*

| Grade | Number |
|---|---|
| A | |
| B | |
| C | |
| D | |
| F | |

a. What are the cut-off scores between the grades A and B and between D and F? Give one reason for arriving at each of the cut-off scores listed.

Cut-off score between A and B  _____
Reason:




Cut-off score between D and F  _____
Reason:



b. Did you make any exceptions to the cut-off scores chosen between any of the grades? If so, list the name of each exception and give the reason for each.

*Student name*                                 *Reason*

_____     _____

                             _____

_____     _____

                             _____

_____     _____

                             _____

# EXERCISE 22
# Gradebook assignment

Maintaining a gradebook is a task all teachers face. You will use the information recorded in your gradebook to arrive at grades for a grading period. This exercise will allow you to use the gradebook information to determine a set of grades. An examination of the decisions you make in this process, along with the reasons used for those decisions, will help you recognize any faulty or unfair logic you used in arriving at your grades.

Directions:

1. Examine the data recorded in the gradebook provided in this exercise. Also examine the data on each student given in Exercise 21. Use any procedures you wish to arrive at a grade for each student. Record a grade in the gradebook for each student.
2. Count the number of A's, B's, etc., given, and record the distribution of grades for the class you graded in the spaces provided.
3. After you have completed giving each student a grade and arriving at a distribution of grades, answer the following questions in the spaces provided.
   a. What are the cut-off scores between the grades A and B and between D and F? Give one reason for each of the cut-off scores listed.
   b. Did you make any exceptions to the cutoff scores chosen between any of the grades? If so, list the name of each exception and give the reason for each.
4. During the next class period, your instructor may have you discuss the following questions either as a small group or as a whole class.
   a. What set of decisions were used in arriving at the cut-off scores? Were different decisions made by different members in your class or group?
   b. How did your assigned grades for selected students differ among members of your class or group? What were some of the reasons for these differences? Were all of the reasons equally valid?
   c. How did your grade distributions vary between members in your group? What were some of the reasons for the differences? Were all of the reasons equally valid?

# Your Gradebook

Name _____

| Student | I | II | III | IV | V | VI | VII | VIII | IX | X | Grade |
|---------|-----|-----|-----|-----|-----|-----|-----|-----|-----|-----|-------|
| Possible points | 50 | 75 | 100 | | | | | | | | |
| Aleck, Smart | 50 | 69 | 75 | B+ | + | + | * | + | C | | |
| Black, Bart | 45 | 71 | 87 | B | + | + | + | + | D | | |
| Bell, Dumb | 29 | 68 | 63 | C− | 0 | 0 | 0 | 0 | B | | |
| Glass, Looking | 44 | 74 | 93 | A− | + | * | + | + | A | | |
| Guy, Nice | 39 | 55 | 72 | B | − | − | − | * | B | | |
| Heavy, Very | 41 | 65 | 77 | A+ | − | − | * | * | A− | | |
| Jones, Davey | 25 | 52 | 66 | D | 0 | 0 | 0 | 0 | F | | |
| Juice, Orange | 38 | 49 | 71 | C | * | * | − | * | D | | |
| Makeit, Willie | 39 | 38 | 65 | D+ | − | − | − | − | A | | |
| Nutt, Ima | 44 | 67 | 82 | B | * | * | * | * | A− | | |
| Ray, Violet | 40 | 57 | 74 | B− | * | − | * | + | C− | | |
| Seedy, Pretty | 27 | 39 | 59 | F | 0 | 0 | 0 | 0 | D | | |
| Sharp, Kinda | 42 | 59 | 83 | A | − | − | − | 0 | B | | |
| Sore, Cold | 34 | 52 | 69 | C− | − | * | − | * | D | | |
| Vendor, Street | 36 | 56 | 72 | B− | * | * | * | * | C | | |
| Welk, Larry | 42 | 72 | 99 | A+ | + | * | + | + | A | | |
| Won't, Betty | 29 | 53 | 58 | D− | 0 | 0 | 0 | 0 | F | | |

Explanation:

| I | Weekly Test | Homework: | |
|---|-------------|-----------|---|
| II | Weekly Test | + | Excellent |
| III | Major Test | * | Acceptable |
| IV | Written Project | − | Unacceptable |
| V-VIII | Homework | 0 | Not turned in |
| IX | Participation | | |
| X | Final ranking | | |

*Grade Distribution:*

| Grade | Number |
|-------|--------|
| A | |
| B | |
| C | |
| D | |
| F | |

a. What are the cut-off scores between the grades A and B and between D and F? Give one reason for arriving at each of the cut-off scores listed.

Cut-off score between A and B _____

Reason:

Cut-off score between D and F _____

Reason:

b. Did you make any exceptions to the cut-off scores chosen between any of the grades? If so, list the name of each exception and give the reason for each.

| *Student name* | *Reason* |
|----------------|----------|
| _____ | _____ |
| | _____ |
| _____ | _____ |
| | _____ |
| _____ | _____ |
| | _____ |
| _____ | _____ |
| | _____ |

# Managing the Classroom 9

When beginning teachers are asked to identify problems they experience in the classroom, discipline ranks the highest of the twenty-four most frequently mentioned problems (Veenman, 1984). Recent research findings have provided a wealth of valuable information about managing classrooms effectively. By utilizing this information, a teacher can make the classroom a pleasant, businesslike, and enjoyable place in which to learn. Failure to manage a classroom adequately can result in confusion, misbehavior, antagonism, anger, and unpleasantness. Fortunately, creating a pleasant environment for the teacher and students is within the ability of most, if not all, beginning and experienced teachers.

Effective management is not, however, an end in itself. A teacher does not manage a classroom solely to control students, but to make it possible to utilize activities that will promote the achievement of his or her goals and objectives. Effective classroom management is necessary but not sufficient for appropriate learning to occur.

## Classroom Management

The management of the physical environment and instructional materials will be called *classroom management* in this discussion. The management of the behavior of students will be called *behavioral management*.

Research has shown that failure to conduct management tasks efficiently and effectively results in confusion, disruption, lost learning time, students failing to complete tasks, and lower achievement (McGarity and Butts, 1984; Sanford, 1984; Evertson and Emmer, 1982; Medley, 1979). Teachers who are poor managers of classrooms also tend to limit the learning tasks to those that involve easy control of pupils, such as having students seated at their desks filling out routine worksheets (Sanford, 1984; Doyle, 1979). Teachers are heard to say, "You can't do _____ with kids. They just can't handle that kind of situation." How sad! In fact, students are able to handle almost any task if it is well managed and within their ability levels. Teachers, not students, are often the ones who can't handle situations.

Effective classroom managers tend to use similar patterns of management regardless of subject area and kinds of students (Sanford, 1984). They tend to have high student achievement and high levels of student engagement and little disruptive behavior or classroom confusion. Such teachers monitor student work closely, communicate directions clearly, make smooth transitions from one activity to the next, pace lessons consistently with the ability levels of the students, establish routine, comprehensive, workable rules and procedures, and deal with even minor inappropriate behavior quickly and consistently (Sanford, 1984; Emmer and Evertson, 1981; Doyle, 1980; O'Leary and O'Leary, 1977; and Kounin, 1970).

While classroom management and behavioral management are often defined as separate entities, they are actually closely related. Poor classroom management results in behavioral problems, while poor behavioral management makes effective classroom management difficult. The purpose for both kinds of management is to increase the time students spend engaged in appropriate learning activities and achieving the teacher's goals and objectives.

## Guidelines for Classroom Management

Analysis of research on classroom management has led to the development of a set of critical guidelines for teachers shown to be related to increased student time-on-task and decreased student misbehavior (Emmer, *et al.*, 1984; Sanford, 1984; Evertson and Emmer, 1982; Emmer and Evertson, 1981; Doyle, 1980; Brophy, 1979; Medley, 1979; Kounin, 1970). Teachers should use these guidelines when planning classroom management procedures.

1. Make procedures simple.

   Management procedures should be as simple as possible. Steps in the procedure should be few and simple. Less complex management procedures take less time to teach to students and increase the chance that students will be successful in completing the procedure.
2. Make procedures efficient.

   Classroom management procedures should minimize the amount of time required for completion. Since the main purpose of any management task is to increase the amount of student on-task time, procedures requiring the minimum of time should be chosen.
3. Avoid dead time.

   When students are left with little or nothing to do, they tend to find something to do that the teacher would rather they not be doing. Minimizing the amount of time that students have nothing to do is important in choosing any classroom management procedure.
4. Minimize student movement.

   Any student movement during an activity is likely to create some problems; therefore, minimize the number of students who need to move during any procedure. Also, carefully choose the kind of movement that students will need to do; avoid movements that require students to congregate around some point or require students to stand and wait.

5. Make procedures routine.

   Attempt to make classroom management procedures routine. Students should use the same procedures consistently from one day to the next and from one activity to the next. When possible, avoid novel procedures because students will lose some time in learning any new procedure.

6. Teach procedures.

   Invest the time needed to teach students classroom management procedures they will be expected to use. Spend some time at the beginning of the school year teaching students the classroom routines they will be using during the rest of the year.

   As with any teaching, check for student understanding of the procedures before the students are asked to use them. Checking for understanding involves more than just asking, "Do you understand?" Before the students are given a signal to begin, the teacher should review the task the students are to accomplish. In order to insure that all of the students can do the task, the teacher should have the class run through an example together; ask a student, or students, to demonstrate the task; or have individual students explain the task.

7. Secure attention.

   Directions should not begin until everyone is listening; otherwise some students will not know what to do when they begin the task. This lack of understanding will result in procedural questions or student misbehavior at the start of the assigned task.

8. Monitor progress.

   Once students have been given the signal to begin a procedure, monitor the procedure to insure that the students are doing the procedure as directed. Avoid being distracted by other tasks when students are carrying out management procedures.

9. Hold students accountable.

   Students are responsible for all tasks. This accountability can take the form of some product to be turned in or demonstration of some behavior during the activity. Rewards or punishments (but preferably rewards) are then given according to whether or not the task was successfully completed.

## Some Common Management Tasks

Applications of these guidelines are found in the following examples. While the examples may seem complex, the processes involved are relatively simple. Once you become acquainted with these processes, their application will become natural and logical.

### Starting Class

It is reasonable to expect students to be in their seats with the necessary instructional materials for the class at the time the bell rings. Prior to the start of class, the teacher could write a class agenda and announcements on the chalkboard. The students would have the task each day of copying off the agenda and announcements into their notebooks when the bell rings to start class. The agenda would include a list of the day's activities and the approximate times. The announcements could include homework assignments and due dates, project due dates, special TV shows or PTA meeting times and dates. The teacher could also have ready one or two questions on the overhead projector that review the previous day's lesson. When the bell for the start of the period rings, the teacher could turn on the overhead projector. After copying the agenda and announcements, students could answer the questions shown on the overhead projector screen. The students should be expected to turn in the paper with their answers to the questions so that they will know they are accountable for answering them. The teacher could have a system of points for making an honest attempt at answering the questions. At the end of a grading period, the students could then be given a grade, credit, or extra credit if they have a minimum of a predetermined number of points.

When class begins the teacher should monitor the students to insure that all are doing the two assigned tasks. If any are not, the teacher should go to the student's desk and find out what might be causing the delay. After ascertaining that the students are on task, the teacher could check attendance from a seating chart and complete any other administrative chores while keeping an eye on the students.

If these procedures are followed each day, and if the teacher takes the time needed at the start of the year to teach these procedures, the students will eventually know what to expect and will not need to be told what to do each day. The tasks the students are asked to do will benefit them. They will know from the agenda what to expect in class that day. Answering the two questions will cause the students to review and think about what they learned the previous day, enhancing achievement. While the students are involved in these tasks, the teacher can accomplish mundane administrative tasks, reducing the time students will be left with nothing to do.

## Transitions

Much time can be lost moving from one activity to the next during a class period. Effective management can considerably reduce this lost time.

When an activity is about to be brought to a close, stop the students and tell them to put away the materials on which they are currently working. If the procedures involved are complex (for example, they may need to leave their seats to return materials to some location), be sure they understand what they are to do. Check their understanding by asking some students to repeat the directions, then review the directions for the start of the next activity. Again check for understanding. Do not allow the students to finish one task and start the next until you know they all understand what it is they are to do. Then give the students a signal to go ahead with the new task.

When the students begin the procedures, the teacher should monitor their progress closely. The teacher should not do things that could distract him or her from monitoring. If some students do not start the tasks immediately, the teacher should go to the students and make sure they do start. Monitoring the students' progress is essential if transitions are to occur smoothly and efficiently. Considerable instructional time can be gained each year through effective management of transitions.

## Seatwork

When students are given individual seatwork to do, establish rules about talking and movement. Students should be instructed to raise their hands if they have any questions, but not to leave their seats. The teacher should go to them. When the teacher goes to a student's desk, he or she should stand in a position so that all or most of the class is visible.

Before the students are given a signal to begin, the teacher should review the task the students are to accomplish. In order to insure that all of the students can do the task, the teacher should have the class run through an example together, ask a student or students to demonstrate the task to be accomplished, or have individual students explain the task.

Students should know they are accountable for some product as a result of the seatwork. Rather than merely have students study or read some assignment, assign some specific written report, such as answering a series of questions. These papers should then be checked for completion and, if possible, accuracy. Grades, point rewards, or some other method of accountability should be attached to the assignment.

The teacher should monitor the students' progress on the assignment. If some student delays starting the assignment, the teacher should immediately go to the desk of that student and ascertain the reasons for delay. The teacher should remain near the student until the student begins the assignment. No student should be allowed not to do the task assigned. A teacher may not need to continually move about the class as students work on the assignment, but at the very least, the teacher should keep good eye contact and immediately go to any student who raises his or her hand or who is not doing the assignment.

Occasional variation in seatwork can be introduced by having students do the work in heterogeneous pairs. This sharing of seatwork can be particularly valuable when students are practicing something that is presenting some difficulty for lower achieving students (Bondi, 1982).

## Homework Assignments

The three basic reasons for assigning homework are remediation, practice, or enrichment. If students have demonstrated some difficulty in learning content or skill, then remedial homework for those students would be indicated. Not all students would be given such an assignment. If the whole class is having a problem learning something, then the best approach would be to provide further classroom instruction. En-

richment and practice on the other hand may be appropriate for the entire class. For example, it may well be that some particularly informative television program is going to be shown. The program may not be available for showing during the day, so an enrichment assignment may be given to the whole class.

All homework should be directly related to class lessons; assigning homework just to keep students busy is inappropriate. Since homework will be directly related to class lessons, and will therefore have some effect on achievement, monitoring homework assignments is necessary. Students should produce something from the assignment. To ask students to read or study something without also requiring a product is to insure that the reading or studying will not occur. Students should be required to turn in some product, and the product should be graded or rewarded. Providing rewards in the form of extra credit can be a more effective strategy than punishment in motivating students to complete assignments. The teacher should keep careful records of students' progress on homework and talk with students who fail to complete homework about how the problem can be worked out.

When homework is assigned, insuring that students are able to do the homework is essential. The same processes as those used when giving directions for seatwork should be followed. Examples should be worked, or students should demonstrate that they understand the directions before they leave the classroom with the assignment. Forming heterogeneous pairs, and then allowing them to do homework cooperatively, can occasionally be beneficial when the task is procedurally complex (Bondi, 1982).

## Collecting and Returning Materials

Much instructional time can be lost by inefficient handling of classroom materials and assignments. Using the same procedures each day for collecting homework or other assignments will save time because explanations of procedures will be unnecessary. For example, having a box available in which students place homework on entering the classroom eliminates the need to use class time for that purpose. Class time can also be saved by planning to return papers during individual seatwork. Using seatwork time for this purpose has the added advantage of allowing the teacher to discuss assignments with individuals when needed.

When passing out instructional materials at the start of activities, avoid having every student go to one central place to pick up the materials. When students are waiting with nothing to do, they will have a tendency to be disruptive. Alternatives include having one of every four or five students pick up the materials for the others; placing all materials for small groups in containers and dispensing the containers, one for each group; having the student at the front of each row pass out materials to the students in that row; or placing the materials on the students' desks before the beginning of class. The last option should only be used when the teacher wants the students to start working with the materials immediately at the start of the period.

## Pacing Lessons

Since student off-task behavior during long periods of teacher talk will tend to increase with time, student on-task time can be enhanced by planning several different kinds of activities during each class period. Breaking the period into shorter segments, each involving a different kind of activity, will help students concentrate on the class activities. For example, the class may start with students working quietly at their seats. The next activity should then involve a change of pace, such as a demonstration, discussion, or some small group hands-on activity. This activity should involve interactions between the students and the teacher, and could last approximately fifteen to twenty minutes. The next fifteen to twenty minutes could be devoted to an activity which involved student-to-student interactions in small groups. The last ten to fifteen minutes would then be devoted to quiet individual assignments. No general agreement exists for the proper number, sequence, or duration of activities for purpose of variety (Sanford, 1984; Brophy, 1979), but activities requiring students to be passive for extended periods should be avoided.

## Ending Class

By scheduling quiet individual seatwork as the last class activity, bringing the class to a close is easier. Teachers should insist on being able to dismiss the class rather than relying on the school bell. By having the students wait to be dismissed by the teacher, the class can be brought to a more orderly ending with less lost time. If all papers have not been turned in, time can be used for that purpose. If instructional materials are not yet all turned in, having the students wait in an orderly fashion until all are turned in insures that none will be lost.

The last minutes of a class should usually involve some scheduled activity. Students should not begin to put materials away until signaled to do so by the teacher. Allow sufficient time, however, for students to return materials. Expecting students to use some of the time between periods for this task is not reasonable. Avoid telling the students they have the last few minutes to sit and relax and talk. Obviously, such a practice may be appropriate on occasion, but allowing such a practice to become the norm is undesirable.

## Grouping Students

Many instructional activities will require the grouping of students either in pairs or other small groups. When forming such pairs, teachers would be well advised to make the pairs or groups as heterogeneous in ability as possible. The evidence is clear that such grouping benefits the lower achievers without any sacrifice to higher achievers (Emmer, et al., 1984; Bondi, 1982) and allows a great deal of peer tutoring to occur. While the benefit to the underachiever is more obvious, the necessity of the higher achiever to explain what he or she knows about something is also of benefit. For example, most teachers recognize how much they learn as a result of planning and teaching lessons.

Grouping students this way also cuts down on the difference in the time it takes different groups to finish a task. Dealing with students who finish tasks long before others is a common difficulty most teachers face. Heterogeneous grouping diminishes this difficulty.

When forming such groups, a teacher is advised to make the procedure appear random. This can be accomplished by placing the name of each student on a separate card and arranging the cards into two stacks. Each of the two stacks is compiled by alternating low and high achievers, with the first card of one stack being a high achiever and the first card of the second stack being a low achiever. The teacher then picks up one card from the first stack and one card from the second stack, pairing a high achiever with a low achiever. Without telling the class how you arrived at

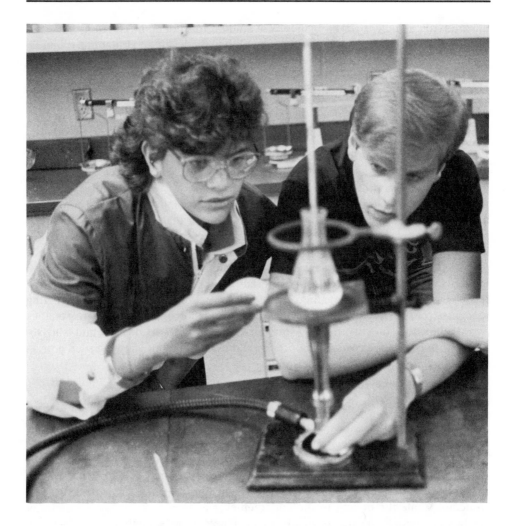

the stacks, begin turning over cards, alternating between each stack. If forming groups of two, then take one card from each of two stacks, one a high achiever, and the other a low achiever. For groups of four take two cards from each stack. If you are forming groups of three, make three stacks; each stack alternating between high achievers, middle achievers, and low achievers. Students will perceive such a process as random, and publicly categorizing students based on achievement may be avoided.

## Student Seating

For most classrooms, assigning seats is preferable to allowing students to choose their own. For example, a student with a visual impairment needs to be placed in a location of optimum viewing, while a student with a hearing impairment needs to be placed in a location of optimum hearing. Such differences need to be accommodated in any seating arrangement. Allowing students to choose their own seats usually will not allow for such accommodations.

Younger students or students in basic classes are easily distracted. Allowing such students to sit where they choose usually means they will sit near friends with the resultant distractions. Highly motivated, more mature students may not experience the same difficulties, and allowing such students to choose their own seats may not cause difficulties. However, even with more mature students, peer pressure may create problems if they sit wherever they choose.

Regardless of how classroom seating is determined, a wise teacher will expect students to stay in the same seats. This enables the teacher to make up seating charts for each class to facilitate roll taking and learning student names.

## Behavioral Management

All teachers are expected to provide a classroom environment conducive to learning. All students should have an equal opportunity to learn, and no student should be allowed to deprive other students of their right to learn. A teacher has the responsibility to insure that the rights of all students are preserved.

Perceiving teaching as the process of merely transferring knowledge of content is too narrow. Teaching also involves helping students to learn ways of behaving that will help them be more effective human beings. Part of the process of learning to behave includes learning how to conduct oneself effectively in group settings. Fundamentally, individuals are born human but not humane; they are not born, for example, with communication and socialization skills. These skills are learned behaviors. One of our responsibilities as teachers is to teach communication and socialization skills. Good discipline, or effective student behavior, should be perceived not as a punitive process but as education.

When thinking of educating students about behavior, effective teachers tend to make certain assumptions.

1. All students are capable of learning and have a desire to learn if we teach things consistent with their levels of ability and teach things that have meaning in the lives of students.
2. All students, with few exceptions, can be taught to stay on-task and not disrupt lessons.
3. Most misbehavior by students is the result of something the teacher has done or has failed to do.

## Causes of Student Misbehavior

### Teacher Causes

Any system of behavioral management will be ineffective if the teacher assumes that the students are the cause of misbehavior (Wayson and Pinnell, 1982). Such a perception on the part of a teacher will likely result in the teacher dealing's with symptoms of misbehavior rather than causes. If basic causes of misbehavior are not altered, then misbehavior is likely to persist.

Most student misbehavior results from things that teachers do or do not do. Inappropriate behaviors by teachers cause or allow students to wander off-task or exhibit disruptive behavior (Emmer, et al., 1984; Wayson and Pinnell, 1982; Grantham and Harris, 1976; Kounin, 1970). Beginning teachers, and some experienced teachers as well, tend to feel anxiety and fear from a lack of confidence in their ability to control a situation. Teachers will do things to reduce the anxiety and fear associated with this insecurity by using inappropriate behaviors. For example, teachers may

1. turn their back on the class
2. maintain poor eye contact with the class
3. ignore problems in the hope that the problems will go away
4. threaten students
5. bluff when they don't know what to do
6. lack body and voice expression
7. behave like a dictator
8. reject student comments when they are unexpected
9. restrict interaction with certain students
10. hide behind the desk and not move about the classroom
11. adopt verbal, facial, and body mannerisms
12. use sarcasm or be defensive

In addition to reactions from feelings of insecurity, other kinds of things that teachers do that may cause problems include

1. using poor eliciting patterns
2. being unconcerned about student motivation
3. teaching too much content in the time available
4. not using students' names
5. being unconcerned about student learning during a lesson
6. overusing presentation (lecture) as a method of teaching
7. praising or criticizing some students more than others
8. utilizing inadequate classroom management
9. failing to provide a variety of activities
10. failing to enforce rules consistently

These lists are not exhaustive. Teachers may also demonstrate a great many other behaviors that cause problems for themselves and children. The important fact is that much of the misbehavior of students results from what we as teachers do or fail to do. If we want our classrooms to be pleasant places where learning can and does occur, then the place to start making needed improvements is with ourselves.

We are not merely passive victims of anything students decide to do in our classrooms. We have control, if we only recognize that fact, and do something about it. This recognition is the first step in effective behavioral management.

### Student Causes

Not all inappropriate student behavior stems from the teacher's behavior. Students initiate inappropriate behavior for a variety of reasons, including

1. an attempt to escape the reality of failure. (By misbehaving some students believe that they can create an excuse for failure such as "the teacher doesn't like me.")
2. the need for attention from teacher and/or peers
3. retaliation because of some earlier embarrassment from peers
4. excitement due to some external event
5. boredom over tasks that are too easy
6. frustration from attempting tasks that are too difficult
7. frustration or uncertainty from not understanding directions for doing a task
8. being emotionally disturbed
9. lack of interest in the ongoing activity

### Preventing Disruptive Behavior

If teachers can recognize some of the causes of misbehavior that result from their instructional practices, then they can reduce the amount of misbehavior that students initiate by

1. keeping good eye contact with the entire class
2. not threatening students
3. not bluffing students
4. treating students with respect and avoiding arbitrariness
5. accepting sincere student comments even when they are unexpected
6. interacting equally with all students
7. moving around the classroom, particularly in the vicinity of students becoming restless
8. avoiding the use of sarcasm
9. using an eliciting pattern of accepting responses only from students called on to respond (Q-N-R)
10. planning the start of lessons with student motivation in mind
11. using students' names
12. not extending activities past the attention span of students
13. monitoring student seatwork
14. planning the management of transitions with great care
15. utilizing interesting and relevant learning experiences

16. giving clear directions and checking understanding of them
17. monitoring the level of difficulty for individual and small group activities

While many others could be listed, these behaviors have resulted in significant differences for many teachers (Emmer, et al., 1984; Sanford, 1984; Evertson and Emmer, 1982; Kounin, 1970). Obviously not all teachers experiencing problems with misbehavior need to modify the same behaviors. Teachers need to analyze what they are doing or not doing that contributes to behavior problems. Such an analysis can then help them identify and change particular behaviors in ways likely to alleviate their problems.

## A System of Behavioral Management

In addition to changing instructional behaviors to reduce the amount of misbehavior in the classroom, teachers can also use a system of behavioral management. The purpose of such a system is to allow teachers to minimize instances of misbehavior as well as to deal effectively with misbehavior when it occurs (Duke and Meckel, 1984). Many systems of behavioral management exist, and no attempt will be made to discuss all of them (Alschuler, 1980; Canter, 1979; Gordon, 1974; Dreikurs, Grunwald, and Pepper, 1971; Glasser, 1969; Glasser, 1965). Rather, one system this author has found to be effective for beginning teachers will be introduced. When elements are taken from several systems to make a modified system, the modified system may be disjointed. The system being recommended takes some of the best aspects from several approaches and puts them together in a combination that, it is hoped, will be a coherent whole.

You need to consider the plan you decide to adopt carefully, regardless of the one you choose. First, choose a plan consistent with your level of skill. Second, adopt a complete systematic plan that deals with more than the immediate symptoms and does not treat every incidence of misbehavior as a unique event. That is, you will want a system that enables you to deal with misbehavior as a matter of education. Teachers who are effective in behavioral management have been found to use such systematic long-term strategies (Brophy, 1982; Medley, 1979).

Also recognize that having a plan to deal with disruptive behavior before you need it is important (Duke and Meckel, 1984). Not having a plan will insure continued difficulty with misbehavior in your classroom. Considerable time would be spent in calling down students, venting anger, threatening students, and other nonproductive activities. Under such conditions, your classroom would not be a pleasant place in which to teach or learn.

Regardless of the system chosen, a rare student may not respond to the system as expected. Some students may be emotionally disturbed or incorrigible and need trained counselors or psychologists. Dealing with them may be beyond the expertise of most teachers, but such students will be the exception in most classrooms.

The system of behavioral management being recommended is a total system, and as such, the essential elements of the total system will need to be used to achieve the desired results—a pleasant classroom for both the teacher and students and one devoid of misbehavior. Consider this system as you would a car. A car works fine when all of its parts are working. If one or more parts are removed or modified by someone not understanding the system, then the car may run poorly or not at all. Some parts may be removed or modified by a person familiar with cars, and the car may run as well or better. But, the likelihood of a person knowing little about cars being able to make modifications successfully is slim. The same is true of any system of behavioral management. If you remove or modify some part of the system you may inadvertently cause it to work poorly or not at all. This plan has been used successfully by other beginning teachers, so if it doesn't work for you, then you have modified an essential part of the system that should not have been modified.

## Establishing Rules

Before students can be comfortable in a classroom, the classroom must have predictability, that is, students need to know what you are going to expect from them. Effective teachers have been found to be those who establish and enforce reasonable rules (Emmer, et al., 1984; Charles, 1981; Gnagney, 1981; Bloom, 1980; Clarizio, 1980; O'Leary and O'Leary, 1977). Students know before they walk into your classroom that rules defining acceptable behavior will be used, but they will not know exactly what you will expect. If rules are reasonable and consistently enforced, students will have no difficulty in accepting them. Students usually prefer that such rules be established (Fisher and Fraser, 1983).

If rules are reasonable, every student in the classroom should be expected to abide by them. Some teachers have the mistaken notion that some students (minorities or special students) cannot be expected to abide by rules. If any system of behavioral management is to be effective, then all students must abide by the same set of rules.

Students will accept rules more easily if they understand the reasons for them. Knowing the reasons for rules makes rules reasonable. Starting with acceptable principles on which rules are based removes arbitrariness from the process and makes acceptance by the students more likely. When discussing these principles, be businesslike, but do not project feelings of hostility. Remember, teaching effective behavior is the same as teaching your content. Both are educational processes, and neither requires feelings of anger or hostility. Rather, a teacher needs to have concern for student learning.

In a classroom, the basic principles you would want to consider include the following:

1. Every student has the right to learn as well as the responsibility not to deprive others of their right to learn.

2. Every student has the right to a safe environment as well as the responsibility not to deprive others of a safe environment.

3. Every student has the right to an environment of mutual respect of persons and property as well as the responsibility not to deprive others of an environment of mutual respect of persons and property.

4. Every student is accountable for his or her actions.

Next, these principles need to be translated into some general rules of behavior and procedures for enforcing the rules, and then the relationships among them should be discussed. Statements of rules should be presented in a positive form rather than as "do nots." The number of general rules should be relatively few (Brophy and Evertson, 1976). *Include no rules unless you actually expect students to follow them, the rules are enforceable, and you are willing to do whatever it takes to enforce them.* Stating rules you do not intend to enforce will result in your loss of credibility with students (Smith and Smith, 1978).

Illustrations of specific behaviors reflecting the rules should be discussed with the students. The number of rules, and the number of specific examples that illustrate them, may need to be more extensive for junior high school students than for upper level secondary students. When first introducing the rules, include only obvious examples or examples of things the students will be expected to do immediately. Other examples may then be introduced as the need arises. Recognize that the specifics may vary with the nature of the activities being used. For some activities you will want the students to talk freely, while for others you will want highly controlled student talk.

Listed here are some general rules that would logically follow from these principles.

1. Students will come to class prepared to learn.
   Specific Rules
   a. Students will come to class with only the materials necessary for that class. This includes having notebooks, pencils, paper, books, and assignments with them when they come to class. They will not bring work from other classes or other materials likely to distract them from the work of the class.
   b. Students will participate in classroom activities by taking notes, responding to teacher questions, and following directions.
2. Students will respect the right of others to learn.
   Specific Rules
   a. Students need to remain in their seats unless given permission to move about.
   b. Students will refrain from talking when this would distract others.
   c. Students will be in their seats and silent when the second bell rings to start class.
   d. Students will make no distracting noises during lessons.
   e. When sharing ideas during a small group activity, students will talk in low tones and will avoid other loud behavior.

3. Students will respect others and their property.
   Specific Rules
   a. Students will raise their hands and wait to be called on to respond and will not interrupt others who are talking during classroom discussions.
   b. Students will ask permission to use the property of others, and they will return such property in good condition.
   c. When an activity has been completed, the students will clean up the area in which they worked.
   d. School property or the property of others will not be defaced or deliberately damaged.
   e. Students will refrain from insults and name calling.
   f. Students will not copy another's work.
4. Students will respect the safety of other students.
   Specific Rules
   a. Students will refrain from striking other students.
   b. Students will throw nothing in the classroom.
   c. Students will handle classroom materials in a way that will not threaten the safety of other students.

Once the rules are identified and discussed, some teachers find it beneficial to have the students read, sign, and return a list of principles and rules. Some teachers also have the rules posted in a conspicuous place in the classroom. You will find these procedures to be helpful at the junior high school level and even at the senior high school level in basic or general classes. Usually in more advanced senior high school classes, such practices are unnecessary. Students in advanced classes know proper behavior, and they tend to be motivated to learn. In these classes, a mere mention of the principles at the beginning of the year, followed by immediate enforcement when misbehavior occurs during the first few days, is often sufficient to deter misbehavior for the remainder of the year.

Once the rules have been discussed, the students then need to be informed of the procedures you intend to use when there are infractions of the rules. Each part of the procedures to be followed needs to be explained fully. This explanation will help you respond more consistently and simply when you need to deal with infractions, which will help you maintain credibility as well as save valuable instructional time.

## What to Do When Students Misbehave

The first part of the plan involves your response to misbehavior that interrupts and disrupts an instructional activity. A plan for your responses to other infractions of rules, such as students' failing to turn in work on time, coming to class late, or not following other established routines, will be explained later. Your responses to disruptive behavior should be based on the following premises:

1. At the first indication of misbehavior on the first day of class and every day follow-ing, the teacher must respond immediately. *To wait any period of time (a few seconds or minutes) will significantly diminish the effectiveness of this system, or most other systems* (Sanford, 1984; Smith and Smith, 1978; Brophy and Evert-son, 1976). When misbehavior first begins, you must do whatever is necessary to insure that the misbehavior stops and does not begin again.

2. You will ignore no misbehavior during the first few weeks with a new class. Later, after students have accepted your rules, it may be possible to relax your rules when you decide that the infraction is relatively minor and is not likely to con-tinue. Allow minor violations only after you have established your predictability.

3. When considering your response to student misbehavior, you should expect the same behaviors from all students. If your limits on behavior are reasonable, then expecting all students to operate within these limits is necessary.

4. You should respond initially in the least overt way necessary to cause the behav-ior to cease.

5. With each continued infraction of the rules by an individual, the teacher's re-sponse should escalate until the behavior is stopped.

6. Do not send a student to anyone else to solve problems of misbehavior in your classroom unless *absolutely* necessary. To do so tells the student that you are ei-ther unable or unwilling to deal with students who do not follow your rules. Both messages are detrimental to your future ability to deal with that student's misbe-havior. Teachers effective in behavioral management follow this practice (Brophy, 1982).

## A Plan for Responding to Disruptions

The following plan can be followed step-by-step, but with practice, you can and should modify the plan to fit your circumstances. If and when you change the specif-ics of any part of the plan to suit your situation, be sure the change is consistent with the premises already listed. The sequence of your responses to misbehavior must make clear that continued misbehavior is unacceptable and that any individual who persists in such behavior cannot be allowed to continue to deprive others of their rights.

*Step 1:*   First disruption by an individual
   The response will be a low key, unobtrusive nonverbal response like a frown, a stern look, a movement placing the teacher in close proximity to the student, or some simple verbal response like mentioning the student's name.
*Step 2:*   Second disruption (regardless of the kind) by the same individual
   Call the person by name and remind him or her that he or she is not abiding by the rules. Tell the student to stop the misbehavior. Demonstrate no hostility, but be calm and insistent. Widespread agreement exists on keeping your responses as mild as possible (Weber, *et al.*, 1983; Howell and Howell, 1979; Soar and Soar,

1979; Tanner, 1978; O'Leary and O'Leary, 1977; and Harris, 1972). For some classes, you may combine steps 1 and 2 in order to keep your response pattern simpler. An effective alternative is to tell students that calling their names is the only warning they will receive before being asked to leave the activity.

*Step 3:*   Third offense by the same individual

Send the person to a seat set off from the rest of the class; that is, remove the student from the ongoing activity. (The seat should be placed in the rear of the classroom, or in some other location not in view of other students, but in view of the teacher.) Again, show no hostility, but be calmly resolved. Anger or hostility on your part may merely breed a hostile, defiant reaction from the student (Howell and Howell, 1979; Kounin, 1970). Removal of a student who persists in misbehavior after being asked to stop has widespread support as an effective strategy (Charles, 1981; Gnagney, 1981; Brodinsky, 1980; Curwin and Mendler, 1980; Wolfgang and Glickman, 1980).

The student removed from the activity takes nothing with him or her and does nothing while seated there. The student also may not take part in the ongoing activity. This removal from the activity is a direct consequence of the misbehavior. Since the student has persisted in depriving others of their right to learn, the student cannot continue as a participating member of the group. The student will remain in the seat for a predetermined period of time (e.g. ten minutes) or until the teacher directs that he or she may return to the ongoing activity.

A student who needs to be removed from an activity should be required to see you for a conference before the next class period. This conference is an important part of helping the student modify his or her behavior in more effective ways (Jones, 1980; Tanner, 1978; Wallen and Wallen, 1978; Gordon and Burch, 1974; Glasser, 1965).

When students break the rules on one day, but not to the point of needing to be removed, and then do the same thing the next day and the next, a teacher may need to modify this system. The usual modification would include telling the student after about the third day to stop, and then adding that you would like to see him or her after class. After class, arrange a conference time. Students should not be allowed to continue misbehavior without experiencing some consequence.

## Description of the Conference

Keep in mind that this conference is for the purpose of helping the student come to recognize more effective behaviors for accomplishing his or her purposes. Students must learn ways of accomplishing their purposes without depriving others of their right to learn. This learning can be accomplished by having the student think about and respond to a series of questions. If the student responds, "I don't know," or remains silent after the question is asked, wait until the student does respond. Explain that the purpose of the conference is to "help you solve your problem, therefore, if I answer the questions for you, you will not benefit from the conference." Approach the conference as an opportunity to help a student with his or her difficulties. Feelings of hostility or defensiveness on your part are inappropriate and should be avoided. A typical conference follows the pattern described here.

*Step 1:*    Student identifies the misbehavior

"What (not why) were you doing that you were not supposed to do that resulted in this conference?"

This question is not meant to provide the student with the opportunity to make excuses but to help the student recognize his or her misbehavior. No excuses for depriving others of their right to learn are accepted.

*Step 2:*    Student identifies the consequences

"What effect did your misbehavior have on the other students? On you?"

The purpose of this question is to help the student associate his or her action with the effects of that action, that is, the consequences of that misbehavior. The student needs to recognize that there were consequences other than, or in addition to, those he or she may have intended.

*Step 3:*    Student is asked to make a value judgment

"Was the effect your behavior had on you or the students helpful or harmful? If harmful, in what ways were you or others hurt by it?"

The student needs to determine how the behavior was detrimental to him- or herself or others. The student needs to see that the consequences of his or her acts can have detrimental effects on others if allowed to be continued. (Steps 2 and 3 may be combined if doing so helps the flow of the conference.)

*Step 4:*    Student formulates a plan

"What could you do the next class period to prevent yourself from doing the same thing, but still achieve your purposes?"

The student should be encouraged to identify several possible alternative plans to accomplish his or her purposes without misbehaving. If the student is reluctant, then be patient and wait until he or she can formulate reasonable alternatives. Telling the student what he or she should do would defeat the purpose of the conference. Do not accept an answer like "I'll try harder." The student must be specific about what he or she will do to prevent the misbehavior and still accomplish his or her purpose.

*Step 5:*    Secure a commitment to a plan

"Which one of the alternatives you suggested would be the one you will try during the next class period?"

Do not accept a vague commitment like, "I don't know which one to try, but maybe the first idea will be OK." Encourage the student to make a definite commitment to follow through on one of the plans discussed.

*Step 6:* Consequences for not following the plan

> "What should the consequences be if you do not follow your plan in the next class period?"

Do not let the student choose additional academic work as a consequence. Avoid punishment. Removing the student from the activity for a longer duration than the time for this last infraction, changing the student's seating, making the student stay after school and help the teacher or another student with an assignment, or sending a note or calling the parents are options. The consequence for the repeated misbehavior needs to be more severe than the initial consequence and needs to be escalated for each succeeding conference if more than one conference is necessary.

*Step 7:* Offer help

> "Is there anything I can do to help you follow your plan or accomplish your purposes?"

Remember that this is a teaching/learning situation, and does not need to be punitive. You are here to help the student with his or her problem. You should sincerely want to help. Also recognize that you may be part of the cause of the student's misbehavior. To the extent that your behavior may have contributed to the student's misbehavior, you will want to modify your practices in order to help that student and others remain on task.

On the surface, having conferences may seem to be a burden on the teacher if many students need them. Conferences would indeed be a burden if that were the case. If, on the other hand, the teacher begins this plan on the very first day of classes and is consistent, then there will very quickly be little or no need for conferences. Students will have ceased their misbehavior. In fact, in most classes, conferences are unnecessary after the first two or three weeks.

When first implementing your plan, explain the steps of this conference to the students. The reasons for each step, along with examples of appropriate and inappropriate responses should be discussed. The time necessary to teach the students the steps of this conference will pay off when the time comes to actually conduct a conference. If students understand each step, then the process will be short.

## A Plan for Other Infractions of Rules

When students do not turn in work on time, do not arrive to class on time, do not bring necessary materials to class, or in some other way fail to abide by class rules, their behavior needs to be modified. The most effective method for motivating students to complete assignments, bring materials to class, and so on, is positive reinforcement (Charles, 1981; Gnagney, 1981; Madsen and Madsen, 1981; Walker and Shea, 1980). For example, you could check at the beginning of the period whether the students have brought the necessary materials. Students should be told that such unannounced checking will occur. All students who bring the required material for that day will get an "A" for effort. A similar strategy for homework also could be applied, but all homework should be checked. You could undoubtedly come up with other forms of positive reinforcement for these and similar tasks students are asked to do.

When reward systems still do not result in students' meeting responsibilities, then other methods need to be used to deal with infractions. The same premises apply to dealing with these infractions as those used in dealing with disruptive behavior: Respond immediately to each infraction and escalate your response with repeated infractions.

*Step 1:* First infraction by an individual

The student should be reminded of the rule that is being broken and told to abide by the rule in the future. The immediate consequence should be one naturally related to the infraction. For example, if the student did not turn in homework on time, then you may choose to have the student complete the work and turn it in the next day without penalty. If the student failed to bring necessary materials to class, then he or she may be given materials. With the first infraction, little or no penalty needs to be assessed. A reminder to the student should suffice.

Also, for certain infractions, the student may have legitimate reasons for not fulfilling the requirement. For example, if the student needed to care for a sick mother in a one-parent family, the student may not have been able to complete the assignment. Penalizing a student by expecting the impossible is not reasonable. When dealing with infractions over which the student may not have complete control, the teacher needs to have compassion and understanding.

*Step 2:* Second infraction by an individual

The student should again be informed that he or she has not followed a rule, and some consequence naturally related to the offense, but stronger than the first, needs to follow. For example, if the student has twice not turned in homework on time, then the student may be asked to stay after school to complete the work. If the student has arrived late to class, then the teacher may have a seat available, set off from the rest, to which the student can go without disrupting others. If the student has failed to bring needed materials, then he or she may not take part in the activity.

*Step 3:* Third infraction by an individual

In addition to the consequences described in step two, the student should be told to come in for a conference before the next class meeting.

## Description of the Conference

This conference will be a somewhat abbreviated version of the conference dealing with disruptions, but the purposes will be essentially the same.

*Step 1:* Student identifies the misbehavior

"What (not why) rule were you not following?"

This step allows the student the opportunity to identify the rule that was not followed. This insures that the student knows the rule that he or she broke. Depending on the nature of the infraction, some discussion could also involve the possible causes of the infraction. If the cause is truly beyond the control of the student, then skipping to the last step may be appropriate. The rest of the conference is based on the premise that the student has control over the cause of the misbehavior.

*Step 2:* Student identifies the consequences

"What effect would continued infractions of this kind have on you, and possibly other students?"

The student is helped by this question to associate his or her action with the effects of that action, that is, the consequences of the actions.

*Step 3:* Student is asked to make a value judgment

"In what ways would (the behavior) be harmful to you or to others?"

The student needs to decide the ways his or her behavior was detrimental to him- or herself or others. The student needs to see that the consequences of his or her acts can have detrimental effects if allowed to continue. (For simplicity, you may wish to combine steps 2 and 3.)

Step 4: Student formulates a plan

"What could you do the next time you face this difficulty to help yourself meet your responsibility?"

The student should be encouraged to identify several possible alternative plans to accomplish his or her purposes without misbehaving. If the student is reluctant, then be patient and wait until he or she can formulate reasonable alternatives. Telling the student what he or she should do would defeat the purpose of the conference. Do not accept an answer like "I'll try harder." The student must be specific about what he or she will do to prevent the misbehavior and still accomplish his or her purpose.

*Step 5:* Secure a commitment to a plan

"Which one of the alternatives you suggested would be the one you will try during the next class period?"

Do not accept a vague commitment like "I don't know which one to try, but maybe the first idea will be OK." Encourage the student to make a definite commitment to follow through on one of the plans discussed.

*Step 6:* Consequences for not following the plan

"What should the consequences be if you do not follow your plan in the next class period?"

Do not let the student choose additional academic work as a consequence. Avoid punishment. Try to help the student recognize consequences that naturally are related to the infraction, such as calling the parents or coming in after school to complete work.

*Step 7:*    Offer help

"Is there anything I can do to help you follow your plan?"

Try genuinely to help the student if the student is willing and you can serve some helpful function.

## Dealing with Misbehavior: Some Reminders

1. Misbehavior, or attempted misbehavior, is an opportunity to teach students more effective behavior. Don't perceive misbehavior as a personal threat—it is not.

2. Misbehavior can be a signal to you for some possible needed change in your teaching. Examine the reasons why students might be disruptive. You may need to change some of the things you are doing that may be causing students to misbehave.

3. Be calm and clinical. You are essentially involved in teaching, so treat misbehavior the same way you would treat the teaching of content. If students lack some knowledge or skills, then you have an opportunity to help them learn new knowledge or skills.

4. Do not ignore misbehavior when beginning your work with a new class. Respond to each act of misbehavior. Ignoring misbehavior can be interpreted by students to mean you were not sincere when you set your rules for behavior, you don't care how the students behave, or you are afraid to deal with the misbehavior. Students expect you to respond. When you don't, you lose credibility. Later, when your limits are well-established and students no longer attempt to misbehave, then some incidents of misbehavior can be ignored without consequence. However, you will always need to respond to any significant infractions.

5. React to individuals. Do not respond to misbehavior by directing your remarks to the whole class. However, if several members of the class frequently attempt to misbehave, then discussing your rules with the whole class may be necessary. The class may need to be reminded of the rules, the reasons for each, and the responses you intend to make when there is misbehavior.

6. Avoid being vindictive about student misbehavior.

7. Avoid feeling hurt by misbehavior, and avoid communicating to students that you feel hurt. Students are not to behave for your benefit but for their own benefit. If students misbehave, this misbehavior is not a threat to you, but it is detrimental to the student and/or to others.

8. Do not send a student to anyone else to solve problems of misbehavior. To do so tells the student that you are either unable or unwilling to deal with the misbehavior. Both messages are detrimental to your future ability to deal with that student's misbehavior. Nonetheless, recognize that on some rare occasions when a student becomes totally belligerent and will not respond to your directions, then others (the principal or assistant principal) responsible for discipline in the building may need to be called on.

9. Avoid feelings of anger or displays of anger. Both are indications to students that their misbehavior is a problem to you. Signs of anger on your part could cause students to react in anger or encourage them to further acts of misbehavior whenever they feel a need to upset you.

10. The basic purpose of responding to misbehavior is to help students recognize when they are depriving others of their rights, recognize more effective ways of letting the teacher know when something is bothering them, and accept more effective ways of behaving in order to accomplish their purposes. Remember, students are misbehaving for some purpose. Try to help them learn more effective ways of accomplishing that purpose.

11. Never use additional work in the subject being taught as a punishment. Using additional work as punishment tells the student that learning your subject is something repulsive or undesirable.

12. Never punish a whole class. Mass punishment is basically unfair because not all students are responsible for the misbehavior that occurs. If misbehavior reaches the point where large numbers of students are involved, then you have been grossly deficient in your behavioral management.

13. Consequences that students experience from misbehavior should be logically related to the infraction. The consequences chosen for dealing with misbehavior should be directed toward helping students discontinue the misbehavior and adopt more effective behaviors. Punishment for the sake of retaliation has no place in this process.

14. The student is responsible for his or her behavior in the classroom as well as the consequences of that behavior. You are responsible for protecting the rights of all of the students to learn. You have no option but to respond when students try to violate others' rights. Students are responsible for avoiding behavior that violates others' rights, and they are responsible for anything that you are called on to do to prevent that violation from occurring.

15. If an individual student decides not to learn, a teacher can do little other than try to encourage that student to learn. Whether or not a teacher should ignore nondisruptive, off-task behavior is dependent in part on the maturity of the student as well as the possible effect such behavior could have on other students if allowed to continue. Usually if a student is quietly off-task, a teacher should at least have a conference with that student to see if the teacher can be of help. If a student persists on not getting involved in the classroom activities, then a parent conference could be helpful. Ultimately, such a student should be either removed from the classroom or separated in some way from the other students.

## Conclusion

You need to explain your rules and the reasons for them, as well as the process you will follow when students break the rules, to all of the students beforehand. Don't keep secrets from the students. They need to know the purpose for each step of the plan. If the plan is clear to them, then you will find that implementing the plan will take much less time in the long run than not having a plan at all.

The behavioral management system introduced may seem like a very involved process and a lot of bother. But you need to ask yourself, "Is it worth the effort to have a relaxed, pleasant environment in the classroom, or do I want to settle for an easier process and then deal with misbehavior throughout the year?" Studies have shown that when teachers do not have an effective *system* of behavioral management, they will spend, on the average, about ten to fifteen percent of class time on dealing with misbehavior throughout the year. The choice is yours.

## REFERENCES

Alschuler, A.S. 1980. *School discipline: A socially literate solution*. New York: McGraw-Hill.

Bloom, R.B. 1980. Teachers and students in conflict: The CREED approach. *Phi Delta Kappan* 61:624–626.

Bondi, E.F. 1982. Two heads are better than one: Peer tutoring makes a difference. *Academic Therapy* 17(4): 401–405.

Brodinsky, B. 1980. *Student discipline: Problems and solutions*. Arlington, Va.: American Association of School Administrators.

Brophy, J., and C.M. Evertson. 1976. *Learning from teaching: A developmental perspective*. Boston: Allyn and Bacon.

Brophy, J. 1979. Teacher behavior and student learning. *Educational Leadership* 37(1): 33–38.

Brophy, J. 1982. Supplemental group management techniques. In *Helping teachers manage classrooms*, ed. D.L. Duke. Alexandria, Va.: Association for Supervision and Curriculum Development.

Canter, L. 1979. *Assertive discipline*. Los Angeles: Canter and Associates.

Charles, C.M. 1981. *Building classroom discipline*. New York: John Wiley and Sons.

Clarizio, H.F. 1980. *Toward positive classroom discipline*, 2d ed. New York: John Wiley & Sons.

Curwin, R.L., and A.N. Mendler. 1980. *The discipline book: A complete guide to school and classroom management*. Reston, Va.: Reston Publishing Co.

Doyle, W. 1979. Making managerial decisions in classrooms. In *Classroom management*, ed. D.L. Duke. 78th Yearbook of the National Society for the Study of Education (Part 2). Chicago: The University of Chicago Press.

Doyle, W. 1980. *Classroom management*. West Lafayette, Indiana: Kappa Delta Pi.

Dreikurs, R., B. Grunwald, and F. Pepper. 1971. *Maintaining sanity in the classroom: Illustrated teaching techniques.* New York: Harper & Row.

Duke, D.L., and A.M. Meckel. 1984. *Teachers guide to classroom management.* New York: Random House.

Emmer, E.T., and C.M. Evertson. 1981. Synthesis of research on classroom management. *Educational Leadership* 38:342–347.

Emmer, E.T., C.M. Evertson, J.P. Sanford, B.S. Clements, and M.E. Worsham. 1984. *Classroom management for secondary teachers.* Englewood Cliffs, N.J.: Prentice-Hall.

Evertson, C.M., and E.T. Emmer. 1982. Effective management at the beginning of the year in junior high classes. *Journal of Educational Psychology* 74(4): 485–498.

Fisher, D.L., and B.J. Fraser. 1983. A comparison of actual and preferred classroom environments as perceived by science teachers and students. *Journal of Research in Science Teaching* 20(1): 55–61.

Glasser, W. 1965. *Reality therapy.* New York: Harper & Row.

Glasser, W. 1969. *Schools without failure.* New York: Harper & Row.

Gnagney, W.J. 1981. *Motivating classroom discipline.* New York: Macmillan.

Gordon, T., and N. Burch. 1974. *Teacher effectiveness training.* New York: Peter H. Wyden Publisher.

Grantham, M.L., and C.S. Harris. 1976. A faculty trains itself to improve student discipline. *Phi Delta Kappan* 57:661–664.

Harris, M.B., ed. 1972. *Classroom uses of behavior modification.* Columbus, Oh.: Charles E. Merrill.

Howell, R.G., and P.L. Howell. 1979. *Discipline in the classroom: Solving the teaching puzzle.* Reston, Va.: Reston Publishing.

Jones, V.F. 1980. *Adolescents with behavioral problems: Strategies for teaching, counseling, and parent involvement.* Boston: Allyn and Bacon.

Kounin, J.S. 1970. *Discipline and group management in classrooms.* New York: Holt, Rinehart and Winston.

Madsen, C.H., and C.K. Madsen. 1981. *Teaching discipline: A positive approach for educational development.* Boston: Allyn and Bacon.

McGarity, J.R., and D.P. Butts. 1984. The relationship among teacher classroom management, behavior, student engagement, and student achievement of middle school and high school science students of varying aptitude. *Journal of Research in Science Teaching* 21(1): 55–62.

Medley, D.M. 1979. The effectiveness of teachers. In *Research on teaching: Concepts, findings, and implications,* ed. P.L. Peterson and H.J. Walberg. Berkeley, Calif.: McCutchan Publishing.

O'Leary, K.D., and S.G. O'Leary, eds. 1977. *Classroom management: The successful use of behavior modification.* Elmsland, New York: Pergamon Press.

Sanford, J. 1984. Science classroom management and organization. In *Observing science classrooms: Perspectives from research and practice,* ed. C.W. Anderson, AETS Yearbook. Columbus, Ohio: ERIC.

Smith, D., and J. Smith. 1978. *Child management: A program for parents and teachers.* Champaign, Ill.: Research Press.

Soar, R.S., and R.M. Soar. 1979. Emotional climate and management. In P.L. Peterson, and H.J. Walberg. *Research on teaching: Concepts, findings, and implications.* Berkeley, Calif.: McCutchan Publishing.

Tanner, L.N. 1978. *Classroom discipline for effective teaching and learning.* New York: Holt, Rinehart & Winston.

Veenman, S. 1984. Perceived problems of beginning teachers. *Review of Educational Research* 54(2): 143–178.

Walker, J.E., and T.M. Shea. 1980. *Behavior modification: A practical approach for educators.* St. Louis: C. V. Mosby.

Wallen, C.J., and L.L. Wallen. 1978. *Effective classroom management.* Boston: Allyn and Bacon.

Wayson, W.W., and G.S. Pinnell. 1982. Creating a living curriculum for teaching self-discipline. In *Helping teachers manage classrooms*, D.L. Duke, ed., Alexandria, Va.: Association for Supervision and Curriculum Development

Weber, W.A., J. Crawford, L.A. Roff, and C. Robinson. 1983. *Classroom management: Reviews of the teacher education and research literature.* Princeton, N.J.: Educational Testing Service.

Wolfgang, C.H., and C.D. Glickman. 1980. *Solving discipline problems: Strategies for classroom teachers.* Boston: Allyn and Bacon.

---

**SUMMARY**

---

### Management

Management is not an end in itself. Management serves the ultimate purpose of helping the teacher achieve goals and objectives. *Classroom Management* is the management of the physical environment and the instructional materials in the classroom. *Behavioral Management* is the management of the behavior of students in the classroom.

### Guidelines for Utilizing Classroom Management Procedures

1. make procedures simple
2. make procedures efficient
3. avoid dead time
4. minimize student movement
5. make procedures routine
6. teach students procedures
7. secure students' attention
8. monitor progress
9. hold students accountable

### Some Common Classroom Management Tasks

1. starting class
2. transitions
3. seatwork
4. homework
5. collecting and returning materials
6. pacing lessons
7. ending class
8. grouping students
9. student seating

### Assumptions on Which Effective Behavioral Management Depends

1. All students are capable of learning and have the desire to learn when teachers use effective methodology and teach appropriate content.
2. Students can be taught to stay on task.
3. Most student misbehavior is the result of something the teacher has done or failed to do.

### Some Reasons Students Initiate Misbehavior

1. attempt to escape the reality of failure
2. need for attention from the teacher or peers
3. retaliation for earlier embarrassment
4. excitement due to some external event
5. boredom over tasks that are too easy
6. frustration over tasks that are too difficult
7. frustration at uncertainty due to poorly understood directions
8. being emotionally disturbed
9. lack of interest in the ongoing activity

### Things a Teacher Can Do to Prevent Disruptive Behavior

1. keeping good eye contact with the entire class
2. not threatening or bluffing students
3. treating students with respect
4. interacting equally with all students
5. moving around the classroom
6. using a Q-N-R eliciting pattern
7. using students' names
8. not extending activities past the attention span of students
9. monitoring student seatwork and behavior
10. planning and utilizing classroom management strategies with care
11. utilizing interesting and relevant learning experiences

### Principles on Which to Establish Rules

1. Every student has the right to learn as well as the responsibility not to deprive others of that right.
2. Every student has the right to a safe environment as well as the responsibility not to deprive others of that right.
3. Every student has the right to an environment of mutual respect of persons and property as well as the responsibility not to deprive others of that right.
4. Every student is accountable for his or her actions.

### Reasonable General Rules

1. Students will come to class prepared to learn.
2. Students will respect the right of others to learn.
3. Students will respect others and their property.
4. Students will respect the safety of other students.

### Guidelines for Rules

1. Include no rules unless you are willing to enforce them.
2. State rules in a positive manner if possible.
3. Keep the list of rules short and to the point.
4. Each rule should be based on valid and reasonable principles.
5. The teacher needs to be clear on the specific behaviors he or she feels would violate the rules and be able to communicate these to the students in a consistent fashion.
6. Every student is expected to abide by the rules.

### Guidelines for Dealing with Misbehavior

1. The teacher should respond to all misbehavior immediately, beginning the first day of class and every day following until rules are firmly established.
2. Misbehavior will not be ignored until rules are firmly established.
3. The teacher should expect the same behaviors from all students.
4. The initial response to misbehavior should be made in the least overt way necessary to stop the behavior.
5. With each continued infraction of the rules by an individual, the teacher should escalate his or her response until the misbehavior ceases.
6. The teacher should not send a student to anyone else to solve problems of misbehavior unless absolutely necessary.

### Guidelines for the Conference on Misbehavior

1. Student identifies misbehavior.
2. Student identifies the consequences.
3. Student makes a value judgment.
4. Student formulates a plan.

5. Student makes a commitment to a plan.
6. Student identifies consequences for not following the plan.
7. Teacher offers to help the student achieve the plan.

## Some Reminders

1. Misbehavior is an opportunity to teach students more effective behavior.
2. Be calm and clinical when dealing with misbehavior.
3. Never use additional work in the subject being taught as a punishment.
4. Never punish a whole class.

# EXERCISE 23
## Using Positive Reinforcement

The purpose of this exercise is to provide some experience in identifying positive reinforcement that could be effective in motivating students to complete homework assignments, bring needed materials to class, and be in their seats at the start of the class period.

*Directions:*   On a separate sheet of paper, briefly describe one positive reinforcement strategy you could use to

1. encourage students to complete and turn in homework assignments on time,
2. bring needed materials to class, and
3. be in their seats at the start of the class period.

   Do *not* use any of the examples already discussed in the textbook.

# *Index*